MW00399784

UNDERSTANDING

the Holy Spirit

UNDERSTANDING

the Holy Spirit

G. Campbell Morgan
Charles H. Spurgeon

WORLD
REFERENCE

Understanding the Holy Spirit
by G. Campbell Morgan & Charles H. Spurgeon
©1995 by AMG Publishers
All Rights Reserved.

Originally published by
Hodder & Stoughton Company, 1900
and by Marshall, Morgan & Scott, Ltd. in London.

ISBN 0-529-10482-2

Printed in the United States of America

Contents

(Note: The Revised Version is used, and the term *Holy Spirit* in preference to *Holy Ghost*.)

Twelve Sermons on the Holy Spirit
by Charles H. Spurgeon

Foreword

Understanding the Holy Spirit contains in one volume the work of two legendary British ministers, George Campbell Morgan and Charles Haddon Spurgeon. In part one, *The Holy Spirit of God*, Morgan presents a clear picture of the relationship of the Holy Spirit with creation, the Scripture, the church, and individuals. Spurgeon, in part two, *Twelve Sermons on the Holy Spirit*, offers twelve eloquent, captivating, and practical lessons on the Holy Spirit's involvement in the lives of believers.

Originally published as separate books in London in the early 1900s, these works are now presented in one volume. In combining them, we at AMG Publishers have made a few minor changes to the original works to help make their content more clear for modern readers. We have updated spelling in accordance with how our language has changed over the years, and, in some cases, unusual forms of punctuation have been simplified. Readers should also note that the points of current history mentioned by Morgan and Spurgeon are from Britain of the late nineteenth century.

Our prayer is that, with the help of this volume, readers will gain a clearer insight into the nature and work of the Holy Spirit and that they will be inspired to deepen their relationship with the Triune God.

The Holy Spirit of God

by Rev. G. Campbell Morgan

In this age of faith in the natural, and disinclination to the supernatural, we want especially to meet the whole world with this credo: "I believe in the Holy Ghost."

WILLIAM ARTHUR

Introductory
Signs of the Times

During recent years two movements have been noticeable in the thought of men outside the Christian Church. First, there has been the development of materialism. The teachings of Darwin, Huxley, Tyndall, and Spencer have tended to the denial of the spiritual in man. Thousands of people who have never read their books have been influenced by their outlook upon life. Moreover, a great many of their first positions have been accepted and taught, and are held until this moment, without any due allowance being made for subsequent statements, which have proved that their teaching consisted in the suggestion of hypotheses, rather than the declaration of ascertained facts. According to such teachers all the phenomena of human life are to be accounted for wholly within the range of matter. It is admitted by them that matter is in itself indestructible, but it is affirmed that the rearrangement of it that takes place at death destroys the identity of human beings. In a more cultured and refined form, and with gleams of hope in the form of doubts, men have been gradually drifting towards materialism; and the effect of this has been seen in the average human life apart from the influence and teaching of Christianity. *Earthly, sensual, devilish,* (James 3:15) are words which fitly describe the vast mass of life apart from God. Some of the old forms of fleshly life have indeed ceased, and there is in the minds of men a new respect for personal character, as a result of the presence of Christianity in the world. A correct view of the condition of the masses of the race would reveal the fact that for the most part life is being lived in the realm of the fleshly, the material, the perishing. Thousands of men, while professing to hold the orthodox creed, are yet living in a practical atheism, and a consequent denial of their own spiritual nature.

The second movement outside the Church has taken the form of a revolt against materialism, and has found its expression in attempts to discover the spiritual—to unfold its laws, and to declare its activities. Spiritualism and theosophy are witnesses to this movement. Mrs. Annie Besant is one of the most remarkable instances of it in individual life. There was a time when she—sickened, alas! by the inconsistencies with which she came into contact within what was called, and falsely called, Christianity—turned her back upon the faith of her early years. She found refuge in denial of high and sacred things; and lived wholly, to all appearance, outside the realm of the spiritual. For her to have found her way back to the acknowledgment of the spiritual in any form is a gain. It is, however, a remarkable fact that one who might have been spoken of as the high priestess of materialism, in a rebound from that position, has taken a leap into the realm of credulity. Belief in a Mahatma, somewhere amid Himalayan heights, who has never been seen, requires a stretch of credence far greater than a belief in the living Christ of God, Whose presence on the earth nineteen hundred years ago is an indisputable historical fact, and Whose abiding presence is witnessed by innumerable transformations of character during the centuries.

This change of front on the part of so gifted a woman is a startling illustration of the fact that, side by side with the materialistic movement that has characterized the past half-century, there has also been a marked revolt against that movement. Indeed, the revolt against materialism has carried a certain section of the community into the opposite extreme. They are declaring that matter is not, and only mind really exists. The tendency of the past was to deny spirit. That has been proved to be absolutely untenable, and now it is the fashion to deny matter. This is evidenced by the vagaries of Christian science, falsely so called.

This groping in the darkness without, has had its counterpart within the churches. A wave of rationalism, originating largely in Germany, has been sweeping over the religious world. Its effect has been the swamping of spiritual ideas and the extinguishing of the fires of Christian zeal. There are churches utterly devoid of the true spiritual tokens of men and women converted to God, and transformed into the likeness of Jesus Christ. Such churches, being destitute of the compassion of the Christ for the needs of men, all too sadly prove that the materialistic element, has crept within their borders, in the form of rationalistic theology, the canker-worm of spiritual life.

But just as outside the Church there has been a spirit of revolt, so within, contemporary with this rationalistic movement, there has been manifested a marked and wonderful revival of interest in the ministry of the Holy Spirit. In 1856 William Arthur issued his *Tongue of Fire*. It was indeed a fiery message to the churches, but it was before its time. Not that it was out of place. Every great movement has its forerunner. Every great development of thought starts with some lonely watchman upon the mountain, who catches the first ray of coming day, and tells the dwellers in the valley of its approach. The book was, in that sense, a book before its time; yet men read it — our fathers tell us — on their knees. There followed a period of waiting, a time during which it appeared as though the book were dead. It was dead as the seed-corn dies, only to issue in a glorious harvest. During the last quarter of the century, men in all sections of the Christian Church have spoken and written upon this great theme of the ministry and work of the Holy Spirit. Dr. Scofield, of Northfield, says: *More books, booklets, and tracts upon that subject have issued from the press during the last twenty years than in all the time since the invention of printing.* The truth thus proclaimed has resulted in new life within the churches; and everywhere eager souls are inquiring after fuller, more definite, more systematic knowledge of this great ministry of the Spirit. The ministries that are forceful in the accomplishment of definite results in the interests of the kingdom of God today, are the ministries of men who are putting the whole burden of their work upon the Holy Spirit of God, of men who, however different their theological outlook may be in certain respects, are nevertheless perpetually realizing that the Holy Spirit is to be thought and spoken of as a Person rather than an influence. Wherever the Spirit of God is being enthroned in preaching and in all Christian work, and having His rightful place as the Administrator of the things of Jesus Christ, apostolic results are seen to follow.

Here, however, as always in the history of fallen man, the Divine movement has had its counterfeit.

The devil has two methods of procedure with regard to the living truth of God. First, he seeks to hide the vision. When that is no longer possible, when truth with its inherent brilliance and beauty is driving away the mists, then the devil's procedure is that of patronage and falsification. Taking it out of its true proportion, he turns it into deadly error.

The Reformation, for which we still thank God, was a return on the part of men, to whom God gave vision, to the great fundamental truth of justification by faith. The central gospel fact, *He that believeth on the Son hath eternal life,* (John 3:36) was rediscovered. For long and weary years Satan had kept that truth out of sight, but when God raised up Martin Luther and others, the devil immediately adopted, adapted, and misapplied it. In the wake of the Reformation came the damnable heresy of antinomianism. Its teaching was, that if men are justified by faith, conduct is of no account; man sins perpetually, and nothing can alter the fact, but being justified by faith, the actual life and character are nothing. Thus a truth taken out of its proper setting, and stretched to undue proportions, became a heresy almost more fearful than that from which justification by faith was a deliverance.

Book I
The Spirit of God

Fountain of Love! Thyself true God!
    Who through eternal days
From Father and from Son hast flow'd
    In uncreated ways!

O Majesty unspeakable!
    O Person all Divine!
How in the Threefold Majesty
    Doth Thy Procession shine!

Proceeding, yet of equal age
    With Those Whose love Thou art—
Proceeding, yet distinct, from Those
    From Whom Thou seem'st to part.

An undivided Nature shared
    With Father and with Son;
A Person by Thyself; with Them
    Thy simple essence One.

Bond art Thou of the other Twain!
    Omnipotent and free!
The consummating Love of God!
    The Limit of the Three!

Thou art a Sea without a shore;
    Awful, immense Thou art—
A Sea which can contract itself
    Within my narrow heart.

And yet Thou art a Haven, too,
    Out on the shoreless sea,
A Harbor that can hold full well
    Shipwreck'd Humanity.

Thou art an unborn Breath outbreathed
    On angels and on men,
Subduing all things to Thyself,
    We know not how or when.

O Light! O Love! O very God!
    I dare not longer gaze
Upon Thy wondrous attributes
    And their mysterious ways.

                        F. W. FARBER

2
The Personality of the Spirit

Before attempting to consider the work of the Holy Spirit through the history of the human race, it is necessary to understand, so far as it is possible, His personality and His relation to the Trinity. Only by a clear understanding of what the Scriptures teach concerning these matters, will it be at all possible to comprehend the mission and work of the Spirit.

Not that it is possible to perfectly understand the personality of the Spirit or His relation to the Trinity. These things are beyond the complete comprehension of minds that are finite. They must be accepted as declarations of a Divine revelation, the final explanation being impossible. It is possible and necessary to discover what the Scriptures of truth have declared about the Spirit in these two respects. This chapter deals with the first point, the personality of the Spirit, under two divisions.

     I. The Holy Spirit a Person.
     II. The Holy Spirit a Divine Person.

The term *Person* immediately introduces an insurmountable difficulty—that, namely, of attempting to express the Infinite in finite terms. It has been argued that personality and absolute existence are contradictions; that God cannot be, at one and the same time, a Person and Infinite. That argument is based upon the assumption that the term *Person* is capable of concise and final definition.

That is a false assumption. It supposes that perfect personality exists in a human being. This is not so. God alone has perfect personality. That of every other being is limited. In other words, God is not a magnified man, rather it may be said that man is a limited god. God is not in the image of man: man is in the image of God. Although, at first, it may appear as though this were a mere play upon words, yet a careful consideration of the statement will prove that no final and definite deductions concerning God can be made from a study of human life.

If man is the one, the final, the absolute unit, then the argument holds that God cannot be a Person and Infinite. If He alone be final and absolute, then personality in man is to be looked upon as being imperfect and limited. When a man declares God cannot be absolute and a Person, he does so because his only view of personality is the view which he has of himself or of his brother. It is possible to form some conception of Divine personality by a study of the human, because men are made in the likeness of God, but wherever the endeavor is made to build up the Divine from the suggestion given in man, it must be remembered that the factors of personality in man are finite, while in God they are infinite.

Four things are contained within the realm of personality—Will, Intelligence, Power, and Capacity for Love. A person is a being who can be approached, trusted or doubted, loved or hated, adored or insulted. These essential parts of personality are limited in human beings: the will has its limitations, the intelligence has its limitations, power has its limitations, love has its limitations.

It is not unthinkable that there may be illimitable will, intelligence, power, and love, and that yet the personality shall remain. Neither is it unthinkable that there may be a Being Who can be approached, trusted or doubted, loved or hated, adored or insulted, having all these elements of personality in infinite measure. Granted that in the Divine there are to be found the elements that exist in other rational beings, it is surely not unthinkable that these may be infinite in the Divine, while yet they are finite in man.

The Christian position is that it is perfectly easy to understand that man, within a circumscribed area, is a picture of the Divine, but that yet, by so much as he is circumscribed and limited, he is not himself Divine. In this sense man was made in the image of God, but that of which he is the image is like him, yet unlike him. It is unlike him in the fact that all that is found in man of essential majesty and grandeur in limited degree, is to be found in God Himself unlimited and illimitable. The Holy Spirit, then, is a Person, possessed of Will, Intelligence, Power, and Capacity for Love.

In the third century of the Christian era, Paul of Samosata advanced a theory denying the Divinity of Christ, and regarding the Holy Spirit as an influence, as an exertion of a Divine energy and power. He attempted to finally explain the terms of the New Testament and of Scripture; and in his attempt to say the last definite, formulated word, he found he must cut away certain supernatural mysteries that surrounded the doctrine of God as contained in revelation; and declared that there was no Trinity, that Jesus was not Divine, and that the Spirit was simply the influence moving out from God, the energy of God exerted upon other people. About the time of the Reformation two men, Laelius Socinus, and his nephew Faustus Socinus, revived the theory, and many accepted it.

The growth and decay of what is known as direct Socinianism is not the subject now under consideration. These facts in the history of the Church are mentioned in order that it may be understood whence came the teaching, the influence of which was like leaven, spreading far more widely through the Church than the circle of those who actually called themselves Socinians. This circle of people had a well-defined doctrine to teach. The great mass of Christian people refused to accept the doctrine, but, alas! passed unconsciously under its chilling influence, and unknowingly almost the whole Church came to think of the Spirit of God as an influence, if not to speak of Him as such!

In the Authorized Version the personal pronoun which refers to the Holy Spirit is translated by the neuter *it*, an index of the trend of thought among Christian people. Men prayed of the Spirit as of *it*, an influence, an energy, proving that the Socinian thought had chilled the zeal and the enthusiasm of Christian doctrine concerning the Holy Spirit.

One of the most remarkable signs in the present time of the revival of the truth of the personality of the Spirit, is the reintroduction in the Revised Version of the masculine pronoun wherever the Spirit is referred to. In that apparently simple and insignificant matter there is a clear revelation of the fact that God is calling His people everywhere to a recognition of this most important doctrine of the personality of the Spirit.

A list of the passages containing the references of Jesus to the Holy Spirit in the Synoptic Gospels and in the Gospel of John will be found as a footnote. Let them be carefully perused.* There are two lines of teaching which run through these utterances. First, the most solemn warning ever uttered in the hearing of men had reference to the Holy Spirit. In the Gospels of Matthew, Mark, and Luke, Christ affirms that His own words may be rejected, that His own Person may be spoken against, and that these things shall be forgiven to the sons of men, but that they who refuse the teaching of the Spirit can find no forgiveness, because the final apostasy of such, the final turning of the back upon the work and mission of the Spirit, constitutes what our Lord speaks of as *eternal sin. Whosoever shall blaspheme against the Holy Spirit hath never forgiveness, but is guilty of an eternal sin* (Mark 3:29)—a deep, searching, and awful thought. The man who can sin against the Holy Spirit, refusing His teaching, deliberately turning his back upon and his will against the message of the Holy Spirit, is in danger of passing into a realm in which his sin is not temporary and transient, but is eternal and abiding. Such were the most awfully solemn words which fell from our Lord's lips. It is not conceivable that a man should sin against a mere influence or energy, so as to bring himself into danger of eternal sin. There is in every word of the warning evidence of an assumption in the mind of Christ of the personality of the Holy Spirit.

---

* Matt. 10:19, 20; 12:28,† 31, 31; 22:43; 28:19;† Mark 3:29; 12:36; 13:11; 14:16;† Luke 4:18;† 11:13;† 12:10–12, 49;† 21:15; 24:48;† John 3:3–8;† 4:10–14;† 5:21;† 7:37, 38;† 14:16, 17, 26;† 15:26;† 16:7–11, 13–15;† 20:22;†Acts 1:5, 8†
(†Peculiar to this gospel.)

The Gospel of John contains Christ's systematic teaching concerning the Holy Spirit. He speaks of Him as the *Paraclete*. This is the title of a Person. It is indeed one of the incommunicable, untranslatable words of Scripture. Neither *Comforter* nor *Advocate* fully expresses its meaning. Both, and even something beyond, would be required to do this. Much would have been gained if no attempt had been made at translation, the word itself becoming the most familiar name of the Spirit.

In these discourses, when speaking of the Paraclete, Jesus does not, in one single instance, use a word which can be construed as indicating thought of the Spirit as an influence. *He shall teach, He shall bear witness, He shall convict, He shall guide* (John 14:26; 15:26; 16:8, 13). These activities attributed to the Holy Spirit must be the activities, not of an influence depending upon another and separate will, but the activities of a Person, of One Who unites within His own Being all the essential elements of personality, Will, Intelligence, Power, and Love. Whether in the solemn warnings of the Synoptic Gospels, or in the teachings concerning the mission of the Spirit in the Gospel of John, the fact is most evidently set forth, that in the mind of Christ the Holy Spirit was thought of, not as an influence, an energy merely, but as One capable of exercising functions and doing deeds which were impossible to any other than a Person.

Again, the Holy Spirit is not only a Person, but a Divine Person. Another heresy arose in the Church in the fourth century. Arius, a presbyter of Alexandria, taught that God is one eternal Person; that He created a Being infinitely superior to the angels, His only begotten Son; that this only begotten Son of God did in His turn exercise His supernatural power by the creation of a third Person, that third Person being the Holy Spirit.

The difference between Socinianism and Arianism lies in the recognition by the latter of the personality of the Spirit, while denying His proper Deity. According to Arius, the Holy Spirit is a Person, a created Person; and if created, then not Creator; and if not Creator, then not Divine. The Nicene Creed was drawn up and adopted as a corrective to this error of Arianism, which had obtained a firm hold in the early Church.

Most assuredly the Scriptures teach not only the personality of the Spirit, but His Divine personality. The unity of two passages in the Old and New Testaments throws light upon this subject.

Then said I, Woe is me! for I am undone; because I am a man of unclean lips, and I dwell in the midst of a people of unclean lips: for mine eyes have seen the King, the Lord of hosts. . . . And He said, Go, and tell this people, Hear ye indeed, but understand not; and see ye indeed, but perceive not (Is. 6:5, 9).

The prophet had come into the presence of God, and was undone by the vision.

The New Testament contains an exposition of that vision of Isaiah.

And when they agreed not among themselves, they departed, after that Paul had spoken one word, Well spake the Holy Spirit by Isaiah the prophet unto your fathers, saying, Go thou unto this people, and say, By hearing ye shall hear, and shall in no wise understand (Acts 28:25, 26).

Paul declared that it was the Holy Spirit Who uttered the words which Isaiah distinctly says were spoken by the Divine Being. Thus the interpretation of the Old Testament by the New reveals the fact of the Divinity of the Holy Spirit.

A new covenant was promised long before the coming of the Messiah (Jer. 31:31–34). In the Epistle to the Hebrews the old promise of the covenant of Jehovah is identified with the new dispensation of the Spirit (Heb. 10:15–17). It is evident that the Persons at first sight apparently different are identical, and that the Spirit spoken of in Hebrews comes in fulfillment of the prophecy uttered by Jeremiah.

Again, the works attributed to the Holy Spirit must be the works of Divinity. Genesis declares that out of the chaos, cosmos was brought by His brooding and force (Gen. 1:2). In the Gospel of John regeneration is declared to be His work (John 3:5). Paul distinctly states that God will quicken our mortal bodies through the Spirit (Rom. 8:11). Creation, regeneration, resurrection, these are works which can only be brought about by infinite power, and therefore the Spirit is not only a Person, but a Divine Person.

Omnipresence, omniscience, and omnipotence, attributes that appertain only to God, are all attributed to the Spirit (Rom. 8:26, 27; 1 Cor. 2:10, 11; 1 Cor. 12:11).

The Scriptures then teach that the Holy Spirit is a Person, having all the Divine attributes and able to do all Divine works. The mystery is acknowledged, and it is very profound. To finally explain it is impossible, but this impossibility of explanation is to be accounted for by human limitation and by the fact that the finite can never grasp the Infinite. The facts must be reverently accepted as forming an integral and necessary part of the system of revealed religion. To deny the personality of the Spirit, and to deny the Divine personality of the Spirit, must eventuate—as it has done in every system where it has been attempted—in denial of the Divinity of the Son, and in the denial of the Divinity of the Son there must also be included—as there always has been—a denial of the atoning work of the Son. The doctrines of the Son—His Cross and Passion—and of the Spirit—His personality and Divinity—are closely connected, and one cannot be interfered with without detriment to the other. Denying these truths, the whole fabric of revealed religion breaks down.

3

The Relation of the Spirit to the Trinity

The doctrine of the Trinity is one of the declared facts of Holy Scripture of which no perfect explanation is possible to minds that are finite. The idea of one Essence subsisting after a threefold manner, and in a Trinity of relationships, finds nothing in the phenomena of nature upon which it can fasten as a sufficient symbol. There have been many attempts to give the mind of man an understanding of this mystery by some such symbol. The mystics attempted, by analogy, to reconcile the doctrine to human reason. They made use of such figures as those of the light, the radiance, and the heat of the sun; the fountain, the flux, and the stream of the river; the root, the stem, and the flower of the plant; the intellect, the will, and the feeling of man; or, perhaps most familiar of all, the human being, consisting of spirit, soul, and body. They declared that in all these things, and indeed throughout nature, there is a perpetual reproduction of that which is the essence of the Divine — Trinity in Unity.

All these illustrations suggest a Trinitarian possibility, but if employed as final symbols, they only serve to mystify. They are insufficient, and differ from the declared facts so radically, that the impression they create, as to the great underlying fact of Divinity —

One in Three and Three in One — is vague and evanescent. As in the case of the personality of the Spirit, so here; the things which are evident are faint and incomplete suggestions of the facts concerning the Infinite. The Scriptures contain a progressive revelation of the doctrine, but when the last word has been said, there is no attempt made to explain the mystery. All that they give is a declaration of the fact, without attempting to give that which would be incomprehensible, a definition or explanation that is final.

The first hint of plurality in the unity of the Godhead is found in the words: *And God said, Let Us make man in Our image, after Our likeness* (Gen. 1:26). To claim that as a definite and final statement of the doctrine of Trinity in Unity would be false. It is the privilege of those who live in the light of the New Testament to view the Old Testament therein. *All things were made by Him; and without Him was not anything made that hath been made* (John 1:3). This refers to the work of the Word, the eternal Son, in creation. It was by His intermediation that the worlds were formed in the beginning.

Thus the Bible story of creation reflects the presence of the three Persons in the Trinity — the Father, as original Source; the Son, as Intermediary; the Spirit, as the Medium through which creation came into being (Gen. 1:1; John 1:3; Gen. 1:2).

The truth is still further developed in the words: *So shall they put My name upon the children of Israel* (Num. 6:27). The emphasis should be laid upon the word, *so* — *so shall they put My name upon the children of Israel*. The method indicated is to be found in the three preceding verses.

The Lord bless thee, and keep thee: The Lord make His face to shine upon thee, and be gracious unto thee: The Lord lift up His countenance upon thee, and give thee peace (vv. 24–26).

This is the trinity of benediction in unity, *My name* in threefold repetition. It is not probable that the priest of the old dispensation, in pronouncing that benediction, had a clear understanding of the truth of the Trinity in Unity, but a hint was enshrined therein which prepared the way for future development. Thus in the priestly benediction of Numbers, there is an advance upon the suggestion of Genesis.[*]

The messages of the prophets contain suggestions on the subject: *In the year that King Uzziah died I saw the Lord sitting upon a throne, high and lifted up, and His train filled the temple. Around[†] Him stood the seraphim: each one had six wings; with twain he covered his face, and with twain he covered his feet, and with twain he did fly. And one cried unto another, and said, Holy, holy, holy, is the Lord of hosts* (Is. 6:1–3).

Isaiah was permitted to have a vision of the King, high and lifted up. He heard the doxology of the hidden place, the cherubim and seraphim chanting the praise of the Eternal, and they sang *Holy, holy, holy, is the Lord of hosts,* a threefold ascription of praise to the one Person.

In this prophecy also is to be found perhaps the most clear statement of the doctrine of the Trinity that the Old Testament contains: *Come ye near unto Me, hear ye this; from the beginning I have not spoken in secret; from the time that it was, there am I: and now the Lord God hath sent Me, and His Spirit* (Is. 48:16). There is an important alteration in this passage from the Authorized Version, which reads: *The Lord God, and His Spirit, hath sent Me.* The *Me* here is the coming One of Whom the prophets wrote and spoke—the great Deliverer, the Messiah, Jesus. The Authorized Version makes it appear as though Christ was sent by God and the Spirit, but in the Scriptures He is never so spoken of. This change in the Revised Version is of the utmost importance; for it contains a prophecy of the coming of Christ and the dawning of the dispensation of the Spirit. *God hath sent Me, and His Spirit.* Here the Trinity is distinctly revealed, not as a doctrine, but incidentally in the midst of prophecy. All that the New Testament unfolds in its beauty is suggested in this

---

[*] This priestly benediction of the Old Testament has its fulfillment in that of the New: *The grace of the Lord Jesus Christ, and the love of God, and the communion of the Holy Spirit, be with you all* (2 Cor. 13:14). Here also the Trinity is named.
[†] *Around,* (not above, as in the English version)—Dr. G. A. Smith.

prophecy, uttered centuries before the coming of the Messiah —
God sending Son and Spirit.

The New Testament takes up the suggestion of the Old, making it clear and plain: *And Jesus, when He was baptized, went up
straightway from the water: and lo, the heavens were opened unto
Him, and He saw the Spirit of God descending as a dove, and coming upon Him; and lo, a voice out of the heavens, saying, This is My
beloved Son, in Whom I am well pleased* (Matt. 3:16, 17). The voice
of the Father is heard from the heavens, announcing His pleasure
in the Son, while the anointing Spirit descends upon Him. This is
a manifestation of the one God in His threefold personality. Thus,
at the outset of Christ's public ministry, the truth of the Trinity was
declared by a solemn manifestation, though the men around did
not then comprehend the deep significance of the event.

The Paschal discourses (John 14, 15, 16) contain the Lord's full
teaching on the subject of the Spirit. This is of sufficient importance to demand special attention, and a subsequent chapter will
be devoted to it.

One more reference claims attention in this section. The Master
having finished His work on Calvary; the Resurrection being accomplished; and the Ascension imminent; He gave to His disciples
the commission under which they were to serve. In connection
with this, He committed to them the great baptismal formula,
which contains the most simple and concise statement of the Trinity that is to be found in the whole of Scripture: *Baptizing them into
the name of the Father and of the Son and of the Holy Spirit* (Matt.
28:19). The phrase *of the,* in each case clearly marks the separation
of personality, but the singular number of *the name,* by which these
are prefaced, marks the unity of the Godhead. That baptismal formula is the consummation of all previous suggestion, and the standard of all subsequent teaching concerning the Trinity.

The declarations of Scripture, then, may be summarized thus:
In one essential Godhead there coexist three Persons, cosubstan-
tial, coequal, and coeternal. This mystery cannot be explained nor
defined, because it is beyond the grasp of the finite; and no explanation is attempted in the inspired Book.

Accepting the doctrine of the Trinity, it is now competent most reverently to inquire what Scripture teaches concerning the relation of the Holy Spirit to the Trinity. The Holy Spirit is always spoken of as the third Person in the Trinity.

In the historical revelation the last personality revealed is that of the Spirit. That of the Father was the supreme point in the creation and history of the Jewish people: *The Lord our God is one Lord* (Deut. 6:4). Then there came the revelation of the Son; and lastly, as the consummation of His mission, came the revelation of the personality of the Spirit.

Again, in the actual facts of the awe-inspiring mystery of the Trinity, the Holy Spirit is not first.

It is distinctly stated that the Spirit is sent; and Christ declared that the Spirit *proceedeth from the Father* (John 14:26; 15:26). This order can never be reversed. The Father cannot be spoken of as being sent of the Spirit, neither can He be said to proceed from the Spirit; therefore, in a sense hard to understand, but distinctly announced, the Holy Spirit cannot be the first Person in this mystery of the Trinity.

Nor can He be the second Person therein. The Son is spoken of as sending the Spirit from the Father, and as Himself sending the Spirit (John 15:26; 16:7). Within the realm of Divinity the Son is never said to be sent by the Spirit. It is said of Jesus that the Spirit drove Him into the wilderness, but that was in His representative capacity as a Man. In His Divinity He is sent by the Father, for the accomplishment of the Father's work, but He is never spoken of as being sent by the Spirit. Consequently, the Spirit, sent by the Son, is the third Person within the Trinity, in the order in which these Persons move in the mighty majesty of their wondrous activities. The great creeds of the Church have caught up the idea of the Spirit proceeding from the Father and from the Son. While there is no direct and positive statement of the kind, still the very argument of the Lord's own teaching, as recorded in the Gospel of John, coincides with that expression of the truth.

The term *third* must be used with most careful limitations. As used with reference to the Persons in the Godhead, it does not imply inferiority. Once in the writing of Paul he reverses the order, and names the Spirit first: *One Spirit, even as also ye were called in one hope of your calling; one Lord, one faith, one baptism, one God and Father of all* (Eph. 4:4–6). Upon another occasion he changes the order again, and places the Spirit in the second place: *Now I beseech you, brethren, by our Lord Jesus Christ, and by the love of the Spirit, that ye strive together with me in your prayers to God for me* (Rom. 15:30). The word *third* is not used in the sense of inferiority. Perhaps that fact will most surely be understood by remembering that the term *third* has here no reference to time. The time element must be eliminated from all consideration of Divine things. It is very difficult to do this. Speaking of the Father, and of the Spirit proceeding from the Father, unconsciously, but none the less certainly, the time element enters into the conception. It may be argued that there can be no procession save that which has a beginning. If that be true, neither can there be a Source from which procession is made, which has no beginning. When dealing with the things of God, time is not; it finds no place in the boundless Being of the Eternal. The procession of the Spirit from the Father is as eternal as is the Father from Whom the Spirit proceeds.

The relation of the Spirit to the Father is declared in the words: *The Spirit proceedeth from the Father* (John 15:26). He is the gift and outmoving of the Divine Essence, the Eternal Spirit. This defies analysis. It is a truth declared, which remains an impenetrable mystery. Men have no right to make any attempt to discover that which is not revealed. It is the simple declaration of the Word of God, that the Spirit proceedeth from the Father; and there the matter must be left.

The relation of the Spirit to the Son is indicated in the words of Jesus in which He declared that the Son receives from the Father, and the Spirit therefore proceedeth through the Son. Professor Swete, in a paper read before the Church Congress several years ago, in well-chosen words stated, with as much clearness as is possible, the great mystery of the Spirit's relationship to the Son. These are his words: *The Son is thus the Intermediary of the self-communication of God. His mediation in creation and in grace rests ulti-*

mately on His mediation in the mystery of the Holy Trinity. The mediation in creation, and the mediation in redemption are based upon the fact, that Scripture declares, that in an inscrutable manner, in a way that defies definition, the Son is intermediary between Father and Spirit, in that great and sublime and magnificent mystery of the Trinity itself.

Here, again, the fact of limitation of language must be borne in mind. These statements refer to eternal attitudes, and consequently they are dateless.

With great reverence and solemnity the question of the function of the Holy Spirit within the Trinity may now be considered.

No such consideration would be possible or proper if it were not based upon the fact that a statement is made with regard thereto in Scripture: *For who among men knoweth the things of a man, save the spirit of the man, which is in him?* (1 Cor. 2:11). This is the apostle's analogy. There immediately follows the statement of a truth of the utmost importance: *Even so the things of God none knoweth, save the Spirit of God.* These words clearly reveal the fact within the mystery of the Trinity—the Spirit is the seat of the Divine consciousness. The eternal Spirit knows the things of the eternal Godhead: *The Spirit searcheth . . . the deep things of God* (1 Cor. 2:10).

That statement leads to the inner heart of this great mystery; and from it a most important deduction is drawn. Seeing that the Spirit of God is the seat of Divine consciousness, He is also the Spirit of revelation. As it is the Spirit of God Who knows the things of God, it must of necessity be the Spirit Who unveils and reveals those things, as much as is necessary and possible, to those outside the marvelous and mysterious circle of the Deity. In that great fact, beyond perfect comprehension, lies the secret of the inspiration of Scripture, and of the presence and work of the Spirit in the Church and in the world.

If any person should accept this attempt to examine one of the greatest mysteries of our most holy religion, feeling that now all is clear, then the attempt has sadly and awfully failed. This subject must be left where God has left it—a revealed mystery, not the revelation of a mystery. That is to say, revelation has declared a mystery;

revelation has not given the explanation of that mystery. The mind of man could never understand, even if the most simple language were used, the Trinity in the Unity of the Godhead, or the relation of the Persons in the Godhead to each other. But, so far as it is necessary and possible for man to see it, *things which eye saw not, and ear hea⁓d not, and which entered not into the heart of man . . . unto us God revealed them through the Spirit* (1 Cor. 2:9, 10).

The statement may thus be made in brief words. There is one God. There are three Persons within the Unity. The Holy Spirit is third in position, forever proceeding from the Father, through the mediation of the Son. That Holy Spirit is the Consciousness of God, and therefore the Revealer of God.

While these things are too high and too wonderful for perfect exposition, yet, so far as is necessary for redemption and life and final perfecting, God has allowed the light of the glory of the inner facts of His own Being to fall upon the human mind.

Book II
Ideal Creation

Fair are the flowers and the children, but their subtle suggestion is
    fairer.
Rare is the rose-burst of dawn, but the secret that clasps it is rarer;
Sweet is the exultance of song, but the strain that precedes it is
    sweeter;
And never was poem yet writ, but the meaning outmaster'd the
    meter.

Never a daisy that grows, but a mystery guideth the growing;
Never a river that flows, but a majesty scepters the flowing;
Never a Shakespeare that soar'd, but a stronger than he did enfold
    him,
Nor ever a prophet foretells, but a mightier seer hath foretold him.

Back of the canvas that throbs, the painter is hinted and hidden;
Into the statue that breathes, the soul of the sculptor is bidden;
Under the joy that if felt, lie the infinite issues of feeling;
Crowning the glory reveal'd, is the glory that crowns the revealing.

Great are the symbols of being, but that which is symbol'd is greater;
Vast the create and beheld, but vaster the inward Creator;
Back of the sound broods the silence, back of the gift stands the giv-
    ing;
Back of the hand that receives, thrill the sensitive nerves of receiving.

Space is as nothing to Spirit, the deed is outdone by the doing;
The heart of the wooer is warm, but warmer the heart of the wooing;
And up from the pits where these shiver, and up from the heights
    where those shine,
Twin voices and shadows swim starward, and the essence of life is
    Divine.

RICHARD REALF

4

The Spirit in Creation

The work of the Spirit in creation, and His perpetual presence and manifestation therein, are subjects full of fascination, and yet strangely neglected. So much attention has been given to the work of the Spirit in its regenerative aspect, that His generative activities have been in a large measure overlooked. The origin and the preservation of everything in nature are spiritual.

> No lily-muffled hum of a summer bee
> But finds some coupling with the spinning stars;
> No pebble at your foot but proves a sphere,
> No chaffinch but implies the cherubim.
> . . . Earth's cramm'd with heaven,
> And every common bush afire with God;
> But only he who sees takes off his shoes—
> The rest sit round it and pluck blackberries.
> Mrs. E. B. Browning

The sacred Writings abound in statements with regard to this aspect of the Spirit's work. What magnificent figures are contained in the words of the Psalmist!

> *He bowed the heavens also, and came down;*
> *And thick darkness was under His feet.*
> *And He rode upon a cherub, and did fly:*

27

Yea, He flew swiftly upon the wings of the wind.
He made darkness His hiding-place, His pavilion
    round about Him;
Darkness of waters, thick clouds of the skies.
At the brightness before Him His thick clouds passed,
Hailstones and coals of fire (Ps. 18:9–12).

It is evident, from a careful reading of this Psalm, that it is a declaration of the perpetual presence of God in all such manifestations. Wherever thick darkness is, it is under the feet of God; whenever the wind passes with swift impetuosity, He flies upon the wings thereof; wherever darkness is, it is God's hiding place, a pavilion round about Him; whenever the darkness is dispersed, it is before the brightness of His rising. In every gleam of the glory of nature there is the evidence of an ever-present God.

The final words of that great doxology which Isaiah heard from the inner temple are of great interest in this connection: *In the year that King Uzziah died I saw the Lord sitting upon a throne, high and lifted up, and His train filled the temple. Around** *Him stood the seraphim: each one had six wings; with twain he covered his face, and with twain he covered his feet, and with twain he did fly. And one cried unto another, and said, Holy, holy, holy, is the Lord of hosts: the whole earth is full of His glory* (Is. 6:1–3). The uplifted Lord is the center of adoration in the courts of heaven, but not there only is His splendor seen—*the whole earth is full of His glory.*

A marvelous declaration of the fact of the presence of God in all nature is to be found also in the great Theophany of the Book of Job (Job 41, 42).

For the purposes of this study, however, it will be sufficient to consider certain definite statements of Scripture, in which the work of the Holy Spirit in creation is clearly set forth in varied aspects.

First compare the earliest reference to the Spirit with one in the prophecy of Isaiah:

And the earth was waste and void; and darkness was upon the face of the deep: and the Spirit of God moved upon [or as the margin gives it, *was brooding upon*] *the face of the waters* (Gen. 1:2).

---

* *Around,* (not above, as in the English version)—Dr. G. A. Smith.

But the pelican and the porcupine shall possess it; and the owl and the raven shall dwell therein: and He shall stretch over it the line of confusion, and the plummet of emptiness (Is. 34:11).

Exactly the same Hebrew words are used in each case to describe the desolation. The word translated *waste* in Genesis is translated *confusion* in Isaiah; the word translated *void* in the one case is translated *emptiness* in the other. This comparison throws light upon the story of creation.

The first picture is that of the Spirit brooding over chaos. Science agrees that the earth must have been in such a condition as this before the appearance of man. How this condition of things arose, whether through some mighty catastrophe whelming a previous order, or through the omnific word of God, no man can tell; both science and revelation are silent. These opening words of the Book of Genesis introduce this planet while yet waste and void, and declare that, for the accomplishment of the change from this condition to that of order, the Spirit brooded over the face of the waters. He acted as the Administrator of the will of God, as expressed by the Word of God. The will of God is that order should supersede disorder. The Word of God announces that will, beginning with the first utterance: *Let there be light* (Gen. 1:3). By the brooding of the Spirit over the chaos the light came. That is the unvarying order of the activity of God in creation.

This is not an account of the first creation of matter. Concerning that, man has no definite knowledge.

In the beginning God created the heaven and the earth. And the earth was waste and void (Gen. 1:1, 2).

How long the interval between these verses no man can tell. Scripture makes no announcement thereupon, and the declarations of science are but surmises. But when the present order was established, it was by the Spirit of God brooding upon confusion and emptiness, as the Power through which the Divine will was realized. The earth as it is today is therefore the direct outcome of the action of the Holy Spirit. Another of the Psalms is full of suggestiveness:

By the word of the Lord were the heavens made; And all the host of them by the breath of His mouth (Ps. 33:6).

The word *breath* here might with perfect correctness be written with a capital letter—*the Breath of God's mouth*. Here again is revealed the will of Jehovah, uttered by the Word of Jehovah, and accomplished by *the Breath of His mouth*, but the sweep of thought is greater than before. It is not a description of the bringing of order to one small planet, but the record in a sentence of the creation of the heavens and all the host of them. The phrase includes all the myriad wonders of the universe around. By the Word of God, and by the Breath of His mouth, came the systems of which man is just beginning to learn that in their entirety they are undiscoverable. The point at which astronomical science has now arrived is an acknowledgment, that beyond the utmost reach of anything which can be studied through the agency of the telescope, lie illimitable space and innumerable worlds.

This has been forcefully stated by Dr. Pierson in his *Many Infallible Proofs*, and the whole paragraph is of such a nature that it is here inserted at length:

> The fact of the vast host of stars is a fact of modern discovery. Hipparchus, about a century and a half before Christ, gave the number of stars as 1,022, and Ptolemy, in the beginning of the second century of the Christian era, could find but 1,026. We may on a clear night, with the unaided eye, see only 1,160, or, if we could survey the whole celestial sphere, about 3,000. But when the telescope began to be pointed to the heavens, less than three centuries ago, by Galileo, then for the first time men began to know that Jeremiah was right when he made the stars as countless as the sand on the seashore. When Lord Rosse's instrument turned its great mirror to the sky, lo, the number of visible stars increased to nearly 400,000,000! and Herschel compares the multitude of them to glittering dust scattered on the black background of the heavens. When John Herschel, at the foot of the dark continent, resolves the nebulae into suns, and Lord Rosse, as with the eye of a Titan, finds in the cloudy scarf about Orion "a gorgeous bed of stars," and the very Milky Way itself proves to be simply a grand procession of stars absolutely without number—how true is the exclamation of Jeremiah, 600 years before Christ, 2,200 years before Galileo: "The host of heaven cannot be numbered"! Who taught Jeremiah astronomy? (Jer. 33:22).

All these unnumbered hosts were made by *the Word of the Lord* and *the Breath of His mouth.* Take now one of the passages in the Book of Job. The words are those of the patriarch himself:

> By His Spirit the heavens are garnished;
> His hand hath pierced the swift serpent (Job 26:13).

The meaning of the passage is obscure, but light is thrown upon it by the context:

> He stirreth up the sea with His power,
> And by His understanding He smiteth through Rahab (v. 12).

That is a perfect picture, in miniature, of a storm-swept sea, over which the dark clouds hang dismally. Then follow the words: *By His Spirit the heavens are garnished.* It is a vision of the bringing back of the blue and the light to the heavens, after the sweeping of a storm; and in this strange expression, *His hand hath pierced the swift serpent,* Job borrows one of the Eastern nature-myths, in illustration of the fact that the calm which follows the storm in nature is—actually and symbolically—the work of the Spirit of God. Job was in fact, or in imagination, looking out upon a storm-tossed sea; he saw it suddenly calmed, the clouds dispersed, and the heavens garnished with beauty. The reference to the flying serpent is difficult to understand. One says that the reference is to the sign of the zodiac; another that it describes the long train of the cloud, as the wind of the Spirit disperses and drives it away; and yet another that the term has reference to the whole arch of heaven, as pierced by the hand of God. Between these views it is not possible to decide, but certainly it is a figure of speech, most probably indicating the driving away of the storm-clouds like trailing serpents, as the heavens smile in sunlight after the storm is spent. The main statement is, however, perfectly clear—that the transformation of beauty is wrought by the Spirit of God.

Another interesting statement is found in the prophecy of Isaiah concerning the agency of the Spirit in nature: *The grass withereth, the flower fadeth; because the Breath of the Lord bloweth upon it* (Is. 40:7). This declaration is at first sight almost staggering. That the Spirit of God comes as a genial summer zephyr upon nature is easy to understand, but it is difficult to believe that He comes also as the fierce blast of God. Yet it is certainly true. He brings death as a process, and a necessity. The pitiless east wind has in it the breath of health. Let there be no more east wind, no more northeast wind, no more biting, keen blast of death, and what would become of nature? Surely Kingsley entered into the spirit of this when he sang: —

> Welcome, wild North-easter!
>   Shame it is to see
> Odes to every zephyr,
>   Ne'er a verse to thee.
>
> Through the black fir forest
>   Thunder harsh and dry,
> Scattering down the snowflakes
>   Off the curdled sky.
>
> Come; and strong within us
>   Stir the Viking's blood,
> Bracing brain and sinew;
>   Blow, thou wind of God.

When the east wind blows, and the flowers are nipped, and the blade of grass is curled and shriveled almost as if by the blast of heat, then the Spirit of God is sweeping the ground and preparing for the springing of life in response to the kiss of His gentler wind.

In close sequence consider the words: *Thou sendest forth Thy Spirit, they are created; And Thou renewest the face of the ground* (Ps. 104:30).

That which follows the death-wind of the Spirit is His life-wind. The first is Winter; the second is Spring. Nothing ever finds its way to Spring save through Winter. The budding of life and the flowers that blossom upon the sod in Spring-time are the result of the cold east wind that swept the hills and the valleys during Winter days. These are not mere figures of speech. The cold and icy wind blows under the direction of the Spirit of God; and the wind which kisses earth, and makes it smile in flowers, is the messenger of the self-same Spirit.

The prophecy of Ezekiel opens with a magnificent piece of imagery, of which no final nor exhaustive exposition is here attempted. There is, however, no more gorgeous vision of the glory of God to be found in the whole of His Book. To Ezekiel, the bard and prophet, there was granted a vision of that glory in the great chariot of Divine movement and life. The vision embraced the creatures of the earth, and the appearances of the heavens. The colors of earth and of heaven were seen. Beryl is translucent and green as earth and sea; sapphire is blue, as of the highest heavens; and over the amber glory in that vision was the appearance as of a Man occupying the highest position. The wheels that turned and went, and the wings that beat the air, were symbolic of the presence of God in every form of nature. *Withersoever the Spirit was to go, they went; thither was the Spirit to go: and the wheels were lifted up beside them; for the Spirit of life was in the wheels* (Ezek. 1:20 margin). Ezekiel was looking at God, so far as man may gaze upon Him. He was beholding the vehicle of the Divine movement, and found that it takes earth and heaven to manifest it. Whether it be in the machinery, the procession, the regular motion of earthly things, or whether it be in the unapproachable and unexplainable light and splendor of the upper world, God is everywhere. Earth's living creatures and heaven's splendors move by the Spirit of God. This is a most inadequate analysis of the vision of that chapter, but it is sufficient to indicate the central truth thereof—that every movement of the wheels of nature, every beat of the wing of created thing, is by the impulse and energy of the Spirit of life.

From the study of these passages it is evident that, as by the power of the Spirit cosmos was produced out of chaos, so by the ever present and active power of the Spirit in the processes of nature cosmos is maintained.

There is yet one more phase of this subject suggested by the apostle Paul: *For the earnest expectation of the creation waiteth for the revealing of the sons of God. For the creation*[*] *was subjected to*

---

[*] The change from *creature* of the Authorized to *creation* of the   [*continued*]

vanity, not of its own will, but by reason of Him Who subjected it, in hope that the creation itself also shall be delivered from the bondage of corruption (Rom. 8:19–21). Paul had no narrow conception of his Master's work. He saw the regenerative work of Jesus, as administered by the Spirit, passing out, not merely into human lives, but into the whole creation.

We know that the whole creation groaneth and travaileth in pain together until now (Rom. 8:22). *We ourselves groan within ourselves* (v. 23). *The Spirit Himself maketh intercession for us with groanings which cannot be uttered* (v. 26).

A trinity of agony is here revealed, nature groaning and travailing in pain; the child of God groaning and waiting for deliverance; and, most wonderful of all, the Spirit of God making intercession with groanings which cannot be uttered.

Thus it is declared that the Spirit is present in creation, and all through creation as a regenerative Force; and ere the work of the Cross of Christ be completed on this planet, every inch of it will be renewed. The whole creation that today *groaneth and travaileth in pain together* will feel the balm, the healing, and the blessing of the work of Christ. Trees and flowers will again realize what they also in some sense have lost by the fall of man. *All the trees of the field shall clap their hands. Instead of the thorn shall come up the fir tree, and instead of the brier shall come up the myrtle tree: and it shall be to the Lord for a name* (Is. 55:12, 13). The Spirit Who created, preserves, energizes, and moves through all nature, is in nature as an intercessory Force—as a Force administrating, by processes which are beyond analysis, the great work of the Christ Himself; and this ministry will eventuate in the removal of the curse from nature, and its consequent renewal, glorious and perfect.

From these seven scriptures certain deductions may be made.

The Holy Spirit is the Director of all order in creation. He is first seen brooding over the primal chaos, and producing order. He is forevermore the Intelligence and Force of all mathematical precision in nature. The old words are still true: *Seedtime and harvest,*

Revised is important. The former word may suggest an individual, the latter embraces all created things.

*and cold and heat, and summer and winter, and day and night shall
not cease* (Gen. 8:22). These processions follow with infinite precision, and mathematical regularity, by the direction of the Holy
Spirit of God. It is by no mere fortuitous accident that morning suc-
ceeds upon night, and that day sinks and nestles into the bosom of
darkness. These things follow because there is an ever-present Spirit
of intelligence, the Spirit of the living God, at work to the utmost
bound of created things.

The Holy Spirit is the Creator of beauty. He is revealed in the
garnishing of the heavens, in the blue of day, and in the darkness of
night with all the splendors of stars scattered in profusion across it.
All these are beautiful, and they appeal to the beautiful in man; for
they were born of God, as man is born of God. Not only is this true
of the beauty which overawes, but also of the form of every leaf and
flower and spire of grass. The stately sweep of the sea and the deli-
cate dome of the dewdrop are alike the outworking of the wisdom
and energy of the Spirit of God. Man, born of the Spirit, in the
grace of transformed life gives evidence of the Spirit's power. So
also, in different degree and kind, but none the less certainly, is it
with the flowers of the field. Put them under microscopic test, and
their exquisiteness and beauty and precision and regularity reveal
the working of the Spirit of God. He in nature not only directs the
order, but creates the varied and varying beauty.

Again, the Spirit is the Breath of renewal. Through death He
ever leads to life. That fact is revealed even in the death of the Son
of God, for it is written that *through the eternal Spirit* He *offered
Himself without blemish unto God* (Heb. 9:14). The Winter wind
that beat upon Him in His dying was but the preface to the Summer wind of Pentecost.

These things are to be seen everywhere in nature because the
self-same Spirit Who works in regeneration works also in generation. This Spirit, the Breath of renewal through death, comes with
manifold glory in the Spring, bringing a renewal of the earth. Winter's cold precedes Spring. Autumn's fire precedes Winter's cold.
Through fire and cold the Spirit ever moves to new life; and the
new forms of beauty, manifold and wondrous, with which the face
of the earth is renewed are His.

To those who live and walk in the Spirit, all creation is seen to be of God. No man can find God through nature, but every man may find nature through God. If man begin with nature, he cannot climb from it to God, but if he begin with God, he may enter into the mystic region, wherein lies true appreciation of the glories and beauties of nature. No man has ever yet seen or understood the beauty of the daisy, save as he has seen that the floweret, blossoming and blooming today, to be trodden underfoot tomorrow, is a part of the work of the same Spirit which is transforming human character and life. The Spirit of God brooded over the chaos and brought forth the cosmos. The Spirit of God has, forevermore, been brooding over nature; and every form of beauty, and every form of order, and every manifestation of renewal are parts of the Divine expression of Himself. All creation is of God, to the man who lives and walks with Him.

One Spirit—His

Who wore the platted thorn with bleeding brows
Rules universal nature! Not a flower
But shows some touch, in freckle, streak, or stain,
Of His unrival'd pencil. He inspires
Their balmy odors, and imparts their hues,
And bathes their eyes with nectar; and includes,
In grains as countless as the seaside sands,
The forms with which He sprinkles all the earth.
Happy who walks with Him, whom what he finds
Of flavor or of scent in fruit or flower,
Or what he views of beautiful or grand
In nature, from the broad majestic oak
To the green blade that twinkles in the sun,
Prompts with remembrance of a present God.

5
The Spirit in Relation to Unfallen Man

A too constant contemplation of man as he is, has resulted in failure to appreciate his original condition. Man today, even at his best, does not realize the full Divine intention. The whole race is suffering from the sin of the past; limitation is to be found everywhere; yet man has endeavored to build up out of the broken fragments of the Divine ideal, an ideal for himself.

In the answer to the Psalmist's question, *What is man, that Thou art mindful of him? And the son of man, that Thou visitest him?* (Ps. 8:4–6).the terms in which man is spoken of are not those of limitation, but those which reveal the perfection of the Divine ideal.

> *For Thou hast made him but little lower than God,*
> *And crownest him with glory and honor.*
> *Thou madest him to have dominion over the works of Thy hands;*
> *Thou hast put all things under his feet:*
> *All sheep and oxen,*
> *Yea, and the beasts of the field;*
> *The fowl of the air, and the fish of the sea,*
> *Whatsoever passeth through the paths of the seas* (Ps. 8:7, 8).

That picture is not fulfilled in the experience of any human being in the present times. There is little about man to suggest that he is but little lower than God—little of the crowning with glory and honor that the Psalmist speaks of; and man has in a large measure lost his dominion. The animal creation is tamed in part, but by far the greater part of it is outside the dominion and the authority of man. The writer of the Letter to the Hebrews claims a partial fulfillment of that ideal of man in the Person of Jesus Christ. He claims the ultimate fulfillment of the whole ideal in the Person and through the work of Christ, but he shows that the larger fulfillment waits for a while. After quoting the Psalm, he proceeds to say: *But now we see not yet all things subjected to Him. But we behold Him Who hath been made a little lower than the angels, even Jesus, because of the suffering of death crowned with glory and honor* (Heb. 2:8, 9). He declares that in the Person of Christ, two of the notes of ideal manhood have been realized: first, *made a little lower than the angels*; secondly, *crowned with glory and honor*. But he has already said, *We see not yet all things subjected to Him*—much lies in the future for fulfillment, but this claiming of the fulfillment of the ideal of the Psalm in the Person of Christ suggests a line of consideration which it is profitable to follow. God's ideal Man and the relation the Spirit of God bears to that Man is discovered by a study of the Person of Christ.

The present inquiry, then, bears upon the ministry of the Spirit in the life of unfallen and ideal man. The consideration is necessarily limited to two examples—Adam and Jesus. The first is valuable in one respect only, as it reveals the essential glory of the creation of man. The life of Adam is not chronicled in detail; and there is therefore no certain knowledge of its character or duration. The relation existing between God's perfect man and the Holy Spirit can only be understood by a study of the life of Jesus.

There are two scriptures which lead into the very heart of the study.

Many persons have a great difficulty about the second account of creation as given in the Book of Genesis (Gen. 2:7). After the apparent completion of the story, at the close of the first chapter, there is a repetition in the second; and a casual observer may imagine that there is not merely repetition, but contradiction. As a matter of fact there is none. The second story is the complement of the first; it is the unfolding of a certain aspect of creation about which nothing was declared in the first.

That reveals three facts:

I. That man was a result of counsel in the Godhead: *Let us make man* (Gen. 1:26).

II. That he was created *in the image of God* (v. 27).

III. That he was given dominion over a previous creation.

In the subsequent story there is an unfolding of his nature. Man is now shown as uniting in his own person the material with the spiritual, the earth with the heavens, the things that perish and pass with the things that abide forever. God made man of the dust of the earth—a material basis—and breathed into him the breath of lives, thus creating a spiritual being. Through that inbreathing by God, the conscious side of man's nature was born, and he *became a living soul* (Gen. 2:7).

The dust which was of the earth was devoid of self-consciousness. Man's power to enter into his new environment, his power to submit to the government under which he was placed, his power to enter into the new companionship, which completed the possibilities of his being—all these were the result of the inbreathing of the Breath of lives by God. Man is not man, apart from the direct ministry and sustaining power of the Spirit of God. Everything that man is, in the essential facts of his being—everything which differentiates between a man and an animal—is due to this peculiar form of inbreathing, whereby man became a conscious soul.

In the illumination of the Breath of God man entered upon a perfect environment. The Garden had been planted by God; the earth had been created by God. Everything that surrounded man, in the moment of his generation, had been prepared by Divine wisdom and infinite tenderness. This being amid the Garden—looking upon the glory of its trees, its plants, its flowers, and all its varied life, comprehending and understanding the whole—is man; and in his powers of comprehension he is distinguished from all lower forms of being, and therein lies his chief glory. He entered thus into the beauty and the glory of his environment, by virtue of the fact that there had been breathed into him the Breath of lives. He was the offspring of God.

In Him was life; and the life was the light of men (John 1:4). The first meaning of this statement is that the living Word of God, the eternal Christ, is the Center and Source of all life. But it also suggests that in man life was different from life anywhere else; in man life became light. There was life in the plant, and life in the lower animals, but when God inbreathed to man the Breath of lives, He bestowed a life in which lay the element of light. In man, creation first looked back into the face of God, and knew Him. No lower form of life knows God. In every flower which decks the sod, there is present the touch of God, but no flower knows it. In all life there are present the power and energy of God; all things live and move and have their being in Him, but apart from man, none are conscious of it. In man life became light, consciousness, knowingness. Man was created to look back into the face of God, and to know Him, to understand in some measure the mystery of His being. Man entered into the perfect environment of the Garden, knew it, appreciated it, and discovered God in it, because there had been inbreathed to him the Breath of lives.

Not only was this inbreathing of light upon his environment; it was, moreover, understanding for his occupation. He was to have dominion over the lower animals, to dress and to keep the Garden. He was able to do this through the inbreathing of the Spirit of life. The energy and the light for wise dominion were the energy and the light of God. The guidance necessary for the further development of the wonderful creation of the earth was provided by the inbreathing of that self-same Spirit.

Man entered not only upon perfect environment, with perfect and sufficient occupation, but he also came under perfect government. *The Lord God commanded the man* (Gen. 2:16) is the statement which marks the Divine sovereignty. Man understood and obeyed the law in the energy of that inbreathing of the Breath of life.

Not only did he enter into environment, occupation, and government, but also into companionship. God made woman to be his companion. He entered into that new relation which created and conditioned the whole social range of human life in the power of that same Breath of lives. When man is thus viewed from the standpoint of original intention as seen in the picture of Edenic beauty and power, it is evident that the natural is spiritual and the spiritual is natural, and that there is no single aspect of human life which is not under the government of the inspiring Spirit of God. Every part of man, the fact of his being, his power to touch his environment with appreciation, his power to follow a daily occupation, his power to submit to government, his power of social relationship and companionship—all are made possible of highest realization by the great inbreathing of God, the work of the Spirit, whereby man becomes *a living soul* (Gen. 2:7).

These are some of the suggestions of the glory of man, gathered from the creation story. They are no more than suggestions, because the story of sin follows quickly thereupon.

Passing over the intervening centuries, as contributing no perfect example of man, the daybreak of the race was reached in the advent of the second Man, Jesus. He was the final and perfect example of ideal human life. *In Him was life; and the life was the light of men* (John 1:4). That is not only a declaration that life becomes light in men; it also claims that the life which is light in man had its most perfect outshining in the Person and character of Christ. It may be said of the Incarnate Word—In Him was life; and His life was the light of men. To know what human life is, He must be known. To have seen Him as the disciples saw Him, was to have seen the perfection of human life in every one of its aspects. In His physical appearance, in His mental life, in His spiritual nature, He was a perfect unveiling of the glory of ideal Manhood.

The art of the great masters seems to have been dominated by a conception of the physical appearance of Jesus which was utterly false. He is represented as pale, thin, wan, emaciated. Perhaps Hoffmann alone has discovered the glory of the beautiful Christ, perfect in form and comeliness, perfect in beauty. Truly it is written of

Him that *His visage was so marred more than any man* (Is. 52:14), but it was the marring of beauty, not of ugliness nor decrepitude. The marks of anguish were evident upon His face, and the lines of sorrow plowed deeply into it, but when the young ruler met Him, fell before Him, and said *Good Master* (Mark 10:17), the exclamation was most probably drawn from him by an overwhelming sense of the beauty and the majesty of the appearance of Christ. Before the surging sorrows of His public ministry rolled over His heart, there is very little room for doubt that He was the most perfectly lovely Man the world had ever gazed upon. Any other conception of Christ dishonors Him. In Him was life, and in Him the life was light; so that men might know, by looking at the Christ, all the beauty and all the glory of the Divine ideal.

This applies also to His mental culture. A sinless soul, living in communion with nature, would understand her to an extent which must be impossible for the sinful one, who attempted to grasp her inner teaching merely on the lines of ordinary study. The men of the synagogue said of Christ, when, after absence from Nazareth, He returned and talked with them: *How knoweth this Man letters, having never learned?* (John 7:15). The emphasis of their question lay, not upon the spiritual teaching of Christ, but upon the illustrations He used, and upon His evident acquaintance with what was then spoken of as learning. It was not that they were overwhelmed by a sense of His spiritual insight; for, then as now, men knew that spiritual insight often belonged to those who had no learning. They were impressed by the beauty of His expression, the wealth of His illustration, and His evident familiarity with those things, to become acquainted with which, men gave themselves up to long courses of study. The mind of Christ was refined, cultured, and beautiful— not through the ordinary process by which limitation and sin endeavor to overcome their deficiencies, but by a pure response to a perfect ideal, and by the inspiring touch and revelation of the Spirit of God.

The relation which existed between this perfect Man of the Gospels and the Spirit, was of the closest. Christ's very existence as a Man was due to the miraculous power of the Holy Spirit. The whole of His perfect Being, spirit, soul, and body, was the creation of the Spirit of God. Therefore, every action of that body, every relation of the body to the mind, and of the mind to the spirit, all the inter-relations of His complex nature, were balanced with the spiritual Power that created them, and were conditioned forevermore by the suggestions, impulses, and energy of that Power.

As Christ passed through childhood and the earlier years of His life, and into those of His mature manhood, all were directed by the Spirit of God. Luke, writing of the time when He went down with His parents from the presentation in the Temple, declares that He *advanced in wisdom and stature, and in favor with God and men* (Luke 2:52). Afterwards, in the course of His public ministry, Jesus said, *Which of you by being anxious can add one cubit unto his stature* (Matt. 6:27). Applying the philosophy of His teaching to His own growth, the fact is clear that His physical growth was the outcome of submission to Divine law, revealed by the inspiration of the Spirit. It is also chronicled that He went down from the Temple with His parents, and was subject to them. That subjection being over, He came forth into public ministry, and with scathing, scorching denunciation testified against the men who excused themselves from caring for the needs of their parents, on the plea that their goods were Corban, or gifts devoted to God. He was angry with them because their action was contrary to Divine law. Subjection to His parents on His part had been a perpetual answer to a perpetual law, written in His heart by the finger of the Spirit of God, as He passed through His boyhood.

How perfectly He was devoted to the law of God as it had been given to His people! He studied it, meditated in it, and became so familiar with it, that when His public ministry began, He knew exactly what it had to teach. In obedience to that law He went up to His Jewish confirmation at the age of twelve, and took His place among the doctors, not, as it is so often represented, as a rude, precocious boy, trying to puzzle old men, but as a sweet boy-disciple, answering their questions with a lucidity which astonished them, and asking them, out of the working of His own pure mind, questions which were amazing, coming from One so youthful. When

He returned to Nazareth, He took up the tools of His reputed father's craft, and mastered their use. Through long years He abode
in that shop, working out the will of God, and revealing in every
piece of carpentry the design and beauty and force of the inspiring
Spirit, by Whom He was created and forevermore sustained.

As the week drew to a close, and the Sabbath came, He went *as
His custom was* (Luke 4:16) to the place of prayer, to worship God
among His people, with His face toward Jerusalem.

All His life, in both its earlier years and maturer manhood, was
conditioned in and by the Spirit, to Whose guidance and direction
He never gave one single moment's slight.

Turning from these earlier years to the account of His public
ministry, Matthew, Mark, Luke, and John give the story of His
anointing with the Spirit for the duties of that ministry. Immediately after the Anointing came the Temptation. Matthew, Mark,
and Luke alike chronicle the fact that He was taken to that Temptation by the Spirit of God. When the Temptation was over, He entered upon the years spent for the most part before the gaze of the
multitudes. Luke declares that He went to that ministry in the
power of the Spirit. He wrought miracles during those three years;
and in his sermon in the house of Cornelius, Peter declared that
these also were performed through the presence with Him of the
Holy Spirit: *Jesus of Nazareth, how that God anointed Him with the
Holy Spirit and with power: Who went about doing good, and healing all that were oppressed of the devil; for God was with Him* (Acts
10:38).

When at last the years of public ministry were ended, and He
went to the exodus of the Cross, He accomplished that in the same
power, for He *through the eternal Spirit offered Himself without
blemish unto God* (Heb. 9:14). After the sojourn in the shades of
darkness He rose again, as Peter declared, through the power and
energy of the Spirit (1 Pet. 3:18). Between His resurrection and ascension He sojourned for a while among His disciples; and during
those days He taught them, organized them, gave them their definite instructions, and this He also did through the Holy Spirit, as
Luke declared in the opening statements of his second treatise: *The*

former treatise I made, O Theophilus, concerning all that Jesus began both to do and to teach, until the day in which He was received up, after that He had given commandment through the Holy Spirit unto the apostles whom He had chosen (Acts 1:1, 2).

The story of the perfect Man of nineteen hundred years ago is the story of a human life, perpetually inspired and energized by the Holy Spirit of God. From birth, through growth, testing, and ministry, on to death and resurrection and the organizing of the apostolate, the whole is a perpetual and unbroken harmony—a harmony created by the moving of the Wind, the Spirit of God, upon the instrument of a perfect human being.

From the glimpse of glory in the first creation, it was evident that creation was of the Spirit; and that the power by which man enters into a perfect environment and occupation, and submits to a perfect government, and continues in the joy of a perfect companionship, is the power of the Breath of lives. This is finally proved by the unfolding of the ideal in the life of Jesus of Nazareth. To know, then, what perfect humanity is, Christ must be known.

Every man's being, in all its complex wonders, exists by the creative energy of the Holy Spirit.

The expressions often used by Paul, *the natural man* and *the spiritual man*, were constantly placed in antithesis. He taught that the natural cannot comprehend the spiritual. A theologian's expressions must be understood in the sense in which he uses them, before his theology can be understood; and this is as true of Paul as of any other theologian. Whenever he spoke of the natural man, he intended to refer to man in the condition resulting from the sin of the race; and therefore, in the higher heights of vision, and in the larger, truer outlook upon humanity, he spoke on such occasions, not of the natural, but of the unnatural. Sin is not natural to man. Men are *shapen in iniquity,* and *go astray as soon as they be born, speaking lies* (Ps. 51:5; 58:3), but the reason for this is that something unnatural has been introduced, which has poisoned every successive generation. The work of the natural Man Jesus is to restore unnatural things to the spiritual, which is the truly natural. No man has discovered the possibilities of his own being, no man understands the glory of his own life, until he has come to see that all he has within himself is of God, save the taint of sin, which has not right to be there, and for the putting away of which the perfect One went into the darkness of His Passion-baptism.

The full and proper use of all the powers of man is made in the energy of the Holy Spirit; and physical health lies within that realm. Here it is necessary to safeguard the position held, even at the cost of repetition. The subject of which this chapter treats is that of ideal man. Under the present order of disciplinary life, sickness is a veritable ministry of infinite love, not only for the sake of those who suffer, but of others, who through their suffering learn more of God, but the man who abides in the will of God, obeys the law of God, and trusts himself wholly to the inspiration of the Spirit of God, that man will touch higher physical conditions than are possible to him apart from such living. That man cannot be compared with another man, because there are many different sets of laws to be considered in any such comparisons, but he may be compared with himself, and, doing this, it may assuredly be declared that, abiding within the realm of the Divine law, his life submitted to the law of the Divine Spirit, he will touch, by such submission and abiding, a higher realm of physical force and power than by any other law of life in which it is possible for him to live.

So also in the mental sphere. Everything that is pure and beautiful in poetry, art, music, and science is the direct outcome of the revealing Spirit of God. Men sometimes affirm that Shakespeare was inspired; and they are right, by no means in the same sense in which the Bible is, but he was inspired nevertheless, and that by the Holy Spirit of God. All pure genius is inspired—not in the same degree as the Scriptures, because not for the same purpose, but by the same Person. All the heights of vision granted to the strong, pure poet, are created for his seeing. Wordsworth, for instance, because he was pure in heart, saw God. All mental magnificence that is pure is an inspiration of the Spirit of God. There may be a prostitution of a Divine gift in this realm also; and a man upon whom God has bestowed the gift of vision, may abuse that gift, and debase it to the purposes of hell. The power to see, whether it be exercised in poetry, art, music, or research, is not born of evil, but is the child of heaven, the flaming, glorious proof of the touch of the Spirit of God upon the mind of man.

Given a man redeemed, regenerated, and wholly possessed by the Spirit, that man has the fullest entrance into all true life. The Divine ideal for man is that he should be spiritual, and that his spirituality should be realized by the surcharging of his whole being with the Spirit of God. That Spirit will turn all the forces of his life into the one direction of true worship. He will employ every power for that purpose for which it was created, and enable a man to worship in the beauty of holiness perpetually. In work and rest, through pathos and humor, by laughter and tears, will be shown, through the Spirit, the glories of creation; and thus God will be glorified in the full life of man.

How far even Christian people are as yet from the realization of this ideal! Toward this the Spirit is working; and at the last there shall not be merely the two men out of all the years as examples of the ideal, but a regenerated humanity, brought into the presence of God by the work of the Savior and of the Spirit, without spot or wrinkle or any such thing.

Book III
The Spirit Prior to Pentecost

Through storm and sun the age draws on
    When heaven and earth shall meet,
For the Lord has said that glorious
    He will make the place of His feet.
And the grass may die on the summer hills,
    The flower fade by the river,
But our God is the same through endless years,
    And His word shall stand forever.

What of the night, O watchman,
    Set to mark the dawn of day?
The wind blows fair from the morning star,
    And the shadows flee away.
Dark are the vales, but the mountains glow
    As the light its splendor flings,
And the Sun of Righteousness comes up
    With healing in His wings.

Shine on, shine on, O blessed Sun,
    Through all the round of heaven,
Till the darkest vale and the farthest isle
    Full to Thy light are given—
Till the desert and the wilderness
    As Sharon's plain shall be,
And the love of the Lord shall fill the earth
    As the waters fill the sea.

Sunday Afternoon Verses
(W. ROBERTSON NICOLL)

6

The Work of the Spirit
from the Fall to the Messiah

By an act of willful rebellion man distanced himself from God, and was alienated from the life of God (Eph. 4:18). The grace of the Divine heart immediately announced a reconciliation. No sooner was sin committed than there was declared the purpose of grace and love, not in detail and in fullness, but in a promise that came to be understood more fully as the ages rolled. Speaking to the enemy, God said: *It shall bruise thy head, and thou shalt bruise His heel* (Gen. 3:15). Necessarily the processes of that reconciliation have been slow, and even yet are not fully and finally accomplished. The Divine love outran in its utterance the actual accomplishment of its purposes. All the arrangements of the old dispensation for the approach of man to God by way of sacrifice were based upon the coming sacrifice of Jesus Christ. The blood of bulls and of goats and the ashes of a heifer never took sin away, but they did help men, amid the twilight in which they lived and worshiped, to understand the principle of sacrifice, without which there could be no remission of sins. In the plan of God, the Lamb slain was the way of reconciliation; and although the Son of His love could not be manifested until *the fullness of the time* (Gal. 4:4), yet for the sake of man, and in the purpose of God, the Lamb was slain *from the foundation of the world* (Rev. 13:8).

The glorious announcement of New Testament ministry is contained in the words, *God was in Christ reconciling the world unto Himself* (2 Cor. 5:19), *but* He was so in purpose, long before the historical fact was accomplished, upon which the larger, fuller dispensation should depend.

The Fatherhood of God was a fact before the coming of Jesus. He illuminated it for men, so that since His coming they have understood it as never before. Though men had wandered and lost their sense of relationship, God was ever their Father, and His presence their home. Even in those old days, before the full light of the glory of God had shone upon man's pathway in the face of the Christ, there were souls who discovered the fact of the Fatherhood, and passed their days homed in God. The same law of procedure is discoverable also with reference to the work of the Holy Spirit.

The whole being of man was conditioned in the energy and the wisdom of that Spirit. The knowledge of this fact man had lost by reason of his sin; and the Spirit, resisted, was separated from the actualities of human life. From the moment of the Fall a new form of His ministry began, which was partial, occasional, special, and prophetic of the great dispensation to be ushered in, when the true light of sacrifice had made plain the way for the clearer apprehension of Fatherhood.

The present age is pre-eminently the dispensation of the Holy Spirit, in which He has a specific work, differing from that of preceding ages. This work is based upon the work of Christ, and was impossible until He had finished that work and ascended on high.

It must, however, be remembered that in the past the Spirit had not a constant ministry. The differences between then and now are most clearly defined. Until after the death, resurrection, and ascension of Christ, the Spirit is not spoken of as creating a Church by His own abiding indwelling. Neither is He spoken of as the one direct and only Administrator of the affairs of such a body. And yet again, He is not spoken of as a Sanctifier. All the other aspects of the Spirit's work are found—not continually and perpetually, and in an abiding sense, as they are today, but as special occasions demanded.

There is also this important distinction between the old, and new dispensations. In the old, the Spirit came upon and filled men for specific work without reference to character. In the new, after the accomplishment of the work of the Cross, this is never so. His filling for service always depends upon His application of the work of the Savior for cleansing and holiness.

Certain phrases of Old Testament Scripture reveal both the methods and character of the Spirit's work during those long centuries.

He is spoken of as coming upon men, as coming mightily upon men, as abiding in men, and as filling certain men for specific work.

There may be a great many subdivisions of the eighty-eight passages in which the Holy Spirit is directly mentioned in the Old Testament,* but, broadly stated, the method of the Spirit is marked by these four statements. It is not stated that He came upon, nor that He came mightily upon the whole nation; nor, again, is it affirmed that He abode in or filled the whole nation. In that fact lies the difference between the old dispensation and the new. At Pentecost the Spirit came upon all, He came mightily upon all, He came to abide in all, He came to fill all. There may be many members of the Church of Jesus Christ who have not realized in their own experience all this fourfold work of the Spirit, but that is not to be laid to the charge of the economy of grace, but rather to the failure of such persons to realize the purpose of God.

The Spirit fell upon Gideon (Judg. 6:34). He had in his own home and family broken down the altar of Baal, in order that he might make a protest against idolatry; and after he had done this *the Spirit came upon him.*

David was doubtful as to the loyalty of Benjamin and Judah. *Then the Spirit came upon Amasai* (1 Chr. 12:18), and he spoke words which convinced David of the loyalty of these tribes.

---

* Dr. Elder Cumming, in his book, *Through the Eternal Spirit,* has compiled a catena of passages in which the Holy Spirit is directly mentioned in the Bible. In the Old Testament there are eighty-eight passages in all.

Zechariah, the son of Jehoiada, the priest, was raised up to protest against idolatry in the holy places; and, in order that he might do it, *the Spirit of God came upon him* (2 Chr. 24:20).

Upon these three men the Spirit came for very different reasons: upon Gideon, after he had broken down the altar of Baal, and in order that he might become the leader of the people to victory; upon Amasai, in order that the loyalty of two tribes might be believed by the king; upon Zechariah, in order that he might utter a protest against idolatry.

The same thought lies within each—*the Spirit came upon them.* The Hebrew word literally means that the Spirit clothed Himself with them—not that the Spirit fell upon them as an anointing, but the Spirit took hold of them, passed into them, and made them the instruments through which He accomplished His work. The thought conveyed to the mind of the Hebrew reader is, that the Spirit clothed Himself with Gideon, the Spirit clothed Himself with Amasai, the Spirit clothed Himself with Zechariah. Here there is a revelation of one of the methods of the Spirit under that dispensation. For the doing of a special work, for the delivery of a special message, for the announcement of the immediate purpose of God, the Spirit clothed Himself with a man, and the Divine energy moved out in speech and in deed; so that through the man was known the will of God, and seen the power of God. These are three instances out of many in which men became the clothing of the Spirit. The distinction must be observed: it was not that these men were clothed with the Spirit, but that the Spirit clothed Himself with them for the doing of specific work.

Take the second thought. The Spirit of God *came mightily upon* Samson (Judg. 14:6), and he slew a lion. Saul joined a company of the prophets; the *Spirit of God came mightily upon him, and he prophesied* (1 Sam. 10:10). Samuel poured the anointing oil upon David, and the Spirit *came mightily upon* him (1 Sam. 16:13).

In these cases an entirely different word is used. It is not said that the Spirit clothed Himself with them, but that the Spirit came upon them; and the thought is that of forcing forward, or pushing. The literal meaning of the word is, that the Spirit attacked these men, came upon them with compulsion, forced them forward to a certain activity. Under the compulsion of the Spirit, Samson slew the lion, Saul joined the prophets and uttered words of prophecy, and David went forward to the work of governing the people. How different is the manifestation of the power! The slaying of a lion, the uttering of the truth of God, and the governing of the people, but in each case the action was under the impulse of the same Spirit.

There are two passages in the Old Testament where it is said that the Spirit dwelt in men. Pharaoh said that in Joseph there dwelt the Spirit of God, and that therefore he was discreet and wise (Gen. 41:38, 39). When a successor to Moses was needed for the government and leading of the people, Joshua was chosen because in him dwelt the Spirit of God (Num. 27:18).

Whether Pharaoh understood his own expression may be very doubtful, but it is certainly worthy of note that in each of the cases cited, the Spirit of God created fitness for government; and this fitness consisted, not in autocratic, tyrannous power, but in discretion, wisdom, gentleness, and beauty of demeanor. Such were the manifestations of the indwelling of the Spirit in these men under the old covenant.

Once again, the Spirit filled certain men; and that expression is only used in connection with the work of the making of the Tabernacle. The Spirit of God filled Bezalel that he might have cunning *to work in gold, and in silver, and in brass, and in cutting of stones for setting, and in carving of wood, to work in all manner of workmanship* (Ex. 31:4, 5). Thus the whole of the work of the Tabernacle, in its exquisite perfection and in its glorious beauty, was the outshining of the wisdom of the Holy Spirit. No man was glorified in that upreared Tabernacle. Perhaps it was otherwise in the times of decadence, but men of spiritual intelligence, who in the early days looked upon the work of the Tabernacle, would not say, *See how cunning a workman was Bezalel,* but rather, *See how wondrously the Spirit of God has wrought through Bezalel, in the accomplishment of the Divine purpose.*

These illustrations go to show that the Holy Spirit was always interested in and working among men; that He did not abide with them, but that, for special purposes and at special points in their history, He equipped them for whatever the particular moment demanded.

As to the character of the Spirit's work through all these years, there is a wonderful development of revelation, concerning the ministry of the Spirit, discoverable in the character of His work as time proceeded: *And it came to pass, when men began to multiply on the face of the ground, and daughters were born unto them, that the sons of God saw the daughters of men that they were fair; and they took them wives of all that they chose* (Gen. 6:1, 2). There were two distinct ideals of life upon the earth, embodied in the seed of Adam through Cain and through Seth respectively, the seventh generation of the one culminating in Lamech, the man who, having committed murder, composed poetry in defense of his sin; and the seventh generation of the other culminating in Enoch, a man of whom it is written that he *walked with God* (Gen. 5:22). Much speculation has been rife concerning the intermarriage of the sons of God and the daughters of men. The exposition of the passage that is most probably correct, is that which treats this intermarriage, as having taken place between people who were godly and those who were godless — between the descendants of Seth and those of Cain. Be that as it may, the condition of things upon the earth had reached a point which is revealed in the words: *My Spirit shall not strive with man forever, for that he also is flesh* (Gen. 6:3). This is, moreover, a revelation of the work of the Spirit of God in the years from the Fall to the Flood. He was striving with men, convicting them of sin.

Then followed another manifestation of the Spirit in history. The chosen people were being organized for the embodiment of a Divine purpose, and as the medium of a Divine revelation; and the Spirit came upon certain men for the carrying out of all the details necessary to the perfecting of the organization. Then, again, in the passages referred to, concerning Samson, Saul, and David, the Spirit of God is seen manifesting Himself as a Spirit of strength. A period of conflict had come in the history of the chosen people, a race of heroes was needed for the accomplishment of Divine purposes among the nations, and deeds of daring that characterized the period were wrought in the power of the Spirit. Men were raised up to do these deeds of heroism by the Spirit falling mightily upon them.

The prophetic books yield yet another manifestation of the presence and work of the Spirit, and that a most interesting one. Both in Isaiah and in Ezekiel there are fifteen distinct references to the Holy Spirit, which for the most part can only have their fulfillment in the present dispensation or in one which is yet to come. Those days were characterized by the failure of kings and priests to fulfill their several vocations. The kings had become entangled with the idol worship of their heathen neighbors; the priests, smitten with the leprosy of the same unfaithfulness, had been superseded by the prophets. These men, devoted only to the will of God, found nothing amid the decadence of the time to satisfy their hearts and minister to their spiritual well-being. But they were men of vision; and beyond the clouds and the mists they saw the gleam of another day, and they foretold the coming of the Spirit in plenitude and in power. An instance of these foretellings is the prophecy of Joel, which Peter quoted upon the Day of Pentecost, to emphasize the historic value of what men saw passing around them. Amid the darkness and the gloom which had fallen upon the nation, the Spirit of God became the Spirit of hope; so that the essential principles of life were not forgotten.

The Spirit of God was the Spirit of conviction while sin worked itself out from Fall to Flood; He was a Spirit of detailed service while the people of God were being organized into a nationality; He was a Spirit of strength while the people were fighting for the land, and were casting out those who had deeply sinned; and He became a Spirit of hope when the peculiar people had passed into a condition of apostasy and wandering. He lit the horizon with the glow of approaching day. He spoke to ears that listened, and revealed to eyes that gazed; and thus, though they did not perfectly understand, men had some dim foreshadowing of the glories of these days of fullness of spiritual power.

Such is a very rapid summary of the work of the Spirit in that whole period from the Fall to the Messiah.[*]

No clear view of present-day aspects of the Spirit's ministry is possible apart from a just and clear conception of His place in history. The Spirit Who brooded over chaos, and Who breathed into nature the life which blushes and blooms into beauty in every branch and leaf and flower—that same Spirit has always been interested in the affairs of men. There is, however, a very distinct difference between the method of His work in those bygone days, and the method of His work today. In those days there was no Church. To speak of the Israelitish nation as a Church in the sense in which that word is used today is to show no true understanding of what the Church really is. Consequently there was no direct, present, actual demonstration of the Spirit to the nation. Most wonderful of all, Old Testament times knew nothing of the Holy Spirit as the Sanctifier of individual lives, in the New Testament sense of cleansing and keeping. Of course Old Testament saints might have sung as truthfully as the saints of the new covenant:

> And every virtue we possess,
>   And every victory won,
> And every thought of holiness
>   Are His alone.

The measure of His work, however, was very different; and the sanctification which embodies all virtue, ensures perpetual victory, and subjects every thought to the obedience of Christ, which is holiness, was unknown. These wonderful manifestations of His power were reserved for the present dispensation. It is full of delightful interest to trace the work of the Spirit through the centuries, preparing the way for the coming of the Christ, until the great moment came which was the fullness of the time. Over all the movements of

---

[*] A small booklet by my beloved and lamented friend the Rev. G. H. C. Macgregor, M.A., entitled *Things of the Spirit*, contains the whole of the passages bearing upon this subject, and thus affords a valuable aid to a careful study of the story of the presence of the Spirit of God among men from the Fall to the days of Jesus.

men the Spirit brooded still, coming as a Spirit of conviction of sin, and as a Spirit of special wisdom for definite service, and yet again as a Spirit of strength for conflict, and continually as a Spirit of hope amid decadence. Thus the things of God were made known amid men, in the measure necessary and possible, by that Spirit of God, Who, within the mystery of the Deity, is the Consciousness of God, and the Revealer of that Deity to man.

7

The Work of the Spirit during the Mission of the Messiah

During the days of Israel's decay, the Spirit, through the prophets, had spoken of the coming One. Hope had been preserved in the heart of the nation through the visions of future glory contained in the wonderful words that had been uttered by the messengers of the King. Even these voices had been silent for nearly four hundred years, from the days of Malachi to those of John the Baptist. During that period, however, a small remnant had kept the hope of Israel brightly burning, by loyalty to the principles of government which had been so often declared.

At last the long silence was broken by John, who announced the advent of One Whose distinguishing work should be that of baptizing men with the Holy Spirit and with fire. To the vast crowds that gathered upon the banks of the Jordan he said: *I indeed baptize you with water, but there cometh He that is mightier than I, the latchet of Whose shoes I am not worthy to unloose: He shall baptize you with the Holy Spirit and with fire* (Luke 3:16). As the Spirit bore a close relation to Jesus as perfect and unfallen Man, so also did He to the office and work of the Messiah. At the commencement of His ministry the Lord claimed as His own the sacred anointing of the Holy Spirit for the fulfillment of His mission:

The Spirit of the Lord is upon Me, because He anointed Me to preach good tidings to the poor: He hath sent Me to proclaim release to the captives, and recovering of sight to the blind, to set at liberty them that are bruised, to proclaim the acceptable year of the Lord. . . .
And He began to say unto them, Today hath this scripture been fulfilled in your ears (Luke 4:18, 19, 21).

The Spirit brooded over the chaos of old, the power of God in creation; the Spirit had been present through all the history of the race, coming specially upon men, for special purposes as God willed. Now that the new dispensation was to be ushered in, and the new order initiated, as the Master began that work which He has not yet completed, but towards the completion of which He is still working, He claimed that the Spirit rested upon Him, as the anointing for His mission. The Lord's view of His own mission is revealed in this quotation. He is anointed

To preach good tidings to the poor:
To proclaim release to the captives,
And recovering of sight to the blind,
To set at liberty them that are bruised,
To proclaim the acceptable year of the Lord.

Standing in the synagogue, reading the words of the prophet, claiming their fulfillment in His own Person, He initiated that new age described by the prophet as *the acceptable year of the Lord.*

The whole of this preparatory work of Jesus Christ was accomplished under the guidance and in the power of the Spirit. The anointing took place at His baptism: Now it came to pass, when all the people were baptized, that, Jesus also having been baptized, and praying, the heaven was opened, and the Holy Spirit descended in a bodily form, as a dove, upon Him, and a voice came out of heaven, Thou art My beloved Son; in Thee I am well pleased (Luke 3:21, 22).

Immediately afterwards He was led by the Spirit in the Temptation experiences: And Jesus, full of the Holy Spirit, returned from the Jordan, and was led by the Spirit in the wilderness (Luke 4:1).

Following this, He entered upon His public work in the power of the Spirit: *And Jesus returned in the power of the Spirit into Galilee* (v. 14).

There is a clearly marked sequence here. Anointed by the Spirit, full of the Spirit, led by the Spirit, in the power of the Spirit—thus He entered upon the specific work of His Messiahship.

During the exercise of that Messiahship He uttered words to His disciples upon one occasion which demand special attention: *If ye then, being evil, know how to give good gifts unto your children, how much more shall your heavenly Father give the Holy Spirit to them that ask Him?* (Luke 11:13). If it were possible to occupy the actual position of the men who heard these words, it would also be possible to understand how startling a statement it was. They knew what the Scriptures of the Old Testament had to teach about the Holy Spirit. They thought of Him as coming on special men for special work, by the direct giving of God apart from human seeking. The thought of asking for the Spirit was absolutely foreign to the whole economy of the past. The circumstances under which Jesus made this statement must be carefully noted. The disciples had watched Him at prayer, and, being attracted by something in His attitude or appearance, said to Him: *Lord, teach us to pray* (v. 1). He immediately gave them a perfect pattern known as the Lord's Prayer, but more correctly spoken of as the disciples' prayer. He then proceeded to teach them, by analogy, how that God was always waiting to answer importunate prayer. He used a contrast to teach the truth, showing how a friend who is unwilling to rise from rest to supply the necessity of another will do so if that other be importunate enough and continue his asking. He summed up the whole thought of importunate prayer in those words that pulsate with meaning: *Ask—seek—knock* (Luke 11:9).

He then led them along another line of thought concerning prayer; and using the relationship of a father to a child as illustration, He declared God's willingness to give the best gifts to men: *If ye then, being evil, know how to give good gifts unto your children, how much more shall your heavenly Father give the Holy Spirit to them that ask Him?* (v. 13). Their request to be taught how to pray

resulted in their hearing the most startling announcement concerning spiritual matters that had ever fallen upon their ears. They
were told that if they asked of God with importunity, and understanding that God would give good gifts only, then they might have
the Holy Spirit.

This statement must have so staggered these men as to surprise
them almost into inaction; for it is evident that they never asked for
the Spirit, and therefore never received Him in answer to their own
asking. This text is perpetually quoted as having a present-day application. This is due to a failure to draw the line of distinction between the various phases of the Master's mission. The words were
spoken to a handful of Jewish disciples gathered around the Jewish
Messiah. He was unveiling to them a great secret in all God's dealings with men—that God would give the Holy Spirit to men who
asked, if they did so according to the law of prayer laid down. There
is not, however, any evidence that they ever had the Holy Spirit,
until that Spirit came along another line of communication. Before the Master left them He said: *I will make request of the Father,
and He shall give you another Comforter . . . the Spirit of truth* (John
14:16 margin.).

On the previous occasion He had said in effect, Ask, and ye shall
receive the Spirit, but they did not ask, and did not receive. They
never truly saw Christ, nor understood His mission, nor entered
into the deep underlying secrets of His life, until after the Spirit
had come upon them in answer to His asking. Our Lord here revealed to them the will of God, the attitude of the Divine heart, the
preparedness of the Father to bestow the wondrous gift of the Holy
Spirit upon them, but there is no evidence whatever that they ever
asked or ever received in answer to their own asking.

One of the most difficult passages to translate, perhaps, in the
whole of the Gospel of Luke is the one which reads: *I came to cast
fire upon the earth; and what will I, if it is already kindled? But I
have a baptism to be baptized with; and how am I straitened till it be
accomplished!* (12:49, 50). The *if* marks the sigh of desire. A paraphrase of the passage may contribute to its elucidation: *I came to
cast fire upon the earth; and what will I? Would that it were already*

kindled! The old acceptation of the verse is most incorrect: I came to cast fire upon the earth; and what will I, if already I find that fire kindled? The passage is a soliloquy? Jesus turned from teaching His disciples, and it seems as though He lifted His eyes and looked out upon the necessities of men, and said: I came to cast fire upon the earth; and what will I? If it were already kindled! or, Would that it were already kindled! Then He proceeded: I have a baptism to be baptized with; and how am I straitened till it be accomplished! As though He had said it was impossible for Him to cast this fire, as He desired, until He had Himself passed through the baptism that awaited Him.

This scattering of fire refers to the baptism of the Holy Spirit which John had already predicted: *I indeed baptize you with water, but there cometh He that is mightier than I, the latchet of Whose shoes I am not worthy to unloose: He shall baptize you with the Holy Spirit and with fire* (Luke 3:16).

In the Acts of the Apostles is chronicled the Master's own Reference after His resurrection to that statement of John: *John indeed baptized with water, but ye shall be baptized with the Holy Spirit not many days hence* (Acts 1:5).

In connection with the baptism of the Spirit at Pentecost it is recorded: *There appeared unto them tongues parting asunder, like as of fire; and it sat upon each one of them* (Acts 2:3). Fire was the symbol of the Spirit, purifying and energizing. Jesus took up the thought of John: John baptized with water, He with fire.

In the light of these passages, it is evident that the fire referred to is that of the Spirit which Christ was waiting to scatter upon the earth, and He declared that until His Passion-baptism was accomplished He was unable to fulfill this purpose.

Jesus, anointed by the Spirit, led by the Spirit, full of the Spirit, was waiting to communicate to other men that fullness which resided in Himself, but He was unable to do this until the Cross was an accomplished fact.

That reveals the character of the years of our Lord's ministry. He was laying foundations, laying them deep and strong, upon the righteousness of God in His own life; He was preparing for the tremendous transactions of the Day of Pentecost, and for all that should follow therefrom. Filled with the Spirit, led by the Spirit, He looked upon men with eyes all lit by tender love, and longed to communicate to them this gift of an indwelling Spirit, yet was unable to scatter the fire until His atoning work was done.

During these years of public life our Lord gave teaching concerning the Holy Spirit which has only been thoroughly understood and valued since He passed through the gateway of death into the larger life beyond. All that it is necessary for men to know about the operation of the Spirit in this dispensation Jesus Christ Himself declared; and this teaching occupied a most important place in His ministry. It is found wholly within the Gospel of John,* and may be divided into two parts—that which is indirect and suggestive, and that which is direct and positive. The indirect and suggestive teaching of Jesus fell from His lips upon different occasions—once to the woman of Samaria, once to a company of Jews, once to the crowds of people who thronged the streets at the Feast of Tabernacles. The direct teaching of Jesus was given, to His disciples only, in the Paschal discourses. These were the last utterances of Christ to them, and contain a perfect statement concerning the work of the Spirit.

In the indirect teaching of Christ, the first instance is that of His conversation with the woman of Samaria: *Jesus answered and said unto her, Everyone that drinketh of this water shall thirst again: but whosoever drinketh of the water that I shall give him shall never thirst, but the water that I shall give him shall become in him a well of water springing up unto eternal life* (John 4:13, 14). The woman had no clear understanding of the depth of that message, nor had

---

* Every reference made in this chapter—and this is not an accident; it is the result of careful analysis of the whole teaching of Christ—is taken from the writings of Luke or of John. There is scarcely anything recorded by Matthew or Mark of the relation of the Spirit to Christ in His work. Matthew views Christ purely as a Jewish Messiah, and necessarily omits the glory of the larger outlook. Mark views Him as a Servant, and sees Him stripped of all supernatural power, but Luke, the Gospel of the universal Savior, and John, the Gospel of a Divine Lord and Master, contain the revelation of the secret forces that made his ministry.

those who heard it from her lips. In common with other words of Christ, it has only come to be understood in the light of the Spirit's dispensation. The water which He gives is the living water of the Spirit, perpetually springing up in the soul of man unto eternal life.

Another statement is contained in a discourse to the Jews directed against materialistic conceptions of communion with God. He declared that it is only in the realm of the spiritual that this communion can be maintained: *I am the Bread of life: he that cometh to Me shall not hunger, and he that believeth on Me shall never thirst* (John 6:35).

The third and last was uttered on the great day of the feast, and is a beautiful statement concerning the ministry of the Spirit and the relation of man to that ministry: *Now on the last day, the great day of the feast, Jesus stood and cried, saying, If any man thirst, let him come unto Me, and drink. He that believeth on Me, as the Scripture hath said, out of his belly shall flow rivers of living water* (John 7:37, 38). Then follows John's inspired exposition of those words: *But this spake He of the Spirit, which they that believed on Him were to receive: for the Spirit was not yet given; because Jesus was not yet glorified* (v. 39).

For this He was preparing by doing a work which would arrest the attention of men and call for their faith; and He declared that men responding to that demand, and exercising faith in Himself, should enter into a new region of life, in which their own personal thirst should be quenched, and out of them flow rivers of living water. All this is condensed truth about the Spirit, uttered by Christ during His life, and only fully understood in the light of subsequent events.

The Paschal discourses are too important to be dismissed hurriedly, and therefore will be considered in following chapters. It will be sufficient here to state their nature. The One of Whom the Spirit was to speak, spoke of the Spirit, by the Spirit. The Spirit's mission is to unfold the glories of the Christ; and men know this to be the case, because the Christ unfolded the glory of the Spirit. There is the most wonderful communion between Son and Spirit revealed in this teaching.

The last point of importance in this connection is the prophetic breathing of the Spirit upon men by Jesus Christ: *Jesus therefore said to them again, Peace be unto you: as the Father hath sent Me, even so send I you. And when He had said this, He breathed on them, and saith unto them, Receive ye the Holy Spirit: whose soever sins ye forgive, they are forgiven unto them; whose soever sins ye retain, they are retained* (John 20:21–23). The place these words occupied in the work of Jesus must be considered, if they are rightly to be understood. He had risen; the Passion-baptism was over. He could no longer say: I have a baptism to be baptized with: and how am I straitened! He had been baptized with that baptism, He was no longer straitened in the same sense, but He had not yet ascended into the presence of God. Not until He had actually taken His place in the heavenlies, in the double right of life and death, standing for Himself in the power of a perfect life, and for us in the power of an atoning death—not until He had represented men in the presence-chamber of the King, could He shed forth that great gift of fire which He had come to scatter upon them.

The former treatise I made, O Theophilus, concerning all that Jesus began both to do and to teach, until the day in which He was received up, after that He had given commandment through the Holy Spirit unto the apostles whom He had chosen (Acts 1:1, 2). For forty days He tarried, giving them commandments, and it is very wonderful to notice that the risen Christ worked in the energy of the Spirit. He gave these men their commandments through the Holy Spirit; and, among other things, He stood in their midst and breathed upon them. The explanation of that act is to be found in what He said immediately before: *As the Father hath sent Me, even so send I you. And when He had said this, He breathed on them* (John 20:21, 22). He declared the law of continuity of service, that these men were to pick up the threads of the work that He had Himself been doing, and were to weave them into warp and woof, until the whole perfect fabric should be completed. *As the Father hath sent Me, even so send I you.* He had been sent anointed with the Spirit; and now He breathed on His disciples, and said: Receive ye the Holy Spirit. As the Father hath sent Me, even so send I you.

He had been sent by the Father in the power of the Spirit, and He sent them in the power of that self-same Spirit.

That this breathing of Christ was a prophetic act is proved by the subsequent facts. Before He ascended He told them that they were not to go, but to tarry until they were endued with power from on high. It was a prophetic breathing. His Passion-baptism was over; He stood among His followers—the little band chosen to carry on His victories and do His work; and, looking at them, He said: *As the Father hath sent Me, even so send I you. . . . Receive ye the Holy Spirit* (John 20:21, 22). It was a typical act, suggesting the power in which they were to go to the work He committed to them.

The whole subject may thus be summarized. The day of new power and of new light was prepared by the ministry of the Son of God and the Son of Man. The light and the glory of the Gospel were created in the mysterious energy, suffering, and agony of the life of the God-man. The Spirit Who brooded over the chaos, Who had visited men, Who had always been interested in men, and Who had ever carried out the work of God among men, came upon Christ, dwelt in Him, energized Him, and prepared, in His Person, for a larger dispensation. Through His life the Spirit prepared for that death of mystery, as the result of which the Spirit should pass into the life of men, for pardon, purity, and power.

Book IV
The Teaching of Christ
Concerning the Spirit

Weary and sad and sorrow-spent were they
    In that still upper room,
While the rich crimson of the closing day
    Was fading into gloom;
And over all, benumbing soul and sense,
Hung the cold shadow of a dread suspense.

The promise of a Spirit yet to come,
    That other Paraclete,
To lead them on to Truth's eternal home
    And guide their wandering feet;
They could not soothe the anguish of their heart,
They ask'd in sadness, *Must their Lord depart?*

Yes, after all, or clear and open speech,
    Or sayings dark and dim,
They yet had much to learn and He to teach,
    Ere they could rest in Him,
Ere they could preach His words with cleansed lips,
Or He impart His full Apocalypse.

E. H. PLUMPTRE

8
The Coming of the Spirit

The little group of men who had followed the Lord during the years of His public ministry gathered about Him at the Paschal board. Judas had left the company. The others were filled with sadness. It is not necessary to attempt an analysis of their sorrow. Probably there was a great deal of selfishness mixed with it, but there is selfishness in all sorrow, save that which is under the constraint of the Holy Spirit. The shadow of approaching separation fell upon them. The Master administered comfort to their hearts. He told them that He was going away, but they were not to be left comfortless, or, as the word really is, orphans. This statement He explained by unfolding for them the great principles of the new dispensation of the Holy Spirit. He gave them a system of teaching on the coming, character, and mission of the Spirit, with the results following—a system which is clear, concise, and sufficient.

His first statement concerning the coming of the Spirit[*] is contained in the words: *And I will pray the Father, and He shall give you another Comforter, that He may be with you forever* (John 14:16). The Holy Spirit is to be the gift of the Father through the Son.

The marginal reading in the Revised Version is, *I will make request of the Father,* but neither rendering perfectly conveys the

---

[*] In this section, by *the coming of the Spirit,* His advent on the Day of Pentecost to usher in a dispensation is referred to.

thought that underlies the word that Jesus used. The conversation of Martha with Jesus, when Lazarus lay dead, throws light on this word: *And even now I know that, whatsoever Thou shalt ask of God, God will give Thee* (John 11:22). Martha used a word for prayer, the word translated *ask*, which Jesus constantly used when speaking of the prayers of other persons, but never of His own prayers. It is a word that conveys the idea of asking as a beggar, as a pauper; and that is how men always pray. The word translated *pray* here is a special one, never used about prayer except in the Gospel of John, and always in that Gospel concerning the prayers of Jesus Christ. This reveals the fact that the prayers of Christ differed from those of other persons. The word suggests, not the petition of someone that asks for something as a favor, but the petition of one who is on a perfect equality with the person to whom it is presented. The thought has within it the idea of perfect fellowship. Perhaps that is better conveyed by the translation: *I will inquire of the Father, and He shall give you another Comforter* (John 14:16). This is by no means a perfect translation, but it approximates more closely to the intention of the original word than either of the other phrases. Christ declared that He was going to the Father, and that He would inquire of, in the sense of conversing or having fellowship with the Father, and, as the direct result, the Father would send them the Holy Spirit. Jesus, the Jewish Messiah, had said to His disciples: *If ye then, being evil, know how to give good gifts unto your children, how much more shall your Father which is in heaven give good things to them that ask Him?* (Matt. 7:11). That was a purely dispensational and Jewish statement; and the men never asked and never received. Now that the Master was leaving them, He said to them: *I will ask, I will inquire of, I will pray the Father, and He shall give you.*

Immediately these great discourses were ended, Christ moved into a higher realm, that of intercession; and John records His words in the presence of God for His people. In that prayer the Lord did not mention the Holy Spirit. The reason for this is found in the fact that the prayer for the Holy Spirit could not be offered until His Passion was an accomplished fact. He could not ask for the Spirit save upon the basis of a perfect fellowship, based upon a finished work, until—no longer straitened—He should stand in the presence of God. Then, in response to the presence in the highest place of the One Who had accomplished the work, God would give.

The teaching then, of this first statement of Christ, concerning the coming of the Spirit, is that the Spirit is the gift of the Father, through the Son, upon the basis of His finished work. In that lies one point of difference between this dispensation and all that have preceded it. The Spirit came upon men in the past for specific purposes, at special seasons, but the Son of His love passed into the presence of God, having accomplished the Divine purpose, and upon the basis of that finished work the Spirit was poured out.

Concerning the Spirit's coming, the Master also said: *These things have I spoken unto you, while yet abiding with you. But the Comforter, even the Holy Spirit, Whom the Father will send in My name, He shall teach you all things* (John 14:25, 26). This reveals that the Spirit is to be the Messenger of the Father in the name of the Son.

Of His own coming Jesus said, *I am come in My Father's name* (John 5:43), and, *I told you, and ye believe not: the works that I do in My Father's name, these bear witness of Me* (John 10:25). Upon two occasions He distinctly stated that He came and worked in His Father's name, that the name of God was the sphere of His work. Now He declared: *The Holy Spirit, Whom the Father will send in My name, He shall teach you all things.* As the Son came in the name of the Father, and as the name of the Father was the sphere of the work of the Son, so the Spirit was to come in the name of the Son, and the name of the Son was to be the sphere of the Spirit's work. This is perfect continuity.

A third statement on this subject is contained in the words: *But when the Comforter is come, Whom I will send unto you from the Father* (John 15:26). This declares the Spirit to be the Messenger of the Son, from the Father.

This reference can only be understood by looking at its context: *He that hateth Me hateth My Father also. If I had not done among them the works which none other did, they had not had sin: but now have they both seen and hated both Me and My Father. But this cometh to pass, that the word may be fulfilled that is written in their*

*law, They hated Me without a cause. But when the Comforter is
come, Whom I will send unto you from the Father, even the Spirit of
truth, which proceedeth from the Father, He shall bear witness of Me*
(vv. 23–26). Jesus had lived among men, unknown, misunderstood
—men had hated Him; and now the Spirit was to be sent by the
Son, as from the Father, in vindication of the character, ministry,
and mission of the Son.

Yet one other declaration follows: *Nevertheless I tell you the
truth; It is expedient for you that I go away: for if I go not away, the
Comforter will not come unto you, but if I go, I will send Him unto
you* (John 16:7). Thus the Spirit is directly the Messenger and Gift
of the Son. He will Himself send the Spirit to His disciples upon
the basis of His union with the Father, a union consummated as
God and Man. He will send the Spirit, in virtue of His ascended
Manhood, and the perpetual reception of that Manhood into the
Godhead.

To sum up. Jesus inquired of the Father, and in answer to the inquiry of the Christ, God gave the Spirit. The Spirit became the Messenger of the Father; and His sphere of work was to be the name of
the Son. This Spirit became God's Messenger concerning the Son,
vindicating His work and His teaching. By virtue of the perfect
union of the Son with the Father, the Spirit is the gift of the Son.

9

The Character of the Spirit

T he teaching of Christ concerning the character of the Spirit
is set forth first in the words: *And I will pray the Father, and
He shall give you another Comforter* (John 14:16). This word
Comforter conveys the first thought concerning the character of the
Spirit. It is indeed impossible to find a translation that will reveal
everything contained within the great word *Paraclete*. It is conceded
that originally the word had what may be spoken of as a passive meaning. It indicated one called to the side of another, and therefore one
who, by his coming, annulled the condition of orphanage or desolateness. But then, in its use, both in Classic and New Testament
Greek, the word passed into another realm, becoming active, and
suggesting the thought of intercession, advocacy, pleading. The
word is peculiar to the writings of John. It occurs four times in his
Gospel, once in his Epistle. In the Gospel it is translated *Comforter*; in
the Epistle, *Advocate*. In the Gospel it is used of the Spirit; in the
Epistle it is used of Christ. The use of it, in the Epistle, is that of
Christ standing in the presence of God, as the Advocate of the believer, the Representative, the Intercessor, the Pleader. That is the
word and idea used of the Spirit in these discourses of Christ. It is,
first, one called to the side of another. That surely was the first
thought in the mind of the Lord. He had ever been accessible to these
men. They had been able to approach Him with their questionings

77

and perplexities. He was about to leave them, but they were not to be deserted. Another was to take His place, and annul the condition of orphanage. The Spirit is therefore the Spirit of love, banishing the sense of despair and desolateness.

The word *Paraclete* also suggests the thought of an active friendship. He will come, not to plead with God for men—that is the work of Jesus—but to plead with men for God, to intercede with men for Christ, and to win, by His intercession, the whole territory of man's being for the dominance of the living Lord Whom He represents. In this great word there are infinite stretches of meaning. To the waiting people of God the character of the Spirit is love; He will come to fill the gap, to take the place of the tender Christ, to be to the orphaned disciples a Comforter nigh at hand—to comfort them, and to do it by pleading within them the cause of their absent Lord and Master.

Another fact concerning the character of the Spirit is contained in the words *the Spirit of truth.* He is the inner life of truth, the fact of truth, and therefore will give the exposition of truth. These subjects necessarily overlap each other. This phrase *the Spirit of truth* (John 14:17; 15:26; 16:13) has its most wonderful explanation in the mission of the Spirit, but it is used here only as revealing His character. How fitting and beautiful this wonderful economy, that the Spirit, Who is Himself the Spirit of truth, should come to be Intercessor for, and Administrator of the affairs of the One Who said, *I am the . . . truth* (John 14:6).

Another fact is declared concerning the character of the Spirit: *the Comforter, even the Holy Spirit* (v. 26). The Spirit of holiness—this reveals the moral character of the Spirit, and so declares the proper use and ultimate issue of truth.

And yet again: *He shall teach you all things. . . . He shall bear witness* (John 14:26; 15:26). He is the Spirit of revelation, the Spirit of illumination.

These sayings of the Master record His teaching concerning the character of the Spirit. He is the Spirit of love, the Comforter; the Spirit of truth, thrice repeated; the Spirit of holiness, the Holy Spirit; the Spirit of revelation, the One Who witnesses and teaches.

10
The Mission of the Spirit

J esus also declared in these discourses the nature of the mission of the Spirit. First, His mission to the disciples: *And I will pray the Father, and He shall give you another Comforter, that He may be with you forever, even the Spirit of truth: Whom the world cannot receive; for it beholdeth Him not, neither knoweth Him: ye know Him; for He abideth with you, and shall be in you* (John 14:16, 17). Here are two great statements.

First, that the mission of the Spirit is to abide with the people of God. The children of God have no need to pray that the Spirit may be given to them: *that He may be with you forever.* Then the Master proceeds to lay emphasis upon the method in which He will abide: *He abideth with you, and shall be in you.* The Spirit abides with the Church, by taking up His abode in the individual. He is no longer a transient Guest, but the indwelling life of the believer; and He creates and maintains, in spite of all apparent breaking up, the one catholic Church of Christ. His work with regard to the believer is revealed: *He shall teach you all things, and bring to your remembrance all that I said unto you* (John 14:26). *He shall bear witness of Me* (John 15:26). *He shall guide you into all the truth. He shall declare unto you the things that are to come. He shall glorify Me* (John 16:13, 14).

Secondly, His mission to the world: And He, when He is come, will convict the world in respect of sin, and of righteousness, and of judgment: (John 16:8–11) of sin, as having a new center—of sin, because they believe not on Me; of righteousness, as having a new possibility—I go to the Father; and of judgment, as being accomplished—the prince of this world hath been judged. This is considered more fully in a subsequent chapter.[*]

---

[*] Chapter 14.

11
The Results of the Spirit's Coming

The teaching of Jesus is clear also as to the results of the Spirit's work: *I will not leave you desolate: I come unto you* (John 14:18). Orphanage is to cease; there is to be no desolateness. This has been dealt with as part of the work of the Spirit. Considered from the side of the experience of the believer, it is indeed full of the deepest comfort. The sense of loneliness never comes to the soul born of the Spirit and living in perpetual obedience to Him. Men hunger after the personal presence of the Christ, but, in proportion as they are yielded to the Holy Spirit, they have that presence, and that in a sense which was impossible to His disciples, while He was here upon earth. He was then limited and localized, and men had to wait for an opportunity of converse. Today He is ever with every member of the Body; and for fellowship, the elements of time and place, with their necessary limitations, are absent.

Again: *But the Comforter, even the Holy Spirit, Whom the Father will send in My name, He shall teach you all things, and bring to your remembrance all that I said unto you. Peace I leave with you; My peace I give unto you* (vv. 26, 27). The two verses are intimately connected. All the sense of peace that resulted from the presence and comradeship of Christ, becomes perpetual in the new and clearer realization of Himself and His teaching resulting from the abiding of the Spirit. The way in which the Master gave His peace was not as the world giveth, because He gave it by the gift of the Comforter. The second result of the presence of the Spirit is that of peace.

Again: *But when the Comforter is come, Whom I will send unto you from the Father, even the Spirit of truth, which proceedeth from the Father, He shall bear witness of Me: and ye also bear witness, because ye have been with Me from the beginning* (John 15:26, 27). The third result of the Spirit's work is power to witness. This declaration is closely connected with that statement of Peter: *We are witnesses of these things; and so is the Holy Spirit* (Acts 5:32). The power to witness, according to the prophecy of Christ, and the testimony of Peter, was by the coming of the Spirit.

One other result: *He shall glorify Me: for He shall take of Mine, and shall declare it unto you. All things whatsoever the Father hath are Mine: therefore said I, that He taketh of Mine, and shall declare it unto you. A little while, and ye behold Me no more; and again a little while, and ye shall see Me.* The Lord did not here refer to His second coming, but to the fact that when the Spirit came He would come by the Spirit, and men would see Him in the ministry of the Spirit. The last result, then, of the Spirit's work is that of vision.

Gather up these four results. Christians are not orphans, and therefore not desolate. Peace is theirs — peace which Christ gives, as the world cannot give, through the ministry of a Person ever present. In the strength of that peace they become His witnesses, because they have a perpetual vision of the Lord.

This is a brief analysis of the Master's teaching concerning the Spirit. The unfolding of all that is contained with in this teaching is to be found, historically, in the Acts of the Apostles and the subsequent history of the Church, and, doctrinally, in the Epistles.

The teaching of Jesus is unified truth; and the interpretation of all that follows must ever be in harmony with the principles laid down in these most wonderful discourses. There is much of glory and beauty revealed in the Acts and in the Epistles, which is the blossoming into flower and fruit of that which is here in root and principle.

Book V
The Pentecostal Age

When God of old came down from heaven,
    In power and wrath He came;
Before His feet the clouds were riven,
    Half darkness and half flame.
        *   *   *   *

But when He came the second time,
    He came in power and love;
Softer than gale at morning prime
    Hover'd His holy Dove.

The fires that rush'd on Sinai down
    In sudden torrents dread,
Now gently light, a glorious crown,
    On every sainted head.

Like arrows went those lightnings forth,
    Wing'd with the sinner's doom;
But these, like tongues o'er all the earth,
    Proclaiming life to come.

And as on Israel's awe-struck ear
    The voice, exceeding loud,
The trump, that angels wake to hear,
    Thrill'd from the deep, dark cloud—

So, when the Spirit of our God
    Came down His flock to find,
A voice from heaven was heard abroad,
    A rushing, mighty wind.
        *   *   *   *

It fills the Church of God; it fills
    The sinful world around;
Only in stubborn hearts and wills
    No place for it is found.

J. KEBLE

12
Pentecost

The Master finished His teaching, and passed to His Cross. Having accomplished its sacred work, He rose from the dead, tarried for forty days among His disciples, appearing to them for special purposes, and giving them *commandments through the Holy Spirit* (Acts 1:2). He then ascended, leaving them one immediate instruction—that they should wait for the advent of the Spirit. He had told them that they were to *go into all the world, and preach the Gospel to the whole creation* (Mark 16:15); He had told them also that they were to *make disciples of all the nations, baptizing them into the name of the Father and of the Son and of the Holy Spirit* (Matt. 28:19). He had given them instructions conditioning all the service that lay before them; and then He charged them that they were not to begin any of the work until they were endued with power from on high. He left upon them that one restricting word: *He charged them not to depart from Jerusalem, but to wait for the promise of the Father* (Acts 1:4). No command was given to these men to pray for the Comforter, nor is it chronicled that they did so. It is somewhat remarkable that commentators almost without exception seem to have taken it for granted that the ten days of waiting were spent in prayer for the Holy Spirit. Neither in the command of Jesus, nor in the chronicled facts, is there any warrant for imagining that such was the case. They were waiting. It is certainly stated that

85

they gave themselves to prayer, but it is not asserted that this was for the Holy Spirit.

During that time they fell into an undoubted blunder, when they endeavored to choose a successor to Judas. Having selected certain men, they proceeded to cast lots to decide which of them should be in the apostolic succession. It is evident that the one upon whom the lot fell never was an apostle in the intention of the Master. The one chosen by the Lord to fill the gap was Saul of Tarsus. When the City of God, described in Revelation, shall be perfect and complete, it is to have twelve foundations, and in the foundations the names of the twelve apostles of the Lamb; and the name of Paul, not Matthias, will surely be the twelfth. Instead of waiting, they proceeded to make appointments. It is no more possible to appoint an officer in the Church, than to preach the Gospel, save by the guidance of the Spirit of God.

After ten days the Holy Spirit was poured out upon the waiting company in that upper room in Jerusalem. As He came, there was a sound like a mighty rushing wind, heard not only by the people there assembled, but by Jerusalem at large; for it is declared that when the people heard the sound they ran together to see what these things could be. Beside this symbolism that appealed to hearing, the coming was one that appealed to sight; fire, parting asunder, sat in the form of a tongue upon the head of each disciple. Beyond this twofold miracle of sight and sound, there was the wonderful bestowment of the gift of tongues, by which the baptized men and women spoke in other languages than their own.

The place Pentecost occupied in the Divine economy was of great importance.

(1) The Holy Spirit was poured out upon the Day of Pentecost as a gift of God. Man had no claim upon God for that great gift; He was not poured out in answer to any prayer of man, nor on account of any merit in man. He was, as was the gift of Jesus, a gift of grace which all received as from God.

(2) The pouring out of the Spirit at Pentecost was dependent upon the presence in heaven of Him Who was dead and is alive forevermore. Because of the work that He had wrought, in which

satisfaction had been given to righteousness, God poured His Spirit upon man, for the initiation of a new movement and the ushering in of a new dispensation.

(3) Pentecost was the coming of God the Holy Spirit to realize His own ideal in human character, by the administration of the work of Jesus, in its redemptive, possessive, and dominant aspects. It was the coming of God as Administrator, in order that the work which He had done as Savior might become a real fact within the experience and the character of men of whom He should be able to obtain full possession, and in whom, therefore, He should be able to exercise absolute control. By the Holy Spirit, Jesus is henceforth to be Lord, while loyal subjects to His dominion are, by the indwelling of the Spirit, to pass into the realization of the will of God. The coming of the Holy Spirit was the dawn of the brightest day the world had seen since the Fall. It was for the actual impartation to his inner being of the power that should realize the purpose toward which man had been moving through every previous dispensation.

Pentecost affected the whole position of the disciples. In the moment when the Holy Spirit fell upon them, the company of apostles and disciples, about one hundred and twenty in number, were changed from being merely followers of the Messiah into members of the risen Lord. The Lord had exercised a purely Jewish Messiahship; He had fulfilled all the prophecies and promises of the past in His own Person. *He came unto His own* (John 1:11) is the word that characterizes His mission up to the Cross; and the Cross is the final emphasis of the other fact—that *they that were His own received Him not.* But out of that great nation, which as a nation thus rejected Him, there had been gathered an elect remnant, in succession to that elect remnant which had always existed, even in the ages most characterized by spiritual decadence. Peter, James, John, and others to the number of about five hundred, were followers of Jesus, the Jewish Messiah; and so they continued up to the Day of Pentecost. When one hundred and twenty of these five hundred souls gathered in obedience to the parting command of their Lord, they were still disciples of the Messiah—the little company of people who, amidst the darkness of the nation, had discovered the light of God, and had been true to it. They were the people who, failing, trembling in the hour of darkness, had nevertheless loved their Lord through all—the people who had been utterly amazed at the miracle of the Resurrection, and who were now waiting in obedience to the new voice of authority that had sounded in their ears, the voice of their risen Lord. These disciples of the Messiah were waiting for something differing entirely from the expectations of the past, but even now they did not clearly understand their position.

When the Spirit came, they were born again. Hitherto they had been followers of the Christ; and in the purpose of God, in company with faithful Abraham and all who preceded them in a life obedient to the measure of light received, were reckoned as sharers in the work of Christ. But, as an actual fact of life, it was only when the Spirit came—outpoured in baptismal flood, as the result of the work of Jesus upon the Cross—that these men began to live. They were then baptized in the Spirit, and filled with the Spirit.

The result of Pentecost was, moreover, one that affected them not as individuals only, but also in their relation the one to the other. By that baptism they were united into one, and Peter, James, and John were no longer three separate individuals, standing apart from each other while holding the same broad sentiment, but they were members of the one catholic Church. In that moment when the Spirit fell upon the one hundred and twenty or more, the mystical Church of Christ was created. Up to the moment of the coming of the Spirit, they were a concurrence of individuals, a company of units, having a bond of sympathy in their common love to Christ, but no actual, vital, necessary, eternal union. When the Spirit came, the concurrence of individuals was fused into a unity, the Church was formed. The catholic Church was created by the baptism of the Spirit. There was no Church in this sense until the Spirit came; and from then until now the Church has continued. God alone knows the limits of His own Church. It today consists of those, in heaven and on earth, who have, by this self-same Spirit, been baptized into the sacred unity of the living Christ. It was when the Spirit fell, that individual disciples of Jesus were transformed from the former association with Him into actual living unity. The mystical Church was formed, by this fusion into unity, of those who were baptized by the Spirit on the Day of Pentecost.

As the result of the great work of the Son of God, in life, death, resurrection, and ascension, there was poured upon a little company of men and women, who had chosen to suffer with Him, the great gift of the Holy Spirit. They were thus created a corporate unity, one with Christ and with each other, and there was brought into the world a new creation, the Church, consisting of Christ and all those thus united to Him.*

The coming of the Spirit and the fusing of these individuals into one great whole affected the relation of the whole race to God. It was the coming into the world of a new temple—the Church. *Ye are a temple of God* (1 Cor. 3:16)—an individual truth, but a collective truth also. It was the coming into the world of that of which the old Temple, with its priesthood, its offerings, and its ritual, was prophetic; it was the building in the world of a dwelling-place of God through the Spirit.

The Temple was the place of praise, whence the song, the chant, and the hallelujah ascended perpetually into the presence of God. Man is created for the glory of God, and *whoso offereth the sacrifice of thanksgiving glorifieth Me* (Ps. 50:23). It is the Divine intention that man should say, not only with his lip, but in every power of his nature, *Hallelujah!* First the Tabernacle, then the Temple, was given to man as a place of praise.

But the Temple meant more than praise; it meant a possibility of prayer. *Is it not written, My house shall be called a house of prayer*

---

* A question arises as to what became of the rest of the five hundred disciples of Jesus who saw Him after His resurrection—*He appeared to above five hundred brethren at once* (1 Cor. 15:6)— but who did not tarry in obedience to His command in Jerusalem. No definite statement can be made concerning them. It is certain, however, that they were not on the Day of Pentecost included in the Church, their disobedience preventing this. It is probable that, as the time passed on, many of them would become more fully instructed, and by submission would receive the gift. Nothing can be said with any certainty, as nothing has been revealed in Scripture.

for all the nations? (Mark 11:17). It was a point to which humanity might come and tell its agony in the listening ear of Heaven, a place where men might pray. Men are, first, to praise, but praise must oft-times cease, choked by the sob of sorrow; then let men pray.

Beyond that, the Temple was the place of prophetic utterance — prophecy being, in its largest meaning, a Divine answer to prayer. Prayer is the voice of man in his need speaking to God: prophecy is the voice of God in His power speaking to man. These things had been symbolized in the Temple.

Now those men and women in the upper room — being no longer simply a company, but Christ's Church — form a Divine institution of praise. Through them there is to ascend from the earth to heaven the praise of men. The outsiders will join the praise as they enter the Church; they will find the opportunity of praise as they come into the new Temple of God given to man.

That company of people, having now become one Church, is also a medium of prayer. They are a kingdom of priests: that is, a company of individuals who will unite prayer to prayer and inter-cession to intercession; a company of men and women who will carry on their hearts the surging sorrow of the earth, and will pour its tale out in the listening ear of Heaven; a company of men and women who will always be conscious of the suffering of humanity, and will tell it out to God. The multitudes outside will begin to pray as they enter the Church. Their prayer will become prevailing as they join the new medium of prayer, which is the new Temple, the Church of Jesus Christ.

The Church will not only praise and pray; all its members have become prophets. They will pass from the upper room, and scatter themselves over the whole earth, reaching out into all the places where men abide. They will not be divided; they will still be the Church. The sigh of Moses long ago, *Would God that all the Lord's people were prophets!* (Num. 11:29) finds its answer in the Pente-costal effusion and the bestowment of the prophetic gift upon the living members of the new Church. Before one hundred years had passed, every known nation and all human institutions had felt the touch of the new power by the prophesying of the Church.

A new Temple was given to men upon the Day of Pentecost —
that is, a new center of praise, a new power of prayer, and a new
power of prophecy. No longer is *Jerusalem the place where men
ought to worship* (John 4:20); no longer is *this mountain,* as Christ
characterized the Samaritan center, the only place, but everywhere
men may worship God. Christ is the Door of the Church; and men
through belief in Him pass thereinto, the Spirit baptizing them into
living union with Him. The Temple grows and expands by this in-
corporation of individual members. Whether in a far-off land or at
home, whether in Jerusalem or at the end of the earth, men pass
into the new Temple by this self-same Spirit Who was poured out
upon the Day of Pentecost for their admission into the relationship
with God which should fit them for praise, prayer, and prophecy.
When Peter handled the keys of the kingdom for the first time, he
opened the door to the Jew, and three thousand entered. Then he
opened the door to the Gentiles in the house of Cornelius, and the
Gentiles began to crowd in. That handling of the keys was not
Peter's peculiar prerogative. It was also the prerogative of every
member of the Church. It is the prerogative of every person who, as
a prophet of the Cross, in the demonstration of the Spirit, speaks
to some soul, so that there opens before that soul a vision of the
things of the kingdom. That is the true exercise of the power of the
keys.* Pentecost meant for the world the creation of a new Temple, no longer limited, localized, and material, but unlimited, to
be found everywhere, and spiritual, for the Spirit is everywhere. Entrance to this Temple is found wherever man in his need and agony
submits himself to Christ.

Before closing this chapter, it is necessary to notice the difference between the events of the Day of Pentecost with the period
immediately following, and the occurrence in the house of Cornelius with the subsequent history of the Book of the Acts. The
whole of the men and women upon whom the Spirit fell on the

---

* This throws light upon the sacerdotal question. With a strange confusion men
have imagined that the keys were the symbols of priestly power. They were not.
They were the insignia of the prophetic office.

Day of Pentecost were Jewish; and the period immediately following Pentecost may be spoken of as peculiarly Jewish. There are two remarkable characteristics of the work of the Spirit during that period that ceased immediately afterwards. This period is dealt with in the first nine chapters, and during it there seems to have been an interval between the acceptation of the good tidings concerning the kingdom of God and the reception of the Holy Spirit. People believed the tidings, and yet they did not receive the Holy Spirit. Moreover, there was some intervention on the part of another disciple before the gift of the Spirit was received.[*]

The Gospel was preached to the Gentiles in the house of Cornelius, and it is never again recorded that those who believed in Jesus received the Holy Spirit as a subsequent blessing (Acts 10). The apostles preached the kingdom of God; and when a Jew heard about the kingdom, he did exactly what had been done in the days of Christ's ministry—he thought of earthly power, had no conception of the spiritual reality, and believed in Jesus as a Restorer of the temporal kingdom. His conception was material; and in every such case it was necessary for some more enlightened disciple to teach him the spiritual reality, in order that he might receive the Holy Spirit.

When Peter preached in the house of Cornelius, he announced good tidings of peace, and the lordship of Jesus, and remission of sins. This the Gentiles heard, not from the Jewish standpoint. The story of the kingdom was not all. They heard also the story of salvation from sin. When they believed, it was the whole Gospel, and the Spirit fell upon them straightway. The was no *second blessing*. This, then, represents the normal condition of things under the present dispensation. Men believe in Jesus as King and Savior, and are baptized by the Spirit into relationship with Him, that being the hour of their new birth, and that in which they become members of the catholic Church of Jesus Christ.

Pentecost, in the economy of God, was the occasion of the outpouring of the Spirit, in answer to the completed work of the Christ,

---

[*] The work of Philip in Samaria and the conversion of Saul are instance. They will be considered in Chapter 15.

in order that the purpose of God might be realized in the character of men.

Pentecost, in the case of the disciple, was the change from being merely a follower, a learner, into that of living union with the living Christ.

Pentecost, in the case of the world, was the advent in the world of a new Temple consisting of living men, women, and children indwelt by the Spirit of God, for purposes of praise, and prayer, and prophecy.

13
The Spirit in the Church

On the Day of Pentecost the coming of the Spirit upon a company of waiting disciples changed them from an aggregation of units into one corporate whole, the Church of the living God. From that moment all the essentials of the Church have been maintained by His abiding therein.

By the creation of the Church a new Temple was given to the world, a new institute for praise, for prayer, and for prophecy. All these functions are fulfilled by the abiding of the Spirit in the Church. The incense of praise is offered by the inspiration of the Spirit; the intercession of prayer is maintained by the whole company of those who pray in the Holy Spirit; the work of prophecy, in its fullest meaning of forth-telling, is carried forward by such as are witnesses, in cooperation with the Holy Spirit, to the eternal verities of God.

The Letters to the Corinthians deal with New Testament Church orders; and in the first, the apostle having discussed certain disorders that had arisen in the church at Corinth, proceeded to deal with ecclesiastical matters; and, in conclusion, he revealed a threefold fact concerning the relation of the Spirit to the whole Church of God. *Now concerning spiritual gifts, brethren* (1 Cor. 12:1). Both in the Authorized and in the Revised Versions the word *gifts* is in italics. The term πνευματικά* covers a subject far wider than that of

---

* πνευματικῶν, Things of the Spirit (v. 1).

the gifts of the Spirit. It is undoubtedly with the gifts that the apostle specially dealt, but he opened his subject by writing: *Brethren, I would not have you ignorant concerning the matters that pertain to the Spirit.* Then he made three main statements concerning these matters. First, he declared the Holy Spirit to be the Defender of the Church's faith: *No man can say, Jesus is Lord, but in the Holy Spirit* (v. 3). In the second place, he declared the Holy Spirit to be the Inspiration of the Church's service: *There are diversities of gifts, but the same Spirit. . . . But all these worketh the one and the same Spirit, dividing to each one severally even as He will* (vv. 4, 11). And, thirdly, he declared the Holy Spirit to be the bond of the Church's unity: *For in one Spirit were we all baptized into one body* (v. 13).

The Holy Spirit is the Defender of the Faith. *No man can say, Jesus is Lord, but in the Holy Spirit* (v. 3). The old desire for authority in matters of faith and of doctrine is still felt, and is perfectly natural and right. It has ever been realized in the history of the Church. It may safely be said that all great crises in Church history have been the result of a division of opinion as to where the seat of authority really lies in matters of discipline and of doctrine.

The Reformation under Luther was a restoration of the lost doctrine of Justification by Faith, but that, in a further analysis, is a statement of the seat of authority in the matter of forgiveness and of pardon. In that wonderful work which Luther was raised up of God to do, he called men back from seeking authoritative absolution from a man, to seek it from God.

The Oxford movement, the outworking of which in the sacerdotal revival today is so manifest, is a startling illustration of this fact. Newman—sweet, strong, sainted soul, from whom those who believe in the alone and undelegated authority of the Spirit radically differ in many particulars, but with whom all saints have communion still in his love for the Master—entered the Roman church because he sought for authority, and his intellect found a species of rest in what he believed to be the authority of that church.

Protestants are perpetually being told that they have no center of authority. This statement is due to the fact that those who make it forget that the one, the abiding, and the only center of authority, in matters of faith and doctrine, is the Holy Spirit. That is the teaching of this declaration, passed over too often as though it were simply a statement of initial matters. That it certainly is, but it is infinitely more. That Jesus is Lord is the center of all Christian doctrine; everything else grows out of it. *No man can say, Jesus is Lord, but in the Holy Spirit* (1 Cor. 12:3). All true systems of theology are but the subdivision and application to varied and varying circumstances of this central fact, that Jesus is Lord.

The same apostle stated: *For to this end Christ died, and lived again, that He might be Lord of both the dead and the living* (Rom. 14:9). The Lordship of Christ is the doctrinal fact which is the center of all others; the Lordship of Christ is the practical fact which is the issue of the doctrine. Doctrine and duty are wedded in the scheme of Christianity. Every doctrine has its expression in some duty; every creed has its out-blossoming in character.

The inner historic fact of Christianity is Christ, living, dying, rising, reigning; and the purpose of His living, dying, rising, and reigning is that He should be Lord both of the dead and of the living. The relation which the ministry of the Holy Spirit bears to that doctrine is of the closest. *No man can say, Jesus is Lord, but in the Holy Spirit.* It is the Holy Spirit Who first reveals Christ to the heart of man so that man says, in response to the revelation: *Thou art my Lord.* It is the work of the Spirit to take this inner, central part of Christian doctrine, and make it real to men so that they respond to the doctrine by fulfilling the duty. That initial work having been done, it is the Spirit Who unfolds the revelation step by step—*precept upon precept; . . . line upon line; here a little, there a little* (Is. 28:10), by so much as men are able to bear it, giving new vision of the beauty and glory of the Master, for life and character. Every vision of Christ granted to the believer has been the result of the presence in that believer of the Holy Spirit, Who alone gives grace to say in new realms of life, in new vistas of outlook, that Jesus is Lord.

Thus, whether the look is backward upon the past of sin, He is Lord, and has *blotted out the bond written in ordinances that was against us* (Col. 2:14); or whether it is at the present condition of our hearts, He is Lord, and will have dominion over the nature until the Divine purpose be realized; or whether it is forward to the end of life, He is still Lord, and fills the horizon, so that souls, homed in His kingdom, wait for His coming; or whether it is round upon the world, He even there is Lord, and

> Through the ages one increasing purpose runs,
> And the thoughts of men are widen'd with the
>   process of the suns—

widened, slowly but surely, nevertheless, to a conception of the Lordship of the Son of God.

The Holy Spirit is the one and only Defender of this Faith; and every fight for orthodoxy other than that which is aimed at bringing men to fullness of spiritual life is futile. Life in the Holy Spirit is the safeguard of purity of doctrine.

In order to emphasize this fact, consider three great landmarks in the history of the Church—the Reformation, the Evangelical revival, and the spiritual movements of today.

The declension that led to the Reformation, and the Reformation itself, are proofs of the fact that purity of doctrine is only maintained by the Holy Spirit. The Reformation was necessary that the truth of Justification by Faith should be restated, because the Church had wandered from spiritual to material conceptions, and the Holy Spirit had been slighted and contemned. To borrow the figure of the old Hebrew prophet, men had gone to Egypt for horses upon which to fight God's battles; they had asked and obtained the patronage of the State in religious matters. Constantine had become the patron of Christianity; the Holy Spirit had been dethroned from His proper position. The result was the materializing of religious thought and character, until men had lost the doctrine of Justification by Faith, because they had lost their loyalty to the Holy Spirit. The doctrine was restored through a man to whom the Spirit gave a new vision of the lost truth. Luther declared the doctrine in the face of the world; the Spirit spoke through him; the eyes of men were opened, and there was a return to the Christian doctrine, because there was a return to the Holy Spirit.

The Evangelical revival illustrates the same thing. This was made necessary by the fact that the Church of God had lost its vision of the truth of Sanctification. John Wesley said that he had been raised up in order that he might promote Holiness throughout the land; and he declared at the beginning of that movement that if he could find one hundred men who feared nothing but sin he would move the world. God gave him his hundred men, and he did move the world. He revolutionized the thought of this country, so that today the spiritual results of the Methodist movement are not measured by the number of its adherents, but by the ever-increasing understanding of the doctrine of Holiness in all the Churches. John Wesley did not discover some new doctrine, save as a man may discover that which had been hidden; it was the old apostolic truth that he brought to light. It had been lost, because the Holy Spirit had neither been acknowledged as a Person nor recognized as the Center of authority in Church life. This land had passed under the deadly blight of material conceptions of Christianity. The fox-hunting parson, who cared neither for God, man, nor devil, but only for tithes and hounds, was the representative of Christianity who cursed the times. He was dismissed by the return of men through John Wesley and his holy club at Oxford to the truth of the sanctification of the believer through the submission of human lives to the government of the Spirit. To borrow Dr. Steele's[*] phrase, *the Conservator of orthodoxy* in every successive age is the Holy Spirit.

Creeds do not ensure orthodoxy, for no individual church holds all the truth of the Church. The great body of truth is the property of the catholic Church, not of any section, nor yet of any individual member thereof. Sometimes one is asked if he *hold the truth.* Certainly not, for no single person can hold the truth. He may see one side of it—and that one side is almost more than he can bear—while another person sees another side. One is not to be angry with the other because neither sees all the facets of the lustrous gem, nor is the other to decline to work with the one because both do not alike include in their understanding all the angles thereof. To this

[*] Daniel Steele, D.D., author of *Milestone Papers*, etc.

man is given a vision of the individual application of the work of
Christ; to another, the vision of its social application; to yet another,
that of the national and international application. And the man who
sees the individual aspect of that work has no right to anathematize
the man who only sees the national aspect. One man feels that
there is laid upon his heart the great message of a Christian doctrine and a living Christ to the nations; and he so feels the impulse
of that upon him, that he must give up his work with individuals,
and appeal, as much as one voice may, to the nation, from the floor
of some legislative chamber. It cannot be said that such a man is
not doing God's work. A man is not necessarily fulfilling the final
and only work of the ministry when he is in the pulpit. Stepping
from the pulpit and from the work of dealing with individual men
about conversion and spiritual upbuilding would be to some a
degradation of life. But if another man has another outlook, and
would speak to masses of men, and to nations of the earth, about
the way in which Christ would have society conducted and nations
order their government, the preacher in his pulpit has no right to
despise that man. Nay, to one is given one vision of Christ, and to
another yet another, but no man holds all the truth, as no man has
all the gifts.

In the catholic Church, by the Spirit, is contained the whole
truth; and in the catholic Church, by the Spirit, is contained all the
gifts necessary for the declaration thereof. The catholic Church, inspired by the Spirit, indwelt by the Spirit, is a divine institution infinitely larger than human sight can compass, human statistics
declare, or human understanding perfectly comprehend.

Life in the Spirit is necessarily, therefore, the inspiration of, and
the equipment for service. Attempts may be made to organize and
apportion to every man has work, giving to one the individual, to
another the social, and to a third the national work; and subdividing
these things, it may be planned that this man shall preach the
gospel of forgiveness, that man the gospel of holiness, and another
the gospel of the coming Christ. For the orderly execution of these
matters there may be distinctions, and degrees, and seasons, and
symbols. The Spirit of God cannot, however, be crowded into small

human channels and ideas. What absolute folly is evidenced by all such attempts! The catholic Church is not bounded by loose ropes of sand, it is not maintained in order by small definitions, but by the Spirit, Who is the Conservator of its orthodoxy and the Inspiration of its service. He gives His gifts severally as He will; and not along such restricted lines of communication as the laying on of hands, but through the broad river of His indwelling of the Church, come the gifts as well as the graces of God.

If the Spirit be the Defender of the Church's faith and the Inspiration of the Church's service, He is also the Bond of the Church's unity. *In one Spirit were we all baptized into one body* (1 Cor. 12:13). The Door of the Church is Jesus Christ; and reverently the figure may be carried further—the Holy Spirit guards the Door. From that Pentecostal effusion to this hour, the Holy Spirit has guarded the entrance to the Church of Christ, and admitted all its members by His own baptism. Men and women have ever passed into the catholic Church by the one Door, and entrance has ever been by the baptism of the Holy Spirit, apart from which it is impossible for any soul to come into living union with Christ, the Head of the Church. Consequently, the whole company of those who are in the Church are energized and impulsed by the same Spirit. There is one body and one Spirit—one body, as the human body is one, having different members, each with its own function, but only one life. The hand has not a separate existence from the foot, but each has the one life; so, in the catholic Church, there are many members having varying functions, but all are impulsed by the one life.

The Holy Spirit is the life of the catholic Church, and in that life lies the great bond of its union. The Church is one undivided. To all outward seeming it is divided, and each division arrogates to itself the name of the Church, until at last one most carefully separated division declares that all the rest are systems and sects, and it alone gives outward revelation of what the true Church is.

The fact is that men do not know the bounds of the catholic Church, which is smaller than the records of the churches show, and is yet greater than them all. There are living members of that Church in all the churches, and it may be that on the rolls of the churches are names which are not on the roll of the catholic Church. Those are members thereof who are baptized into union with Christ by the Holy Spirit. The Lord knows them; and being members of His one Church, they can sing the words of Baring-Gould's hymn in a far higher sense than some people imagine:

> We are not divided;
> All one body we,
> One in hope and doctrine,
> One in charity.

It may be objected that the Church is not one in doctrine. The catholic Church is one in doctrine, and this is its central word: Jesus is Lord. Whether men express that truth to swing of censer and swell of music, or to the beat of the drum and the blare of the trumpet, or without any of these accompaniments, matters far less than is imagined.

The life of the Church came, not by the will of man, nor by a ceremony of human invention, but by the baptism of the Spirit; and the great unity of that Church is still maintained by the indwelling of all its members by the Holy Spirit. The true consciousness of this unity of the Spirit, is the love concerning which Paul wrote, and which finds its manifestation toward the unit and the aggregate of units which make up the whole. The unity of the Church can only be realized in full spiritual life. Acts of Uniformity cannot make the Church one: that is the original and continuous work of the Spirit. Of that great Church of Christ some of its members are at home with the Lord, some are passing through the earth, and some are coming up out of tomorrow; and the Spirit is the Keeper of the unity, which cannot be broken. Presently out of all the seeming disagreement and disruption will come the glorious Church of the First-born, without spot or wrinkle or any such thing.

14
The Spirit in the World

T he ministry of the Spirit in the present age is by no means con-
fined within the limits of the Church. Scripture very clearly
reveals the intention as being far wider; and the history of the
centuries proves the accomplishment to be in keeping with the intention.

There are three portions of Scripture which may be examined
as throwing light on this subject. First, a prophetic utterance, the
fulfillment of which Peter claimed as being accomplished on the
Day of Pentecost; secondly, the express declaration of the Lord concerning the Spirit's ministry in the world; and, lastly, the teaching of
Paul and John concerning the work of the Holy Spirit as opposed to
the work of the spirit of evil. All these deal with a present ministry of
the Spirit which in some sense is united to the work of the Church,
but is also apart from and beyond it.

First, the prophecy: *These are not drunken, as ye suppose; seeing
it is but the third hour of the day, but this is that which hath been
spoken by the prophet Joel; And it shall be in the last days, saith God
I will pour forth of My Spirit upon all flesh: and your sons and your
daughters shall prophesy, and your young men shall see visions, and
your old men shall dream dreams: Yea and on My servants and on
My handmaidens in those days will I pour forth of My Spirit; and
they shall prophesy* (Acts 2:15–18).

The term *all flesh* is an expression which is uniformly used in the Old Testament Scriptures with reference to the whole race. The exceptions are to be found repeatedly in the Pentateuch and once in the Book of Daniel, where the expression *all flesh* refers not only to the human race but to everything having life (Dan. 4:12). The sense of the phrase cannot be narrowed to anything smaller than the whole human family; and the statement here is clear and distinct—the utterance of the prophet long years before Pentecost, and the utterance of the apostle on the Day of Pentecost, claiming the fulfillment of the old prophecy, that the Spirit should be poured upon *all flesh*.

The link between the prophecy and its fulfillment is revealed in the Gospel of John: *In the beginning was the Word, and the Word was with God, and the Word was God. . . . And the Word became flesh, and dwelt among us* (John 1:1, 14). The eternal Word took upon Him a nature common to the race, and therein wrought righteousness and accomplished redemption. Consequently, when He ascended on high to receive gifts for men, He received the Spirit, and by His outpouring upon disciples, the Church was formed. The Pentecostal effusion had, however, another and far wider significance. The Spirit was poured upon all flesh, so that the whole human race was thereby brought into a new relationship with Him as the result of the work of Jesus Christ. Just as the Word took the common flesh of humanity, and associated Himself with the whole race; so, as the result of the work He did while thus associated, the Spirit was poured not merely upon the company of disciples, but also upon *all flesh*. This is the larger outlook upon the mission of the Spirit. Let there be no minimizing of the value of this great statement.

There is, however, a distinct difference between the relationship that the Spirit bears to the believer and to the unbeliever. The Spirit is in the believer, and he by that indwelling is kept in union with Christ. The Spirit strives with the unbeliever as a Spirit of conviction, of reasoning, wooing him in patience to the way of God. The difference is most marked, yet the ministry of the Spirit is a ministry which touches all men.

Secondly, the declaration of Christ in the Paschal discourses: *And He, when He is come, will convict the world in respect of sin, and of righteousness, and of judgment: of sin, because they believe not on Me; of righteousness, because I go to the Father, and ye behold Me no more; of judgment, because the prince of this world hath been judged* (John 16:8–11). This is the first aspect of the ministry of the Spirit among men. He came not merely to reveal the things of Christ to the Church, but *to convict the world of sin, of righteousness, and of judgment.* In the Authorized Version the word convict is rendered reprove. It is a word the inner thought of which is not revealed by the translation *convict.* Bishop Westcott, in his luminous exposition of the Gospel of John, says that this word has in it four shades of meaning: first, an authoritative examination of the facts; secondly, unquestionable proof; thirdly, decisive judgment; and, lastly, punitive power.

The mission of the Holy Spirit with men is that of revealing to them the truth on these subjects, in such a way that they shall be convinced that it is the truth. Concerning sin, men seek to excuse themselves, try to evade the facts, but when the Spirit deals with a man about sin, he cannot escape; and under His illumination man has the same clear vision of righteousness and judgment.

Passing from the word itself to the subject, *He . . . will convict the world in respect of sin, and of righteousness, and of judgment* (v. 8), it is clear that these three words cover the past, the present, and the future of the outlook of man as a sinner—the history of past sin, the present demand for righteousness, and the fear of future judgment. The Spirit takes these three cardinal facts and places them in their true light, so that men may make no mistake concerning them. The Master declared the testimony the Spirit would bear on these subjects. . . . *Of sin, because they believe not on Me; of righteousness, because I go to the Father, and ye behold Me no more; of judgment, because the prince of this world hath been judged* (John 16:9–11). That is the threefold revelation which the Spirit is giving to the world today, and it demands a closer examination.

Three persons are spoken of: Man, Christ, and Satan—Man in the realm of sin, Christ in the realm of righteousness, Satan in the realm of judgment. Observe next the inter-relation of these three: Man in his relationship to himself, to Christ, and to Satan; Christ in His relationship to Himself, to man, and to Satan; Satan in his relationship to himself, to man, and to Christ.

First, Man in his relationship to the three. Man's relationship to himself is that of a sinner having lost his life, whose sin ceases and is put away when he believes in Jesus. Man's relationship to Christ is that of a sinner for whom He has procured salvation, and through Whose triumph of righteousness man may himself do righteously. Man's relationship to Satan is that of a slave under the prince of this world, but from whose power he is set free, for this prince has been defeated.

Secondly, Christ in His relationship to the three. Christ's relationship to Himself is that of righteousness, for He declared His personal triumph when He said: *I go to the Father* (John 16:17). His relationship to man is that of a Savior, and therefore man's sin consists in refusal to believe on Him. Christ's relationship to Satan is that of Conqueror, for *the prince of this world hath been judged* (v. 11).

Lastly, Satan in his relation to the three. Satan, concerning himself, is conquered—*hath been judged*—and is powerless; concerning man, is conquered—*hath been judged*—and therefore can no longer claim man's service; concerning Christ, is conquered—*hath been judged*—and therefore even he must own Him King. There is no other outlook for evil than that of conquest.

Once again: He, when He is come, *will convict the world in respect of sin . . . because they believe not on Me* (vv. 8, 9). With the coming of the Spirit upon all flesh, sin had a new center. Henceforth sin consists in the refusal to accept the Divine provision of healing and power. No longer is the root-sin that of impurity, or drunkenness, or lust, or pride, or even law-breaking; the root-sin is the refusal to believe on Jesus. If men will believe on Him, in that relationship to Christ which springs from belief is to be found healing for wounds, and strength which issues in victory. The Spirit declares that the sin lies, not in the fact of passion, but in the refusal to let the Master master the passion.

The Spirit has also come to reveal the truth about righteousness. If the revelation of sin be that of a new center, the revelation of righteousness is, consequently, that of a new possibility. *Of righteousness, because I go to the Father* (John 16:10). In the height of that glory, which mortal eyes may by no means look upon, is God's perfect Man, the One Who said, *I go to the Father.* Not simply by virtue of His own righteousness did He go, but bearing into the presence of the Father the marks of that death on the Cross, by which He liberated His life, that it might become the force of renewal for man. The Spirit comes to bring to men the gospel of a new possibility of righteousness.

Lastly, the Spirit's revelation of judgment is concerned with a new exercise thereof. A common mistake in quoting this passage is that of adding the words *to come* after *judgment*. The confusion of thought which this reveals is obvious; for the judgment here referred to is not that which is to come, but that which is already accomplished. The Judgment Day is not to be one of twenty-four hours, but of long duration, an age in itself, of which the closing event will be the final assize before the Great White Throne. That stupendous transaction will simply be the unfolding of the facts which are present today, because the prince of this world hath been judged. Righteousness has had its conflict with evil, and has won in the fight. The head of the enemy of the race had been bruised, even though the heel of the Victor was wounded in the process. *The prince of this world hath been judged*; and the things that must pass and perish are evil things and unrighteous things, while the things that cannot be shaken and that will remain are righteous things, pure things, and beautiful things, yea, all the things of God. Judgment is fixed, doom is marked, destiny is sealed, by the Cross of Jesus Christ. If men fling in their lot with things which are doomed and judged, then they must share the doom and judgment which have been passed upon them by the Cross of Calvary, but if they turn their backs upon doomed things, and lift their eyes toward the things that abide, the heavenly things where Christ is, the upper things, the conquering things, then for them judgment was borne upon the Cross, and they have entered into justification-life. Thus the ministry of the Spirit in the world today is that of revealing the truth concerning sin, righteousness, and judgment.

Thirdly, the teaching of Paul and John is clear that the Spirit has yet another ministry in the world today—that, namely, of hindering the full manifestation of sin. Paul and John in their Epistles give testimony to the fact that the Holy Spirit is the ever-present Force denying, hindering, thwarting, the outworking of evil. This is clearly revealed by comparison of certain of their writings.

The man of sin . . . the son of perdition, he that opposeth and exalteth himself against all that is called God or that is worshiped; so that he sitteth in the temple of God, setting himself forth as God (2 Thess. 2:3, 4). That is a description of antichrist as he will be. *The mystery of lawlessness doth already work. . . . And then shall be revealed the lawless one* (vv. 7, 8). The apostle thus states that there is a mystery of iniquity, *a mystery of lawlessness,* at work among men, and that there is a day coming when that mystery will have a manifestation in an actual person, *the lawless one will be revealed.*

John, writing on this same theme, says: *Who is the liar but he that denieth that Jesus is the Christ? This is the antichrist, even he that denieth the Father and the Son* (1 John 2:22). *Every spirit which confesseth not Jesus is not of God: and this is the spirit of the antichrist, whereof ye have heard that it cometh; and now it is in the world already* (1 John 4:3). This is practically the same teaching—namely, that there is a spirit of antichrist, a spirit of the *mystery of lawlessness* in the world, and that at some period in the future it is to have a manifestation in a person. It is the spirit which denies God, not necessarily with the blatant blasphemy of public speech, but it may be with all cultured correctness of life. It is that which denies God, that which denies Christ.

Paul distinctly states that there is another force which holds this force of evil in check: *And now ye know that which restraineth. . . . The mystery of lawlessness doth already work: only there is One that restraineth now, until He be taken out of the way* (2 Thess. 2:6, 7). This is a plain declaration that the spirit of evil is at work, and also that there is a Force which restrains. He does not say it is the Holy Spirit. There has been a great deal of controversy about this partic-

ular passage, and attempts have been made to show that it had regard to the Roman power in the past. John, however, makes it clear
Who the One that restraineth is: *Hereby know ye the Spirit of God:
every spirit which confesseth that Jesus Christ is come in the flesh is of
God: and every spirit which confesseth not Jesus is not of God: and
this is the spirit of the antichrist* (1 John 4:2, 3). Here the two things
are placed in opposition: the spirit of antichrist, which denies Jesus
Christ and denies God; the Spirit of God, Who announces the
Christ of God, and teaches men how to call Him Lord.

These two forces are still at work in the world—the spirit of evil,
the leaven that is undoing men everywhere; and the Spirit of God,
Who restrains and holds in check the force of evil.

All the great forces which are antagonistic to God have been
thus hindered, restrained, checked, flung back upon themselves
during the last nineteen hundred years.

The ministry of the Spirit is larger than His ministry in the
Church; it is worldwide, and is always based upon the work of the
Christ. Whether to the Church or to the world, the Spirit has no
message but the message of Jesus Christ. To the man in the Church,
and to the whole Church, He is revealing the Christ in new beauty
and new glory. To the world He is revealing sin, righteousness, and
judgment in their relation to the Christ. The Spirit is poured upon
all flesh; and, in cooperation with the Church, He convinces of sin,
and of righteousness, and of judgment. Therein lie the heart, the
center, and the responsibility of foreign missionary work. *How shall
they hear without a preacher? and how shall they preach, except they
be sent?* (Rom. 10:14, 15). The Holy Spirit is waiting in the far-dis-
tant places of the earth for the voice of anointed man to preach, in
order that through that instrumentality He may carry on His work of
convicting of sin, and of righteousness, and of judgment.

Beyond that, there is this other marvelous ministry which is too
often lost sight of. By His presence in the world He is restraining
the outworking of iniquity, and is checking, hindering, and driving
back every attempted combination of the forces of evil for the
swamping of the Church, and the hindering of the kingdom. The
Spirit's restraining work will go forward until the moment has come

when the number of the elect is complete. Then shall the Spirit be withdrawn when the Church is called away, in order that iniquity may be manifested and smitten to its final doom, and the glorious kingdom of our God be set up.[*]

---

[*] The only sense in which the Spirit is withdrawn is that which characterizes His special work in this age—that, namely, of conserving the Church and preventing the progress of evil to finality. He will carry on His work of striving with men as He did prior to the Deluge, but with results more glorious. This, however, is another subject and a part of prophetic study.

Book VI
The Spirit in the Individual

Thou Breath from still eternity,
     Breathe o'er my spirit's barren land—
The pine-tree and the myrtle-tree
     Shall spring amidst the desert sand,
And where Thy living water flows
The waste shall blossom as the rose.

May I in will and deed and word
     Obey Thee as a little child;
And keep me in Thy love, my Lord,
     Forever holy, undefiled;
Within me teach and strive and pray,
Lest I should choose my own wild way.

O Spirit, Stream that by the Son
     Is open'd to us crystal pure,
Forth-flowing from the heavenly Throne
     To waiting hearts and spirits poor,
Athirst and weary do I sink
Beside Thy waters, there to drink.

My spirit turns to Thee and clings,
     All else forsaking, unto Thee,
Forgetting all created things,
     Remembering only God in me.
O living Stream, O gracious Rain,
None wait for Thee, and wait in vain.

                              G. TERSTEEGEN

15
The Baptism of the Spirit

In dealing with these matters of the Spirit, it is wise to keep, as far as possible, to the terms of the New Testament; and it would be an enormous gain if they were used only as they are used in Scripture. The term *the baptism of the Spirit* has been very generally misunderstood, and therefore misapplied. It has been used as though it were synonymous with *the filling of the Spirit*; and, consequently, some persons speak of the baptism of the Spirit as *a second blessing.* They teach that it is necessary to ask for, and to wait for, and to expect this baptism of the Spirit, as something different from and beyond conversion. That is a view utterly unauthorized by Scripture. The baptism of the Spirit is the primary blessing; it is, in short, the blessing of regeneration. When a man is baptized with the Spirit, he is born again. There is, however, an essential difference between that initial blessing and the blessing into which thousands of God's people have been entering during recent years—the difference between the baptism of the Spirit and the filling of the Spirit.

In the majority of cases in the experience of believers, the filling of the Spirit is realized after the baptism. They are identical in the purpose of God, but there is a difference in the experience. So important is it that Christian people should have a clear understanding of what the baptism of the Spirit really is, that it will be well to review the whole of the passages in the New Testament in which the

words are used, in order to get a correct appreciation of the true significance of the phrase.

John . . . when he saw many of the Pharisees and Sadducees com-
ing to his baptism, said unto them . . . I indeed baptize you with
water unto repentance: but He that cometh after me is mightier than
I, Whose shoes I am not worthy to bear: He shall baptize you with the
Holy Spirit and with fire (Matt. 3:4–11).

John . . . preached, saying . . . I baptized you with water, but He
shall baptize you with the Holy Spirit (Mark 1:6–8).

John answered, saying unto them all, I indeed baptize you with
water, but there cometh He that is mightier than I, the latchet of
Whose shoes I am not worthy to unloose: He shall baptize you with
the Holy Spirit and with fire (Luke 3:16).

John answered them, saying, I baptize with water: in the midst of
you standeth One Whom ye know not, even He that cometh after me,
the latchet of Whose shoe I am not worthy to unloose (John 1:26,
27). *. . . And John bare witness, saying, I have beheld the Spirit de-*
scending as a dove out of heaven; and it abode upon Him. And I
knew Him not: but He that sent me to baptize with water, He said
unto me, Upon Whomsoever thou shalt see the Spirit descending,
and abiding upon Him, the same is He that baptizeth with the Holy
Spirit (John 1:32, 33).

It is more than remarkable, it is almost startling to discover that
the Gospels which chronicle the life and ministry of Christ, have
no account of this baptism of the Spirit, save the prophecy of His
coming uttered by John the Baptist, who spoke of it as something
beyond himself, his message, and his age.

What the baptism of the Spirit is may be gathered from the word
of the Master to Nicodemus: *Jesus answered, Verily, verily, I say unto*
thee, Except a man be born of water and the Spirit, he cannot enter
into the kingdom of God (John 3:5–8). The inference is, that if a
man be born of water and the Spirit, he can enter into the kingdom of God. But follow the words still further: *That which is born of*
the flesh is flesh; and that which is born of the Spirit is spirit. Marvel
not that I said unto thee, Ye must be born anew. The wind bloweth
where it listeth, and thou hearest the voice thereof, but knowest not

whence it cometh, and whither it goeth: so is everyone that is born of the Spirit.

Except a man be born of water and the Spirit is a passage about which there is great diversity of opinion. The Master is here linking His own teaching and dispensation to the teaching and dispensation that is concluding with the mission of John. The water baptism is the baptism of John, and the Spirit baptism is the baptism of Jesus, the gift of life. That which is symbolized by the first is necessary, for repentance must precede life, but the baptism of the Spirit is the gift of life by which a man is admitted into the kingdom of God.

In the Gospels, John, standing as the forerunner, declared: *I indeed baptize you with water, but there cometh He that is mightier than I . . . He shall baptize you with the Holy Spirit* (Luke 3:16). Years passed, John's ministry was ended, the earthly ministry of Christ was ended, the Cross and Resurrection were accomplished facts. Jesus now stood amid His disciples, and before He ascended on high He said to them: *John indeed baptized with water, but ye shall be baptized with the Holy Spirit not many days hence* (Acts 1:5). There had been as yet no baptism with the Holy Spirit; and, consequently, these men gathered around Christ had not yet entered into the final relationship with Him that characterizes the Christian dispensation, and forms the holy catholic Church. They had been the disciples of a Jewish Messiah, but now that relation was passing away, and the living Lord in resurrection glory was about to pour upon them the baptism predicted by John. Christ took up the words of His forerunner, and claimed that they were to be fulfilled in the experience of these men: *John indeed baptized with water*—that is as far as they had gone at the moment, but the greater blessing was coming—*ye shall be baptized with the Holy Spirit not many days hence.*

And as I began to speak, the Holy Spirit fell on them, even as on us at the beginning. And I remembered the word of the Lord, how that He said, John indeed baptized with water, but ye shall be baptized with the Holy Spirit. If then God gave unto them the like gift as He did also unto us, when we believed on the Lord Jesus Christ, who was I, that I could withstand God? (Acts 11:15–17). Peter, in giving account of the conversion of Cornelius, declared that these men were baptized with the Spirit when, as he preached, they believed on Christ. The teaching of both these passages evidently is, that the Spirit's baptism is that by which men pass into the new relationship. In both places a contrast is drawn between the baptism of the Spirit and the baptism of John, showing that the baptism of the Spirit was the power which took men beyond the legalism of the old dispensation into the vital relationship of the new.

Are ye ignorant that all we who were baptized into Christ Jesus were baptized into His death? We were buried therefore with Him through baptism into death: that like as Christ was raised from the dead through the glory of the Father, so we also might walk in newness of life (Rom. 6:3, 4). This is the only direct reference to the baptism of the Spirit in the Letter to the Romans. Certainly the baptism referred to is the Spirit's baptism, for surely no man is baptized by water into the death of Christ. Water baptism may be a symbol of the great fact that a man has passed from death unto life, but the baptism by which men are actually brought into relationship with the death and the life of Christ is the baptism of the Spirit; and it is quite evident that in this argument of the Epistle a reference is made to the beginnings of spiritual life—to the initial blessing, to the blessing of regeneration.

For in * *one Spirit were we all baptized into one body, whether Jews or Greeks, whether bond or free* (1 Cor. 12:13). Here again the reference must be to the moment when men entered the Church of Christ; and the statement is that then they were baptized in the Holy Spirit.

For ye are all sons of God, through faith, in Christ Jesus. For as many of you as were baptized into Christ did put on Christ (Gal. 3:26, 27). Faith was the condition of the baptism by which these people put on Christ and became sons of God, that baptism being, undoubtedly, the baptism of the Holy Spirit.

One Lord, one faith, one baptism, one God and Father of all (Eph. 4:5, 6). *One Lord*—the object of the sinner's faith; *one faith*—

---

* Notice the slight alteration of the Revised Version—not *by one Spirit*.

centered upon the one Lord; *one baptism*—the baptism of the Holy Spirit, by which the sinner becomes the Lord's; *one God and Father*—the new relationship that God bears to the sinner when, baptized by the Spirit, he passes into the place of adoption. Here baptism takes its place at the beginning of the Christian life, immediately succeeding faith in the revealed Lord, and succeeded by the new relationship to God.

When the long-suffering of God waited in the days of Noah, while the ark was a preparing, wherein few, that is, eight souls, were saved through water: which also in the antitype doth now save you, even baptism, not the putting away of the filth of the flesh, but the interrogation of a good conscience toward God, through the resurrection of Jesus Christ (1 Pet. 3:20, 21 margin.).

Peter says that in the days of Noah the people were saved by water; and that men are saved today by that of which water is a figure—that is to say, men are saved by the baptism of the Holy Spirit.

This is a review of the whole of the passages in the New Testament that refer to the question of the baptism of the Spirit. In every case the reference is, not to some blessing subsequent to regeneration, but to regeneration itself—to that supernatural miracle by which a soul passes from darkness into light, out of death into life, from the thraldom of sin and Satan into the glorious liberty of a child of God.

This sweeps away the view that the baptism of the Spirit is a second blessing. There is absolutely no warrant in the whole teaching of Scripture for such a view; and therefore there is, further, no warrant for the popular and prevalent idea that the Holy Spirit must be asked for, or waited for.

Referring to the oft-quoted words of the Master, *If ye then, being evil, know how to give good gifts unto your children, how much more shall your Father which is in heaven give good things to them that ask Him?* (Matt. 7:11). it has already been shown[*] that these words were spoken while He was fulfilling His work as the Jewish Messiah to Jewish disciples. They never asked, and therefore never received the Spirit through their asking. He came in reply to the asking of Jesus,

---

[*] Chapter 7

upon the ground of His finished work. The Spirit is never given in answer to human asking, but upon the ground of repentance and faith, man is baptized therewith, and from that moment the Spirit of God takes possession and dwells within. The believer may check Him, hinder Him, thwart Him, and grieve Him, but from the moment of the new birth he is a temple of the Holy Spirit. It is, then, in the initial miracle of regeneration that souls are baptized with the Holy Spirit.

On the same ground it is not right that Christian people should profess to be waiting for the baptism of the Spirit. The words, *Tarry, . . . until ye be clothed with power from on high* (Luke 24:49), have no application to newborn souls at all; or if they have an application, it is one that is a sad revelation of a condition of life that dishonors the Lord. If men have to tarry until endued with power, it is not because God has not given the Spirit, but because there is something in the life which will not let the Spirit work. Every believer is a temple of the Holy Spirit; and if there be tarrying, it is on account of some disobedience, and not on account of any unreadiness on the part of God to bestow full blessing upon all His children. Such tarrying is not the waiting of man for the Spirit, but the waiting of the Spirit for man.

There are certain passages in the Acts of the Apostles which are used to show that the gift of the Holy Spirit, or the baptism of the Spirit is subsequent to conversion.

Philip went to Samaria and preached there; people believed in Jesus, and were baptized in His name. After that the apostles visited these believers, and they received the Holy Spirit. Therefore, it is asserted that people believe on Christ, and are baptized, but the Holy Spirit has to be received as a second blessing.

Carefully notice what actually took place. Philip came to Samaria, preached in the name of Jesus, and men believed in some intellectual sense, and were baptized. Among the number was Simon Magus. It is impossible to distinguish between Simon Magus and the rest, because the statement that Simon Magus believed is as distinct as is the statement that the others did so, and the Scriptures as distinctly state that he was baptized because he believed, as that the others were baptized because they believed. But when the apostles came, Peter thus described Simon Magus: *Thou hast neither part nor lot in this matter: for thy heart is not right before God. . . . For I see that thou art in the gall of bitterness and in the bond of iniquity* (Acts 8:21–23). As to the others, Peter unfolded to them the full meaning of the Gospel message, and those that heard it received the Holy Spirit. None of them had received the Spirit, and therefore none of them were born again. These people of Samaria, it must be remembered, held the Jewish view of Messiahship, and their belief in Jesus, was in Him as having come for the establishment of the earthly kingdom. They had given an intellectual assent to the story of Jesus, and, having believed it, had consented to go through an outward form and ceremony, but not until the apostles came, and the Spirit of God fell upon them, were they members of the Church or converted souls.

Again, the story of the conversion of Saul of Tarsus is used in the same way: *And Ananias departed, and entered into the house; and laying his hands on him said, Brother Saul, the Lord, even Jesus, Who appeared unto thee in the way which thou camest, hath sent me, that thou mayest receive thy sight, and be filled with the Holy Spirit. And straightway there fell from his eyes as it were scales, and he received his sight; and he arose and was baptized; and he took food and was strengthened* (Acts 9:17–19). Concerning this case there is certainly room for doubt. The probability, however, is that the procedure is in harmony with all the rest, and that Saul was arrested and convinced of the kingship of Jesus on the road to Damascus, but did not enter into the Church by regeneration until the fuller light came from the instruction of Ananias. Even if it be granted that there were certain people who believed in Jesus, yet did not immediately receive the Holy Spirit, it must be remembered that cases like these are not to be found in the subsequent story of Acts.

The passage most often used in this way is the question Paul addressed to certain people at Ephesus: *Did ye receive the Holy Spirit when ye believed?* (Acts 19:2). The Authorized Version, with less accuracy, translated it: *Have ye received the Holy Spirit since ye believed?*

This, it is alleged, gives a clear case of people who had believed and yet had not received the Holy Spirit. But here again the facts of the case must be carefully examined. Paul came to Ephesus, and found there a little company of believers in Jesus. There is no record as to why he put this question to them, but he asked them: *Did ye receive the Ho¹y Spirit when ye believed?* (Acts 19:2). The question evidently carries with it the thought that they ought to have done so. *And they said unto him, Nay, we did not so much as hear whether the Holy Spirit was given. And he said* [most probably in surprise], *Into what then were ye baptized? And they said, Into John's baptism. And Paul said, John baptized with the baptism of repentance, saying unto the people, that they should believe on Him which should come after him, that is, on Jesus. And when they heard this, they were baptized into the name of the Lord Jesus. And when Paul had laid his hands upon them, the Holy Spirit came on them* (vv. 2–6).

These people were not Christians, they were not born again; they were the disciples of Jesus as He was heralded by John. It was therefore necessary for them to receive the Holy Spirit, in order that they might pass from that region of water baptism into the region of the baptism of the Holy Spirit. But it may be wondered how there came to be disciples of John as far away as Ephesus. The explanation is found in the context: *Now a certain Jew named Apollos, an Alexandrian by race, a learned man, came to Ephesus; and he was mighty in the Scriptures. . . . Being fervent in spirit, he spake and taught carefully the things concerning Jesus, knowing only the baptism of John* (Acts 18:24, 25). That accounts for the presence of disciples at Ephesus. When Apollos came there, he himself did not know the baptism of the Spirit; and these were people baptized with the baptism of John, and knowing therefore only so much of Jesus as John himself had been able to declare. Apollos himself had to be instructed in *the way of God more carefully* (v. 26); and when the apostle came, this handful of believers in John's baptism had also to be taught. Therefore to interpret this text as teaching that beyond the day of conversion there is some other gift of the Holy Spirit necessary, is to wrest it out of its proper setting and to set up a new standard of Christian life, for which it gives no warrant.

There are many moral people who admire Christ, and have perchance even been baptized with John's baptism, but they have never been born again: to them this text has a direct application. But to people born again of the Spirit of God, there can be no application of this message, because by the new birth they have received the Holy Spirit, and into that Spirit they have been baptized.

The baptism of the Spirit, then, is that miracle of regeneration whereby a man passes into the new realm of life in which Christ is supreme in the power of His own communicated life.

In the great commission, *He that believeth and is baptized shall be saved, but he that disbelieveth shall be condemned* (Mark 16:16), most assuredly the baptism referred to is that of the Holy Spirit. The words declare the condition of salvation and the promise thereof: *He that believeth* [that is the human condition] *and is baptized* [that is the Divine miracle] *shall be saved*. When the negative side is stated, baptism is omitted, as being unnecessary; for he that disbelieveth cannot be baptized. If it is water baptism, he can, but if it is the baptism of the Spirit, he cannot. Thus in that commission the Lord most evidently puts the baptism of the Spirit at the very entrance of the kingdom. Men believing (one faith), and being baptized (one baptism), are saved; while he that believeth not is condemned.

By this baptism of the Spirit the individual becomes a temple of the Holy Spirit; and the message that ought to be delivered to Christian people today is: *Ye are a temple of God* (1 Cor. 3:16); do not desecrate the temple, but let the Divine One Who indwells, govern absolutely the whole being. Not that the heart should be opened to admit the Spirit; for God's children are such because the Holy Spirit has already taken possession, and even though defiled, they nevertheless are the temples of the Holy Spirit; for it was not to sanctified people, in the usually accepted sense of the term, that the apostle said: *Ye are a temple of God*. The central fact, the great and almost appalling miracle of Christianity, is that persons baptized by the Spirit become temples of God. They also become members of the catholic Church, parts of the Body of Christ. Moreover, by that baptism they are sealed unto a consummation, sealed unto the final day of redemption.

It is to be feared that many, in emphasizing what is spoken of as the second blessing—an idea and an expression to be found nowhere in Scripture—insult and degrade the blessing of regeneration, which holds within itself all subsequent unfoldings of blessing and of power.

16
The Filling of the Spirit
(The New Testament Ideal)

In discussing this subject, the one matter of importance is the discovery of the sense in which the term *the filling of the Spirit* is used in the New Testament.

In one form or another it occurs four times prior to the Pentecostal effusion:

For he shall be great in the sight of the Lord, and he shall drink no wine nor strong drink; and he shall be filled with the Holy Spirit, even from his mother's womb (Luke 1:15).

And it came to pass, when Elizabeth heard the salutation of Mary, the babe leaped in her womb; and Elizabeth was filled with the Holy Spirit; and she lifted up her voice with a loud cry (vv. 41, 42).

And his father Zacharias was filled with the Holy Spirit, and prophesied saying (v. 67).

And Jesus, full of the Holy Spirit, returned from the Jordan, and was led by the Spirit in the wilderness during forty days (Luke 4:1).

John, the forerunner of the Christ, was filled with the Spirit from his birth. Elizabeth was filled with the Spirit for the singing of a sacred song. Zacharias was filled with the Spirit for the uttering of prophecy. The Lord was filled with the Spirit for the exercise of His Messianic ministry.

This filling of certain persons, prior to the Pentecostal effusion, was a continuation of the Spirit's work, in keeping with the methods which had characterized the whole of the dispensation then drawing to a close. Just as in the past the Spirit had filled men for the accomplishment of special work for God; so, as the dispensation drew to a close, and Messiah approached, He again equipped those who were to do the special work the occasion demanded.

A clear line is drawn between the old and the new dispensations; and the teaching of the New Testament concerning the filling of the Spirit in the dispensation which had its birth at Pentecost is very distinct.

The expression occurs in the Acts of the Apostles eight times, and once in the Letter to the Ephesians. These passages practically contain the whole system.

The sum of that teaching is that the Spirit-filled life is the normal condition of the believer. There are those who believe that the filling of the Spirit is something which is not merely a *second blessing* in the experience of the majority of Christians, but in the purpose of God. But just as the baptism of the Spirit is never spoken of as a second blessing, but always as the initial blessing of regeneration, so in the economy of God the filling of the Spirit is coincident with conversion. When a man is baptized with the Spirit, he is born of the Spirit, and is filled with the Spirit. There are many who do not enter into the realization of that blessedness at conversion. In the purpose of God, however, the normal condition of Christian life is that of being baptized by the Spirit into life, and filled with the Spirit for life.

Nothing can be clearer than the statement of what happened on the Day of Pentecost: *And there appeared unto them tongues parting asunder, like as of fire; and it sat upon each one of them. And they were all filled with the Holy Spirit, and began to speak with other tongues, as the Spirit gave them utterance* (Acts 2:3, 4). In the moment when the group of Jewish disciples was transformed into the Church, the Spirit was not only given to them, He filled them. It is evident, therefore, from the account of the opening of the dispensation, that in the purpose of God those who passed into its new life, new glory, new breadth, and new beauty were baptized and filled with the Spirit.

An illustration of this occurs in the history of the early days. Saul of Tarsus, *breathing threatening and slaughter against the disciples of the Lord* (Acts 9:1), was on his way to Damascus, when he was suddenly arrested by the shining of a light from heaven; he heard the voice of Jesus, and yielded to the claim of the Master, saying: *What shall I do, Lord?* (Acts 22:10). He remained blind; and having been led to Damascus, the Master sent Ananias to him: *And Ananias departed, and entered into the house; and laying his hands on him, said, Brother Saul, the Lord, even Jesus, who appeared unto thee in the way which thou camest, hath sent me, that thou mayest receive thy sight, and be filled with the Holy Spirit* (Acts 9:17). It may be a matter of opinion as to whether that was the moment of his conversion or not.* Even if he were born of the Spirit on the way to Damascus, the filling of the Spirit, according to this teaching, came immediately, and was part of the very earliest experience of his Christian life.

It follows, therefore, that the will of God for His people is that they should be filled at once; that God does not give a man the Spirit today, and then make him, as a necessity, wait for perhaps a number of years before he is filled with the Spirit, but that the supreme miracle by which a man is born of the Spirit, and so baptized of the Spirit into new relationship with Christ, is also the miracle by which he becomes filled with the Spirit of God.

There is another use made of this same phrase in the Acts of the Apostles: *And when they had set them in the midst, they inquired, By what power, or in what name, have ye done this? Then Peter, filled with the Holy Spirit, said unto them, Ye rulers of the people, and elders, if we this day are examined* (Acts 4:7–9). The sense of the word *filled* in this case is that of being specially filled for special work. It does not describe a normal condition of life, but a specific filling, in order that he might be specially prepared for work that awaited him at that moment. Filled with the Spirit, he spoke the words.

---

* Chapter 15

Another instance of the same kind is chronicled in the words: *But Saul, who is also called Paul, filled with the Holy Spirit, fastened his eyes on him* [that is, on Elymas the sorcerer], *and said, O full of all guile and all villainy, thou son of the devil, thou enemy of all righteousness, wilt thou not cease to pervert the right ways of the Lord?* (Acts 13:9, 10). A special work of discipline had to be performed: a man who had wronged the truth and the faith had to be rebuked, and Paul was suddenly filled with the Holy Spirit for the doing of that particular work.

Again the term is used in a way that includes the filling for life and service, the former being viewed as the condition for the latter: *Look ye out therefore, brethren, from among you seven men of good report, full of the Spirit and of wisdom, whom we may appoint over this business. . . . And the saying pleased the whole multitude: and they chose Stephen, a man full of faith and of the Holy Spirit, and Philip* (Acts 6:3–5). These men were chosen for work in the Church because they were full of the Spirit.

It is written of Barnabas that *he was a good man, and full of the Holy Spirit and of faith: and much people was added unto the Lord* (Acts 11:24).

These are the occasions where the term is used in the Acts of the Apostles with reference to service. Twice in the case of the deacons, and also in the case of Barnabas, it is evident that the condition for service is that men should be full of the Spirit—not that there should be a special gift, but that they should be living the life that is Spirit-filled. Where that is so, they are fit for the office of deacon; where that is so, they are fit, as was Barnabas, for visiting the churches and for administering spiritual comfort. But from the other instances of Peter and Paul, it is equally clear that the term is used with reference to a special filling for a special work.

The phrase is also used in a sense proving that though the filling of the Spirit is the normal condition of the believer's life, yet it may be lost and restored: *And when they had prayed, the place was shaken wherein they were gathered together; and they were all filled with the Holy Spirit, and they spake the word of God with boldness* (Acts 4:31). This has been erroneously spoken of as *the second Pen-*

tecost. There can be no second Pentecost. Pentecost came once and forever. Undoubtedly a second manifestation of the Spirit is here referred to, but it was rendered necessary because these men had passed into a realm of fear and trembling. Peter and John were imprisoned, and the disciples were gathered in fear and trembling, hardly daring to open the doors or show themselves. When Peter and John were miraculously restored and came into their midst, they gave themselves to prayer, asking that they might have boldness. The answer to their prayer was the shaking of the house in which they were assembled, and their refilling with the Spirit. These men had not lost the Spirit. They had been sealed unto the day of redemption. Born of the Spirit, the Spirit remained in them, but through their own fear, unbelief, and lack of loyalty to Jesus Christ, the blessing of the Spirit's fullness had been lost. When they returned to the Lord, the filling was granted to them anew.

Another instance is recorded which gives yet another light on the subject. Of Stephen it is said: *But he, being full of the Holy Spirit, looked up steadfastly into heaven, and saw the glory of God, and Jesus standing on the right hand of God* (Acts 7:55). Passing through martyrdom, Stephen was strengthened in his suffering by a vision of his Master in the glory. The condition for seeing the vision was the fullness of the Holy Spirit.

These are the only instances in the Acts of the Apostles where the term *filling of the Spirit* is used. The sum of their teaching may thus be stated. The Spirit-filled life is the normal condition of the believer; it may be lost; it can be restored. Newborn souls, baptized by the Spirit into union with Christ, are filled, but very often, for lack of clear teaching and full understanding of the law of the Spirit, the fullness of the blessing is lost.

There are thousands whose memories go back to some convention, to some service, to some hour of loneliness with God, when they became Spirit-filled in a sense which they had never experienced before. The explanation of this fact is that at some point in their Christian life, preceding the experience of which they speak as a *second blessing*, they had been disobedient to the Divine purpose; and therefore the blame of the low-level life preceding that blessing is to be laid, not upon the economy of God, but upon the disloyalty of the believer. There is no reason why a man should not immediately from the moment of regeneration enter into all the blessedness of the Spirit-filled life: that is the Divine intention, and that is the Divine purpose. This is a question of condition and not of finality. The law of growth is that the believer should be Spirit-filled.

For special service there is, however, a special filling of the Holy Spirit, and whether it be Peter or Paul or any other servant of Christ having a special work to do for Him, that servant may be specially filled with the Spirit for the accomplishment of that special work.

There is one other passage demanding attention: *And be not drunk with wine, wherein is riot, but be filled with the Spirit* (Eph. 5:18). The injunction *be filled with the Spirit* is in the imperative. It is a command; and the fact that it is a command lays responsibility, not upon God, but upon the believer. In the commencement of the Epistle the whole scheme of thought which was here in the mind of the apostle is stated: *In Whom ye also, having heard the word of the truth, the gospel of your salvation—in Whom, having also believed, ye were sealed with the Holy Spirit of promise, which is an earnest of our inheritance* (Eph. 1:13, 14). The sealing of the Spirit is identical with the baptism of the Spirit. The apostle is writing to people who are sealed with the Spirit, and he charges them to be filled with the Spirit. Here are two distinct things—the sealing of the Spirit, and the filling of the Spirit. Though the filling be coincident with the sealing, it is necessary to enjoin these people to be filled, because that is the point of their responsibility. That responsibility is revealed in the words: *Grieve not the Holy Spirit of God, in Whom ye were sealed unto the day of redemption* (Eph. 4:30). Here is a solution of the mystery that gathers around the experience of thousands of Christians. They are born of the Spirit, and none will deny that they are Christians. They are not, however, filled with the Spirit, for the fruit of the Spirit is not manifest in their lives. The reason for this is that they have grieved the Holy Spirit of God somewhere in the past. The path of obedience has been clearly marked, and they have disobeyed. Christian people who are baptized by the Spirit into new relationship with Christ have grieved the Spirit by disobedience, lukewarmness, indifference to the claims of Christ, worldliness, or frivolity, and they are therefore not filled with the Spirit. The subject of responsibility, showing what are the conditions of the filling and what is the result of the filling, will form the subject of a subsequent chapter.*

Dr. Erdmann, of Philadelphia, has given a formula of the law of the Spirit in these words—*One baptism, many fillings*; and perhaps no statement of the case could be more helpful. It is borne out by New Testament teaching and history. One baptism—the moment of the new birth, when the Spirit comes upon the repenting and believing soul and unites that soul to Christ. Christians may be disobedient and lose the filling of the Spirit, and by repentance and obedience it may be restored; and in the experience of multitudes of believers this formula is proved to be correct—One baptism, but many fillings.

This is also illustrated, as has been already shown, by the filling of the apostles at the baptism of Pentecost, and by their refilling subsequently, which was by no means a second baptism. The specific fillings for service are the fillings to overflowing, of which the Lord Himself declared: *He that believeth on Me . . . out of his belly shall flow rivers of living water* (John 7:38). This third phase of blessing, the specific work of the Spirit for service, has sometimes been spoken of as an anointing of the Spirit, but without Scripture warrant. The term *anointing of the Spirit* is used only twice with regard to Christians (2 Cor. 1:21; 1 John 2:27). In both places the reference is to regeneration. There are those who are perpetually declaring that Christians must follow in the steps of Christ, and that, as He was anointed for His work, so must they be for theirs, but there is no perfect analogy between the dealings of God with Christ, and His dealings with believers, because Christ was sinless and spotless, while they have always to be dealt with as those who have failed, and must be restored to the divine pattern. It would be just as incorrect to speak of a second anointing as of a second Pentecost, or of a second Pentecost as of a second anointing. The anointing which is

---

* Chapter 19

on the child of God is that which was received at regeneration. What is needed for life is the perpetual filling of the Spirit which is the normal condition of those who are living in the way of God, and the specific fillings to overflowing which may always be counted on when special service demands.

Every believer on the Lord Jesus Christ having vital relationship with Him, became a Christian when baptized with the Holy Spirit, and at the moment of baptism was filled with the Spirit. If not filled with the Spirit now, the blame is to be laid, not upon the Master, but upon personal disobedience. Somewhere in the life of relationship to Christ there was a moment of disobedience, a moment of disloyalty, a moment of rebellion against government; and by that rebellion the filling of the Spirit was lost. It may be restored by restoration to obedience, the new yielding of the life to the Spirit. He will enter and will take possession of the territory from which by disobedience He has been excluded. Dr. Handley Moule, who is perhaps one of the most lucid exponents of the Scriptures upon this subject, says that the difference between a soul that is filled with the Spirit and one that is unfilled, is the difference between a well in which there is a spring of water choked, and a well from which the obstruction has been removed, so that the water springs up and fills the well. In every child of God the Spirit is present, waiting to fill; and if He does not fill the whole life to its utmost bound with His own energy, light, and power, it is because there is something which prevents Him, and which must be removed before He can do His blessed work.

The filling of the Spirit is indeed an experience far beyond that of which the majority of Christians know anything, but it is the purpose of God that every child of His should be filled, not a year, nor two years, nor ten years after conversion, but at the moment of conversion, and perpetually until the consummation of his sojourn upon the earth.

17

The Power of the Spirit

The first chapter of the Acts of the Apostles is of great interest, as giving the last glimpse of the disciples of Jesus apart from the indwelling of the Holy Spirit. The picture is full of instruction, revealing with clearness the enormous difference there must ever be between man in his fallen nature, and man as he may be through the baptism and indwelling of the Spirit. One cannot look at this picture, incomplete though it may be, without seeing that these men were still ignorant and selfish. There is no comparison between the men of the first chapter, and the men of the subsequent history contained in the book.

They came to the risen Lord with the old question: *Lord, dost Thou at this time restore the kingdom to Israel?* (Acts 1:6). They had made no progress. The events of the past weeks had not been sufficient to reveal to them the great essential verities of the Christian faith. They were still bound by the materialism of Judaism; the spiritual vision had not yet fallen upon them; they did not understand the mission of Christ. They were still looking for a temporal kingdom which should be immediately set up. They had no appreciation of the fact that Jesus was passing to a hidden throne and a hidden crown, and that the work to which they were now to be committed was not temporal, external, and material, but eternal, internal, and spiritual.

They had not yet escaped from the narrow, national prejudices which had been the curse of the nation for so long. *Dost Thou at this time restore the kingdom to Israel?* They had no idea of the worldwide kingdom of the Messiah. Their vision was still limited by the horizon of their own people. The Master had ever looked beyond the confines of the nation. Not so the disciples, neither were they yet able to do so.

They did not understand that the work He had come to do was something absolutely new. They dreamed of the restoration of the old. *Restore* was the word they made use of.

Their love was deep, and true, and intense; their knowledge during the days of discipleship was far in advance of that of the men of their age; the Resurrection was to them a fact, for the living Christ was in their midst. Yet they were absolutely unfit for the work they had to do, for they were still looking for the temporal kingdom to be set up in the same way that other earthly kingdoms had been.

To these men Christ said: *Ye shall receive power, when the Holy Spirit is come upon you: and ye shall be My witnesses both in Jerusalem, and in all Judea and Samaria, and unto the uttermost part of the earth* (Acts 1:8). This word answers and corrects the false idea contained in their question. They said: *Dost Thou at this time restore the kingdom?* They thought of a return to old things. He replied: *Ye shall be My witnesses.* He directed their thought to the new Center. They said: *Dost Thou at this time restore the kingdom?* Their minds were fixed upon earthly things. He said: *Ye shall receive power, when the Holy Spirit is come.* His mind encompassed the spiritual relationship. They said: *Dost Thou at this time restore the kingdom to Israel?* They were bound by the idea of the nation. He replied: *Jerusalem, and in all Judea and Samaria, and unto the uttermost part of the earth.* He included the world in His vision.

This was a new beginning, moving out from Himself as Center, having the Holy Spirit as Administrator, and the disciples as channels of communication.

There is a sense in which these words of the Master cannot be addressed to Christian people today. These men had not yet been baptized with the Holy Spirit; they were not yet born again. Those that are Christians today are such by that baptism and new birth; and, consequently, they possess the power promised to these men.

The central principle declared is that fitness for service in the new covenant lies within the realm of the power of the Holy Spirit. This is of perpetual application, and it is therefore important that a chapter should be devoted to its consideration. There are three matters to be noted: first, the power needed; secondly, the nature of the power available; and, thirdly, the purpose for which the power is bestowed.

For the accomplishment of their work these men needed a fourfold force. They needed intellectual power, because of their ignorance and inability to appreciate the meaning of the Master's mission. They needed spiritual power, in the sense of ability to do righteously, notwithstanding the carnal possibilities still resident in their own lives. They needed a new power of the affection and will, because of the tremendous forces which would be arrayed against them in the prosecution of the work that was before them. They needed power for the accomplishment of the results at which they aimed, because the forces hitherto used in great movements would be denied them.

It is not necessary to deal at length with the first phase of this need, having already referred to it, but their lack of understanding of the Cross must be remembered. The apostle in writing to the Corinthians described the Cross as being *unto Jews a stumbling block* (1 Cor. 1:23)—that is, something in the way, an obstruction; and up to this point their outlook was purely Jewish. Think how they had followed the Master, and how they had learned to love Him. Then remember how swiftly doom fell upon Him, their Teacher, their Friend. They had seen Him overcome by the detested Roman power, and nailed to the Cross. It is only as their place is occupied in imagination, and the prejudices of their birth and education are in some measure understood, that it will be possible to appreciate how completely the Cross must have extinguished hope for them, and how sincere and sad was the sigh of the men who walked to Emmaus: *We hoped that it was He which should redeem Israel* (Luke 24:21).

Of the mysteries that are the essential grandeur of Christianity—death, the entrance to life—life won through death; defeat, the way into victory—victory won through defeat; darkness, the price of light—light dawning out of darkness—they had no appreciation. They saw only the death, the defeat, and the darkness. The Cross was to them a stumbling block. Afterwards they told the story of the Cross as being the story of love, of liberty, of light, but before they were able to do this, they needed a new intellectual grasp upon the things of God. The power they were to receive after that the Holy Spirit came upon them was the new power of intelligence, enabling them to comprehend the true meaning of the facts they were to publish.

The second phase of the need is the power for holy living. In the purpose of God the force and meaning of the Cross were to be revealed to men not merely by the words of His servants' lips, but also by the transformation of their lives. Man had been the slave of his own carnality, dominated by the evil forces within him. Henceforth he is to be free from this power; in union with Jesus Christ he is to be master of the things that have mastered him. The essential message of the Gospel is the declaration that through the Cross and Resurrection of Christ a new dynamic is at the disposal of men, in the power of which they may be victorious, trampling under their feet the lust of which hitherto they have been the slaves. Witness to this truth is to be borne not only by a testimony of the lips, but by the triumph of lives, proving the accuracy of the testimony. First, a clear appreciation of the meaning of the Cross; secondly, the personal apprehension of its power; behind the testimony the triumph—the testimony proved by the triumph, the triumph accounted for by the testimony. Such is the Divine ideal of the work that lay before these men. If this indeed be true, it is evident that they needed this power of Holiness that their lives might be transformed. It is this power that He promised to them when He spoke of the coming of the Holy Spirit.

Further, they needed new power of the affection and will. Persecution awaited them. All the forces that had been against their Master would oppose them. The doctrine of deliverance which they were to announce was revolutionary, and the powers that held men in slavery would array themselves to silence their voices and stop their progress. If they were to continue bearing witness to Him through darkness as well as through light, when the way was rough as well as when it was smooth, through the perils of popularity as well as through the dangers of ostracism, they needed some new power of the affection and the will, which should make their love burn as a flame, and set their faces as flint.

They had already been in one place of testing, and with what dire results! Oh the tragedy of that simple sentence, *They all left Him, and fled* (Mark 14:50)! If they had done that while He was yet with them, while the power of His personality was upon them, how would they act when the clouds had hidden Him from view and the sound of His voice was not to be heard? They stood in need of a power that should keep love burning, and the will to accomplish their work unconquered.

> They cannot drive the world
> Until themselves be driven.

This power is precisely what Jesus promised in the indwelling Spirit. Ever revealing the fact of the Christ to the disciples, He would capture the soul by the vision of love every moment, and make the will to do His work invincible as the very will of God.

Once more, they needed a new working power. Said the Master: *Ye shall be My witnesses both in Jerusalem, and in all Judea and Samaria, and unto the uttermost part of the earth* (Acts 1:8). They were to tell the story of His life and death to all men; they were to urge His claims upon the attention of men; they were to win men for Him. And all this was to be done without the aids that human wisdom would immediately think of. The conquests of the past had been the conquests of argument, and policy, and the sword. These were all denied them. They had no commission to persuade men by argument. Policy had no place in their program. Of the sword the Master Himself had said: *Put up . . . thy sword . . . for all they that take the sword shall perish with the sword* (Matt. 26:52).

By other methods they were to accomplish their work. The propagandists of the new kingdom were sent forth in the name of an absent King, with no sign of power recognized by the men of the world. They needed some new power, and this is exactly what the Master promised them when He spoke of the coming of the Holy Spirit. Having that power, they should pass into all lands, and do deeds and win triumphs more mighty and marvelous than any that the world had ever seen or known.

So far the first disciples have been under consideration, but the teaching is permanent. No man can do the work of God until he have the Holy Spirit, and is endued with power. It is impossible to preach the Gospel save in the power of the Spirit, because none can comprehend the true meaning of the Cross of Christ unless taught by the Spirit of God. Neither a knowledge of the letter of the New Testament, nor a system of theology, is sufficient to equip for preaching the Cross. Nothing short of the immediate, direct, personal illumination of the Spirit is sufficient equipment. Witness for the Master is impossible save to those who cooperate with the supreme Witness. The keenest intellect and the most cultured mind are unable to understand the mystery of redemption, and therefore cannot explain it to others. Whoever can say light has broken upon the Cross and the eternal morning has dawned is able to do so through the direct illumination of the Holy Spirit; and apart from that, there can be no witness and no service.

It is equally true that there can be no witness in the life but by this constant indwelling of the Holy Spirit. The nature is still capable of sin; and if it pass from under the Divine government, all manner of evil will follow. Men can only live the life that is in harmony with the teaching of Christ as they are possessed and energized by the Holy Spirit of God.

It is also necessary that the affection and will should be under the dominion of the Spirit. Perpetual love and perennial joy are only possible where the Spirit of God abides at the center of being, energizing the will that else would fail, and strengthening every step in the path of obedience. Save as the life is lived under the dominion of the Spirit, temptation will prove too strong and the sacred Name will be dishonored.

Again, in all service for God, the power of the Spirit is still needed. Much has been done since the apostolic days for making the work of the preacher easy. The Canon of the New Testament is complete; theology has been systematized; the necessity for the thorough equipment of the preacher educationally, wherever possible, is realized: these and many other advantages which the early Christian preachers had not, contribute to the smoothness of the pathway of the preacher today. All these, however, are insufficient. Beside them all, and as the power which alone makes them of real use, the Holy Spirit must equip the preacher, or preaching will degenerate into lifeless rhetoric, or heartless argument. This is equally true of every form of Christian service. It is pre-eminently the day of organization. Societies have multiplied on every hand, and the machinery of the Church is complex and multitudinous. This is all cause for thankfulness, but it cannot too often be repeated, that apart from the Holy Spirit's control and direction, all is dead. The advantages of the moment are not to be despised. Those who would go back to primitive simplicity must deny the guidance of God in the centuries. Let all be yielded to the fire and power of the Spirit for cleansing and energy, and the pulpit will be the greatest force in all human life, and every organization of the Church will throb and pulsate with Divine energy.

The nature of the power is evident. It is the coming of God to man for the accomplishment of a Divine purpose in this sacred partnership. Man is helpless apart from this immediate cooperation with God. God chooses to be helpless apart from cooperation with man. Within the next thirty years from Pentecost the whole known world was influenced by this handful of men who had been gathered by Jesus, and taught by Him with such matchless patience and gentleness, preparatory to the Spirit's baptism. Yet the world failed to comprehend the meaning or to explain the mystery of this new movement. The younger Pliny, in a letter to the Emperor about the Christians, said that after inquiries he found that they sang hymns about One called Jesus, and that they paid the taxes. A most excellent testimony. May it still be borne concerning all those who take the name of Christ! Yet what a remarkable analysis for an educated mind to offer! It was simple and sublime—simple, in that it revealed his failure to comprehend the deep meaning of Christianity and his inability to do more than read the externals; sublime, in that it unintentionally, yet surely revealed the fact that joy and righteousness resulted from the worship of God in Christ, and the characters of men were so transformed that they sang and paid taxes. As a rule human nature is hardly capable of doing both these things, but these men accomplished it because righteousness itself had become a joy in the power of the name of Jesus. It is not to be wondered at that they were not understood. The usual signs of power were absent altogether. These people had no visible Head. The Founder had perished by the ignominious death of the Cross. They were gathered and marshaled and led, not to arming and battle by the cry of a warrior, but silently and surely, to the undermining of empires, and the downfall of dynasties. This element of mystery lasts until this hour. The man of the world is still unable to account for it. Proof of this is to be found in a perusal of his magazine articles occasionally. The secret of it all is that within the Church, God has taken up His abode within every individual member thereof; and in a perpetual comradeship and cooperation He moves on towards the purposes of His heart, through all the forces that oppose and the obstacles that hinder. Wherever Christianity has been a real force, working to success, it is because it has been spiritual. The wheels of the chariot are clogged by all attempts to make arrangements to help God. They are speeded when, self forgotten, the Spirit that indwells is permitted to have unquestioned and absolute control.

Yet let it be remembered that, if the force of Christianity is not of man, it operates through man. God has so chosen to work. This was symbolized on the Day of Pentecost by the cloven tongues of fire: *There appeared unto them tongues parting asunder, like as of fire; and it sat upon each one of them* (Acts 2:3). *Tongues,* diversities of gifts; *fire*, the one Spirit. *Tongues*, the human instrument; *fire*, the Divine energy. Man, the instrument; God, the Worker.

Much of the lack of power in service today is due to the fact that the true conception of what service should be has been lost. The only reason that those who are born again of the Spirit are left in the world is that they may be His witnesses. Paul distinctly teaches in his Letter to the Ephesians that the supreme vocation of the Church lies not in the present age nor in present circumstances. Her final work will be the manifestation of the wisdom and the grace of God to principalities and powers in the heavenly places. The reason why the Church is not at once removed to this higher service is that in the midst of the darkness and death around, she may profess to others her absent but living Lord.

Light is thrown upon this work by a consideration of the word *witness*. The word actually used is *martyr*. This word is used today almost exclusively of those who suffer persecution for the truth. That use of the word, while dignifying it, is in danger of obscuring its first intention. A martyr is one, convinced of truth, manifesting that truth in life. The fires of persecution never made martyrs—they revealed them. A man who was not already a martyr never laid down his life for truth. The noble army of martyrs died, not to become martyrs, but because they were martyrs. This is the distinctive service of all believers in this age. They are to reveal in transformed and transfigured lives the glory and beauty of the teaching and character of Jesus Christ. This ideal of service flings men back at once into the place of conscious dependence upon the Holy Spirit, for none can witness of Christ save in actual cooperation with Him. Two simple sentences will be helpful in order to understand the law of that cooperation:

The Holy Spirit witnesses of Jesus only.

Only the Holy Spirit witnesses of Jesus.

It is very important to remember the first of these. The Spirit has nothing to say of Himself. His whole mission and message has to do with Christ. Many people today are waiting for a manifestation of the Spirit Himself. They are doomed to disappointment. When

He obtains full possession of any individual, it is not His own Person and personality He makes real, but that of Jesus.

The second point is of equal importance. Everything that is known of the Savior is known as the result of the illumination of the Holy Spirit. He is the Revealer of the Revealer. There can be no communication with Jesus until the Spirit reveals Him to the heart. There is no vision of the loveliness of His face save as the Spirit anoints the eyes. Herein lies the blessedness of this Pentecostal age. The power for witnessing is the birthright of every believer. The Spirit reveals Christ to the consciousness. This new sense of the Master captivates the will and transforms the entire being into likeness to Himself. This development of character is also increased capacity for the reception of revelation. To that increased capacity the Spirit is able to make still more glorious revelation, which yet further increases capacity, and prepares the way for still more glorious revelation. Thus, in a proportionately increasing ratio, life under the control of the Spirit is manifesting the glory of the Master, and thus witnessing for Him.

For such witnessing the world waits today. Humanity amid its sobbing, and its sighing, needs a manifestation of the sons and daughters of the King; and in proportion as the temples of the Spirit are yielded to the Spirit, that great need of the race is being met.

Book VII
The Practical Application

Breathe on me, Breath of God,
  Fill me with life anew,
That I may love what Thou dost love,
  And do what Thou wouldst do.

Breathe on me, Breath of God,
  Until my heart is pure,
Until with Thee I will one will,
  To do and to endure.

Breathe on me, Breath of God,
  Blend all my soul with Thine,
Until this earthly part of me
  Glows with Thy fire Divine.

Breathe on me, Breath of God,
  So shall I never die,
But live with Thee the perfect life
  Of Thine eternity.

E. Hatch

18

Ye Must Be Born Anew

No person can be a child of God but by the renewing work of
the Holy Spirit. The entrance to Christianity is perpetually
and jealously guarded by the words of Jesus to Nicodemus:
Ye must be born anew (John 3:7). The reason for this is to be found
in the very nature of Christianity. It presents an ideal of life, and
enunciates an ethical code, of such a nature as to demand something more than themselves. Its ideal is Jesus. Its code of ethics is
His teaching. These are united in a sacred and wondrous union, for
all He taught men to be, He was Himself. So wondrous was He in
beauty of character, and so searching and severe in the requirements
of His law, that man in his impotence is absolutely unable to copy
the one, or to obey the other. If Christianity, therefore, has nothing
more to offer men than these, it is an impossible and impracticable
ideal, a mere mirage of the desert, suggesting growth and fertility, but
ever eluding the grasp of those who, weary and desolate, stretch out
longing hands after its fruits. The something more required is the essential gift and power of Christianity. It comes to men with life which
is the very life of the Ideal, and is therefore the dynamic of obedience
to the code. Nothing short of actual participation in that life constitutes any human being a Christian. Admiration of the Person and
character of Christ, together with patronage of His teaching, are insufficient, and indeed do but insult the purpose of Christianity, whose

mission it is, not so much to captivate the admiration, as to remake and beautify the character.

These words of Jesus to Nicodemus were the more remarkable because spoken to him. He was no profligate sunk in the mire and filth of bestiality. Nor was he a self-centered and self-satisfied Pharisee. He was a sincere seeker after truth, and the question he put to Jesus revealed the working of his mind. He came to a Teacher from God, and therefore he came with an open mind willing to receive truth. He was perhaps the most perfect example of the highest possibilities of the old covenant, which had instructed men in the things of God and had led them to the highest act possible in the energy of fallen nature—that, namely, of submission to a baptism which symbolized repentance. Christ's answer cast no aspersion upon the past. It revealed its limitations. It was as though He had declared that John, the last of the magnificent line of the Hebrew prophets, had done all that was possible in leading unregenerate men to the door of the kingdom. To enter, there was necessary the new and essential miracle of Christianity—that man should have a second birth, without which he could neither see nor enter in. Times have not altered human nature, nor have they changed the essential character of Christianity. To every seeker Jesus still says: *Ye must be born anew.* The first chapter of the practical section of this book is therefore devoted to a study of the New Birth, its necessity, nature, evidence, and method.

The teaching of Christ was unified. He said in a sentence, what other teachers under the inspiration of the Holy Spirit, would unfold in volumes. This conversation with Nicodemus deals fully and finally with this whole subject. The teaching of the Epistles is, however, valuable, in order that the sayings of the Master may be fully comprehended.

As to the necessity for the new birth, He declared: *That which is born of the flesh is flesh* (John 3:6). This statement must never be construed into a condemnation of the physical and material side of man's nature. That matter is inherently evil is a doctrine of devils, that finds no warrant in the teaching of Christ or His apostles. Every pulse and fiber of physical being owes its creation and preservation to the thought and power of God. That which He created in His own image, and which, when redeemed, He inhabits as a temple, is not in itself evil. The condition of human life apart from God is evil, because it has passed into limitation and prostitution. Those wondrous material bases of life upon which, for a time, essential being was to manifest itself, and be prepared for the final and perfected life, have become the prison-house of the spirit, and man is attempting to live by bread alone, to condition his being in the flesh. That is the condition of life which Jesus describes as flesh, and of that He says: *That which is born of the flesh is flesh.* The same guarding of terms is necessary in turning to the Epistles. The writers place the natural and spiritual in perpetual antithesis. This is not because the spiritual is unnatural, or the natural unspiritual. The deepest fact of human nature is that the natural is spiritual, and only when all the being is dominated by spirit is man natural. A concrete illustration may be found in the early chapters of Genesis. The man in the garden, himself a spirit tabernacling in physical dwelling, and yet holding unafraid communion with that God Who is a Spirit, is the natural man. He, who presently is seen bending back to earth, and entering upon the bread life which is ever through the sweat of the brow, is unnatural, because it is contrary to the Divine purpose and thought. When New Testament writers speak of the natural man, they are not condemning that which is natural in the sense now described. They are using the phrase in exactly the same way the Lord here used the word *flesh*, to describe the condition of being which is enslaved by the things temporal and material, as in opposition to those eternal and spiritual. This is the condition under which men are now born, and herein lies the necessity for the new birth.

What this condition really is may be gathered from a consideration of certain of the words of Paul. Take, first, his description of the Gentiles before they are brought into union with Christ: *Darkened in their understanding, alienated from the life of God* (Eph. 4:18). That is the root-trouble. Man has lost his vision of God. He has no true conception of God. Man has ever been attempting to construct a deity out of the imaginings of his own heart, and the result has been the idea of God as an enlarged man, and a consequent mis-conception of His true being. A flesh-conditioned life cannot dis-cover God. Hence the necessity for the new birth, which is first of all new vision.

Then consider the apostle's description of the heart of the unre-generate: *The mind of the flesh is enmity against God* (Rom. 8:7). How man fears God—nay, hates Him! To disturb the peace and mar the pleasure of the worldling, it is only necessary to introduce a conversation concerning Divine things. The one constant and successful endeavor of the flesh-homed life is to keep God out of conscious touch. There may be no open blasphemy, no avowed ha-tred, but the unvarying law of life, and the unchanging order of its activities, reveal that man has no desire for God, no joy in His com-pany. A flesh-conditioned life cannot love God. Hence the necessity for the new birth is that of a new possibility of love.

Again, notice the description the apostle gives of the purpose, and set, and impulse, of the unregenerate: *They that are after the flesh do mind the things of the flesh* (Rom. 8:5). It would be a star-tling revelation to some persons if they would take the time to ex-amine their own lives for any given week, registering the occupation of all the hours. One hundred and sixty-eight hours in all—so many given to the spiritual side of life, so many to the mental, so many to the purely physical; the vast majority devoted to *What shall we eat? . . . What shall we drink? . . . Wherewithal shall we be clothed?* (Matt. 6:31). This is so in many and varied ways, and must continue until man is born of the Spirit, and a higher view of life, and conse-quently other impulses, are produced.

Once again, notice his statement concerning the true govern-ment of such lives: *Ye walked . . . according to the prince of the power of the air* (Eph. 2:2). They are the slaves of Satan, accomplishing his designs, yielding their allegiance to him. All unconsciously, man apart from God becomes the abject slave of the devil, and through the flesh hears the suggestions and proposals of hell, and yields to them, and becomes more and more fast bound.

This fourfold description explains the meaning of Jesus' words to Nicodemus, and gives the necessity for the new birth: *That which is born of the flesh is flesh* (John 3:6). The understanding is darkened; the heart is at enmity; the life is set on the things of the flesh; the being is enslaved by Satan. The hopelessness of man is still more clearly seen when it is observed that this fourfold description is a sequence. The understanding dark, and therefore a false conception of God. Then it is not to be wondered at that man hates. No man could hate the true and living God. The hatred of the human heart is for the monster of its own imagination. There can be no love for God until all the false views are swept away by the new vision that breaks with the new birth. If man turn away from God in hatred, it follows that, in order to satisfy the craving of his nature, he will turn to fleshly things and earthly things, because he has no vision of the higher. The man with the muck-rake is proving his capacity for the unseen crown by the very devotion with which he is searching amid the baubles at his feet. There will be no deliverance until a new life gives him the sense of those higher possibilities. The man thus enslaved is enslaved by Satan. God's perpetual work is to bring man near to Himself, that man may love. Satan ever enslaves through agencies and intermediaries, lest man, seeing the corruption, should be afraid and escape. This is no flattering tale of the need of human nature, yet it is the account which alone is true to the facts of history, and the present state of men. There is neither light, nor life, nor love, nor liberty save in the power of the regeneration of the Holy Spirit. *Ye must be born anew*, for *that which is born of the flesh is flesh* (John 3:7, 6).

The nature of the change necessary is perhaps most sublimely described by the simplicity of the words of which Jesus made use: *Except a man be born anew* (v. 3). A birth is a beginning. It is not the reconstruction or renovation of something already in existence, but the commencement of a new thing. That is what a man needs, if he would see or enter the kingdom. This statement of the case immediately lifts the possibility of being a Christian out of the realm of the human as to initiation. God only can begin a new thing. Men may manipulate the things that are, may replace in another order, may imagine they have started, begun something, but give a man nothing and tell him to begin a new thing, and the only new things will be the old nothing. Born: that is the supreme fact; it is the commencement. As every living being is a work of God, so, if there is to be new birth, that also must be of God. If man must be born anew, then is he helpless until the Spirit of God work the creative miracle.

This view of the Christian life as a new thing was that which the apostles clearly enforced: *If any man is in Christ, there is a new creation: the old things are passed away; behold, they are become new* (2 Cor. 5:17 margin.). A new creation, having a new vision of God, out of which springs a new love for God and a new devotion to Him—this is beyond the possibility of analysis. It is the mystery of life, and, like every other phase and form of life, is beyond the explanation of any teacher or scientist the world has produced.

The result of the new birth Christ declares as clearly and as simply in the second half of the verse Coverfirst quoted: *That which is born of the Spirit is spirit* (John 3:6). Again it must be restated that He is not undervaluing the physical side of man's being, and certainly He is not putting it out of count altogether. The vision presented by the statement is that of human life in which first things are first, and second things are second, and last things are last—life in which spirit is dominant, the lord of being, and soul and body are subservient and sanctified. It is a perfect contrast to the old life, but it is a contrast which consists, not in the exaltation of one side of the being at the expense of the others, but in the restoration of the true balance of power and proportion. The change is summarized in the words of Christ, and light is thrown again upon this summary from the Epistles.

Following a law of nature, Christ placed the antidote in juxtaposition to the poison. Immediately after His summary of the facts of human life in the words *That which is born of the flesh is flesh,* He gave as brief and graphic a description of the changed life: *That which is born of the Spirit is spirit.* This method is followed through the New Testament, and a second reference to the statements of the apostle concerning the natural man will reveal a statement in each case side by side with them, giving the antitheses in the spiritual man. Those *darkened in their understanding* become *taught in*

Him, even as truth is in Jesus (Eph. 4:18, 21). Those of whom it was declared that *the mind of the flesh is enmity against God* (Rom. 8:7), being born again of the Spirit, and indwelt by the Spirit, look into the face of God and cry, *Abba, Father* (v. 15). They that being *after the flesh* did *mind the things of the flesh,* now being *after the Spirit* do mind *the things of the Spirit* (v. 5). Those who *walked . . . according to the prince of the power of the air* (Eph. 2:2), now *sit with Him in the heavenly places, in Christ Jesus* (Eph. 2:6).

The whole form and fashion of the life is changed, and the change is so radical and complete that the only way in which it is possible to account for it, is by the acceptation of the teaching of Christ, that it has been brought about by a new creation, a new beginning, a new birth.

As there was a sequence of thought in the description of man's condition in his sinful nature, so also is there in the antitheses just glanced at. The first effect of imparted life is to give man a true vision of God. That which could not be found by the flesh life is discovered directly; the new life restores the lost sight. Then the spirit of man, seeing God, cries, *Father.* Fear passes, and the life—tremblingly, it may be, at the beginning, but none the less surely—takes hold upon God with intense satisfaction and ever-deepening love. That is the cure for the minding of earthly things. To revert to a former illustration, let but the man with the muck-rake see the higher things and know they are his own, he will forget all the empty trifles that have captivated him before. Again, the man satisfied with the things of God, becomes, by that very sense of satisfaction, master of Satan, and invulnerable against all his attacks.

The method of the new birth is most definitely stated in this same conversation. The miracle itself is a Divine work. The condition upon which it is wrought is the point of human responsibility. In the words *born of the Spirit* the Master claims the essential act as Divine, and most clearly does He show that work to be beyond our comprehension. *The wind bloweth where it listeth, and thou hearest the voice thereof, but knowest not whence it cometh, and whither it goeth: so is everyone that is born of the Spirit* (John 3:8). Just as the power of the wind is beyond dispute by the evidences of its blowing that appeal to the senses, while the law of its coming and going abides a mystery, so the fact of the regenerating power of the Holy Spirit is proved by the phenomena of grace, while all the sacred mystery of its operation is beyond the discovery of any human mind. Men are called upon to accept the fact in each case, and to wait for the explanation of the mystery. Granted the possibility of the miracle, it is for man to seek to know the condition upon which it is wrought. This Nicodemus felt, and hence his question: *How can these things be?* (v. 9). The answer is perfectly clear: *And as Moses lifted up the serpent in the wilderness, even so must the Son of Man be lifted up: that whosoever believeth may in Him have eternal life* (vv. 14, 15). Man needs life. The Son of Man is to be lifted up that it may be provided. Pointing this seeker to the kingdom, the Master sets His Cross as the gate of life. On the place of awful uplifting, through the mystery of His Passion, He would liberate His life that this man might share it. The life-giving work of the Spirit is to be that of communicating to souls, dead in trespasses and sins, the very life of the Son of God. This can only be done as the corn of wheat dies to live, and there is no new birth for individuals or the race, but by the death of the Son of Man. That death has been accomplished, and now *whosoever believeth may in Him have eternal life*. The one condition of life is that of belief. What this belief is has explanation in the opening part of this Gospel: *But as many as received Him, to them gave He the right to become children of God, even to them that believe on His name* (John 1:12). Here two terms are used in explanation of each other. To believe on Him is to receive Him: to receive Him is to believe on His name. To believe is the condition upon which the Holy Spirit imparts the life by the coming of which old things pass away, all things are new. Thousands believe in the historic Christ, and are yet dead in trespasses and sins. No weak trembling soul in all the centuries has ever yet believed on Him in the sense of receiving Him as the Way, the Truth, the Life, with unquestioning surrender and abandonment, but immediately the new life has been imparted. In this, as in everything, God is a God of method, and this is His law of grace, by observance of which man appropriates the blessings of the Cross.

Ye must be born anew (John 3:7). Apart from this there is no escape *from the corruption that is in the world by lust* (2 Pet. 1:4). Save through this, there is no becoming *partakers of the Divine nature*. While living in the full tide of spiritual possibilities, men shall yet pass through the years of probation barren and dead, unless they surrender to the Infinite Love; and receiving Him Whom they crucified in blindness, become *heirs of God, and joint-heirs with Christ* (Rom. 8:17).

19
Be Filled with the Spirit

They fall far short of the truth who speak of the filling of the Spirit as the privilege of believers. The word of Paul *Be not drunk with wine, wherein is riot, but be filled with the Spirit* (Eph. 5:18), is a present imperative, being of the nature of a command, rather than a counsel of perfection. Not merely for an elect few, but for all those born of the Spirit, the will of God is that they should be filled with the Spirit. And the necessity for this filling is proved by the fact that, apart from it, there can be no full Christian life, and no powerful Christian service.

The apostle declares that *no man speaking in the Spirit of God saith, Jesus is anathema; and no man can say, Jesus is Lord, but in the Holy Spirit* (1 Cor. 12:3). The Lordship of Jesus is the basis of all Christian life. The Christian graces and virtues all spring from the recognition of that Lordship, and from absolute surrender thereto. It is only as man is born again of the Spirit that he can call Jesus Lord; and it is only as he is under the perfect dominion of that Spirit that he can live under the Lordship of Jesus.

Not only is this true with regard to the first step in life, but also in reference to the whole subsequent course. *The fruit of the Spirit is love, joy, peace, long-suffering, kindness, goodness, faithfulness, meekness, temperance: against such there is no law* (Gal. 5:22, 23). These are the evidences of Christian character looked for in all those who profess to belong to Christ, the things that differentiate between a Christly and a worldly soul. There can be no manifestation of them save under the perpetual control of the Spirit. Neither is it possible to work for God except in the energy of the Spirit. There may be a great deal of what appears to be Christian work, but it is absolutely devoid of power unless thus energized.

No man can live the Christian life, and no man can serve in the Christian dispensation, save he is filled with the Spirit.

It is, then, of urgent importance that there should be clear understanding of the law which governs this filling. That there are scores of Christian people who are not filled with the Holy Spirit is an all too evident fact. Bring that cluster of the wonderful *fruit of the Spirit* side by side with the actual life and achievement of scores of professing Christians, and this fact must be at once confessed.

To Christian people who really want to be such as God would have them be, who are tired of all that is merely formal and mediocre, and are anxious to live in the will of God at all costs, there is no question of more importance than that of the conditions upon which the believer, born of the Spirit, may live that life which is filled with the Spirit.

These conditions are of a twofold nature—the initial, and the continuous; that by which blessing is first realized, and that by which it is maintained.

The first is that of abandonment.

The second is that of abiding.

The word *abandonment* is used intentionally. Consecration is a great word, but it has been so much abused that it has lost much of its deepest significance. This word *abandonment* is perhaps out of the ordinary run of theological terms, but it is full of force. Wherever whole-hearted, absolute, unquestioning, positive, final abandonment of the life to God obtains, the life becomes filled with the Spirit.

The thought is contained in Paul's words: *Neither present your members unto sin as instruments of unrighteousness, but present yourselves unto God, as alive from the dead, and your members as instruments of righteousness unto God* (Rom. 6:13). The whole life, according to this conception, is to be handed over to the control of

God, in order that, through that life, His will may be realized, His work may be done, His plans may be carried out. That is the abandoned life.

There are two passages which bear on this subject. The first reads: *Grieve not the Holy Spirit of God, in Whom ye were sealed unto the day of redemption. Let all bitterness, and wrath, and anger, and clamor, and railing, be put away from you, with all malice* (Eph. 4:30, 31). This is the abandonment of the life for purification. Abandonment to God is not merely the act of enlisting as soldiers to fight battles—that is a secondary matter; it is first the abandonment of self to the Spirit of God, that He may purify and cleanse from everything that is unlike His own perfection of beauty.

The apostle did not say: *Put away bitterness, and wrath, and anger, and clamor, and railing.* The believer is not called upon to put these things out of the life: that is not the New Testament conception of purification. He said: *Let these things be put away.* The verse preceding explains the responsibility: *Grieve not the Holy Spirit.* The work of putting out of the life this unholy brood of evil things—bitterness, wrath, anger, clamor, railing—is not man's work. Man is to let Him accomplish it.

The second passage is as familiar as the first: *I beseech you therefore, brethren, by the mercies of God, to present your bodies a living sacrifice, holy, acceptable to God, which is your reasonable service* (Rom. 12:1). This is another aspect of abandonment. It is not merely assent to purification; it is also the presentation of the whole being to God for sacrifice. There are very many who seem to imagine that the apostle is calling Christians to sacrifice themselves to God, but he is rather calling upon them to present themselves to God as a sacrifice, which the High Priest will lay upon the altar. The abandonment asked for is a twofold one—first, abandonment to purification by the Spirit; and, secondly, abandonment of the whole being to Jesus Christ, that He may offer it to God.

The theory seems easy. The practice is a very definite thing. The life which is thus abandoned to God for the filling of the Spirit is a life that has given up its own plans, and purposes, and hopes; and has taken instead the plan, and the purpose, and the hope of God.

If God wills to alter what appear to be Divine arrangements for today, so that the desire and the hope of today are disappointed, the follower of the Master should yet be able to say: *I delight to do Thy will, O my God* (Ps. 40:8). The will of God should be the supreme matter, beyond the doing of which the soul should have no anxiety. How often men promise God that they will do certain things if He will do something for them—an iniquitous attempt to bargain with the Most High, which is very popular, and as old as Jacob.

The difference between the Spirit-filled life, and the life that is not filled with the Spirit, is the difference between a life abandoned wholly to the will of God, and a life that wants to have its own way and please God too. Abandonment is that of which it is most easy to speak, and yet it is the one thing from which all men shrink. Men are quite prepared to sign pledges, to do any amount of work, even to sign checks or give money, if only God will let them have their own way somewhere in their life. If He will not press this business of abandonment, if He will not bring them to the Cross, they will do anything, but they draw back from the place of death.

Yet it is only in that place that the Holy Spirit is able to flow out into every part of the life and energize it, until in all conduct Jesus is crowned Lord, and the fruit of the Spirit is manifest in character. Nothing can take the place of abandonment. Some there are who attempt to put prayer where God has put abandonment. Others profess to be waiting until God is willing to fill them. Both are wrong! While they think they are waiting for God, the fact is God is waiting for them. At any moment, if they yield to the Spirit, He will sweep through every gate and avenue and into every corner of the life.

The filling of the Spirit is retained by abiding in Christ. A great deal has been said about abiding, and many have endeavored to define the term. Some beautiful definitions have been given, mystical and poetical, and yet for the most part out of the reach of the ordinary life of the believer.

It is well, where possible, to have definitions of Scripture from Scripture; and John gives a definition of what it is to abide in Christ: *He that keepeth His commandments abideth in Him, and He in him*

(1 John 3:24). Nothing can be simpler. The mistake which may be made is that of trying to explain that passage until it is robbed of its simplicity. The definition is the very embodiment of clearness, and may be stated in a brief sentence: To abide is to obey.

The *commandments* referred to are given in the preceding passage, but are spoken of there, as one commandment, having two applications: *And this is His commandment, that we should believe in the name of His Son Jesus Christ, and love one another* (v. 23). The whole law of Jesus Christ is summed up in that verse. The commandment is that of faith and love. Faith is the absolute dependence of the soul upon Him, and the consequent life of obedience to Him. Faith in the Lord Jesus begins when a guilty soul submits itself to Him for pardon, but it does not end then. It is not by that one act of faith that men abide, but by continuing in the course begun, by making Him Lord always—by entering into no transaction of business or of pleasure without taking Him into account; by treating Him as the ever-present King, by believing in Him; and by saying to Him, at all seasons and hours and everywhere: *Master, is this Thy will?* Faith in Him is belief on His name at the beginning for pardon, and constantly for purity and direction. Then every moment the soul lives in dependence upon Christ, and is able to sing:

> I dare not take one step without Thy aid.

Not faith merely, but love: *That we should . . . love one another.* That is the life of service. *He that keepeth His commandments abideth in Him* (1 John 3:23, 24). The conditions for abiding in Him are those of always believing in Him, always loving someone and serving someone. If men are filled with the Spirit by abandonment, they continue filled with the Spirit by abiding.

While it is true that there can be no full life and no powerful service apart from the filling of the Spirit, it is equally true that the Spirit-filled life must manifest the fruit of the Spirit and be powerful in service for God. These broad principles, however, are granted. The present subject is rather the conscious experience of a soul that is filled with the Spirit. Here a word of warning is necessary. A vital

mistake is made by persons who formulate a code of sensations, and
wait for them as evidences of the Spirit's filling. Some expect a mag-
netic thrill, some an overwhelming ecstasy. These experiences may
be realized, they may be utterly absent. Others wait for an experience like that of someone else. That they will never have. There are
many people who have read the Lives of good men like Fletcher of
Madeley, Finney, and Bowen, and who expect to realize just what
these men describe. Such hopes are doomed to disappointment. It
may safely be said that the experience of the filling of the Spirit is in
no two cases exactly identical, any more than the consciousness of
ordinary life can ever be the same in any two persons. There are
points of resemblance, great fundamental facts which are identical,
but in the light and shade there is variety. Surely, if this be true of ordinary life, it is also true of the higher spiritual blessing. The Holy
Spirit fills one and another. The realization of the one differs from
that of the other. *There are diversities of workings, but the same God*
(1 Cor. 12:6).

There is, however, a common consciousness to those who are Spirit-
filled. It is the consciousness of Christ. The Holy Spirit, coming in His
fullness, will give men to know the Lord as they never knew Him before. The consciousness of Christ in the experience of believers will be
as varied as are the saints themselves; for the full consciousness of the
Head can only be realized by the whole Church. His greatness is such
that He cannot give Himself wholly and utterly and finally to an individual; He needs the whole Church for the display of His perfect glory,
and the unfolding of the majesty of His Person. Let no one narrow down
his consciousness of the Christ to the consciousness of any single person.
He is one thing to one man, He is another thing to another, but the
men are united in the fact that it is the Master of Whom they are all
conscious by the Spirit. The Lordship of Jesus as a reality, is the first result of the Spirit-filled life.

It follows that Christ's victory over evil will be shared by His people; His point of vision of the affairs of men and the needs of men
will be theirs also; and the impulses of service which bore Him to
Calvary, against all opposition, and made Him Victor in its darkest
hour, will likewise be their impulse of service, so that no longer will

they offer Him the service of mechanical arrangement, but in the passion of His life they will serve, even though that be a consuming passion, as it was with Him.

Again, Christ's revelation of God to men will in measure be their revelation of God to men. As the Spirit fills the children of God, He will reproduce in their lives such likeness to the Christ, that men, seeing them, will begin to understand Him, and be led into a clear apprehension of the glory of the Father.

This subject brings all to the point of personal responsibility. The whole study culminates here for the individual. That Divine Spirit Who worked in creation, Who was the Spirit of revelation and of service through every age, dwells now in each believer. The individual question is whether He is indwelling in all His fullness. Or is He grieved and quenched by disloyalty to His government? If that has been the case hitherto, let the whole life be yielded to Him, that He may reproduce the Master Himself, to the glory of God, and for the good of men.

20
Resist Not, Grieve Not, Quench Not

New privileges always bring new responsibilities; and it follows, necessarily and naturally, that these new responsibilities create new perils. If this age is the most favored in the history of men, it has therefore to face greatest and gravest perils. They are the perils of resisting, grieving, and quenching the Spirit. The terms do not refer to the same danger. There are those who have not resisted the Spirit who yet are grieving Him; there are also those who have not resisted and have not grieved Him in the sense in which the apostles used the word, who are nevertheless in perpetual danger of quenching Him. The peril of resisting the Spirit is that of those who are not born again; the peril of grieving the Spirit is that of those who, born of the Spirit, are indwelt by Him; the peril of quenching the Spirit is that of those upon whom He has bestowed some gift for service.

To Nicodemus Jesus said: *Ye must be born anew* (John 3:7). That refers to the first act of the Spirit in man. To the woman of Samaria He said: *Whosoever drinketh of the water that I shall give him shall never thirst, but the water that I shall give him shall become in him a well of water springing up unto eternal life* (John 4:14). That refers to the second aspect of the Spirit's work in the believer, as a perennial and perpetual spring. To the crowds at the feast He said: *He that believeth on Me, as the scripture hath said, out of his belly shall flow rivers of living water* (John 7:38). That refers to the work of the Spirit, in its outflow through the believer, for the refreshment and renewal of other lives.

The three aspects of the Spirit's work, regeneration, indwelling, and equipment, reveal the perils of the dispensation.

In reference to regeneration the peril is marked by the word *resist*. In reference to indwelling the peril is marked by the word *grieve*. In reference to equipment for service the peril is marked by the word *quench*.

The first of these words occurs in the defense of Stephen. After having enumerated the acts of rebellion which had characterized the history of his people, he exclaimed: *Ye stiff-necked and uncircumcised in heart and ears, ye do always resist the Holy Spirit* (Acts 7:51). Resisting the Holy Spirit consisted in a determined hostility to His purposes and work. At the moment it was not always apparently willful; the sin lay in the fact that they did not perceive their opportunity when it came. When his brethren sold Joseph, they did not understand that they were selling their deliverer into slavery. It was a sin of blindness. When the people failed to understand Moses, and refused him, and murmured against him, they did not comprehend all the Divine mission for which he was raised. They were hostile to the work of the Holy Spirit of God, and their hostility was the result of blindness. Resisting the Holy Spirit, therefore, is not necessarily willful—it may be the result of blindness, but when God deals with men, He takes into account that which causes the blindness, and where the cause is of their own creation, He holds them responsible. Jealousy and hatred blinded the brethren of Joseph to his true position; and the same spirit of malice lay at the root of the opposition to Moses. They were blinded, and out of the blindness grew the hostility. The reason for the blindness was disobedience to the heavenly vision at some earlier point in their history; and for that disobedience they were guilty.

Men need perpetually to examine themselves as to whether they are in the faith. There are many who would vehemently deny the charge of being hostile to Divine purposes, whose lives are out of all harmony with the movements of the Spirit. He Who has come to set up in the heart of man the kingdom of God, He Who has come to bring righteousness and love into human lives as forces that transform and transfigure, has not yet been able to accomplish these purposes in them. By so much as that is a fact the Holy Spirit is being resisted. To the Corinthians the apostle wrote: *Try your own selves, whether ye be in the faith* (2 Cor. 13:5). It is a solemn warning, occurring as it does after the expression of a fear on his part: *I fear, lest by any means, when I come, I should find you not such as I would, and should myself be found of you such as ye would not; lest by any means there should be strife, jealousy, wraths, factions, backbitings, whisperings, swellings, tumults* (2 Cor. 12:20). The whole unholy brood may be summed up in the one thought of lack of love. Among the things of which the apostle was afraid, there were none which were deeds of open impurity. It was the spirit of faction, schism, and division that he feared; and his fear gave rise to his warning. *Try your own selves, whether ye be in the faith.* That was a word spoken, not to the outside world, but to professing Christians. The question as to whether men are resisting the Spirit, as to whether they are a part of the force that is hostile to the Spirit in the world, is to be settled, not by the judgment that neighbors pass, but by the judgment that falls clear as the light and searching as fire, when in the place of loneliness with God the prayer is sincerely offered:

> *Search me, O God, and know my heart:*
> *Try me, and know my thoughts:*
> *And see if there be any way of wickedness in me*
> (Ps. 139:23, 24).

There is perpetual need for rigorous self-examination as to whether those professing loyalty are still in the faith; for it may be that, by disloyalty to God, the mind has been blinded to the correct perception of the work of the Spirit; and without intending it, there may be hostility to His work, there may even be resistance to the Holy Spirit.

The second peril is that of *grieving* the Holy Spirit. There is no word in the New Testament that more clearly and beautifully reveals the tenderness of the heart of God. The word means literally, *to cause sorrow to.* Dr. Beet has said that the word *grieve* is one of the most striking instances of anthropomorphism in the whole Book. It certainly is a remarkable instance of the way in which God graciously uses the being of man for the illustration of His own activity of affection and thought. There is a sense in which it is difficult to think of God as sorrowing; and yet He stoops to this great word, to teach that it is possible for a child of His, indwelt by the Spirit, to cause sorrow to His heart. Let no one minimize the value of the word. Grieve not, do not cause sorrow to, do not make sad the heart of God.

The words occur in the midst of a most magnificent argument concerning the high calling of God for His people, and are connected with the statement: *In Whom ye also, having heard the word of the truth, the gospel of your salvation — in Whom, having also believed, ye were sealed with the Holy Spirit of promise, which is an earnest of our inheritance, unto the redemption of God's own possession, unto the praise of His glory* (Eph. 1:13, 14). The Holy Spirit seals the believer unto the day of redemption. When He takes up His abode in the heart of the trusting soul, it is not only for present blessing, it is also for a consummation. When the Holy Spirit takes possession of a soul and imparts life, that life is the prophecy and the promise of an eventuality. For those who are children of God, the full meaning of the fact is not yet: *Beloved, now are we children of God, and it is not yet made manifest what we shall be. We know that, if He shall be manifested, we shall be like Him* (1 John 3:2). What the glory of the coming One will be, none can imagine; nor can they yet know what will be the glory of the children of God, when the work of God is finished in their lives. The Holy Spirit within, seals unto that glorious issue. The sealing consists not merely in setting a possession mark upon the property, but in the outworking in the life of all the beauty and all the grace of Christ Himself. As when our blessed Lord was transfigured upon the mountain it was not the transfiguring of a glory that fell upon Him, but that of a glory that was already resident within Him, outshining through the veil of His flesh; so, when the Spirit seals, He does so by the gift of life, which is able to transform the character.

Out of that second aspect of the work of the Spirit grows the second peril. Whenever He is thwarted, whenever He is disobeyed, whenever He gives some new revelation of the Christ which brings no response, He is grieved. The heart of God is sad when, by the disobedience of His children, His purpose of grace in them is hindered. Alas! How often has the Holy Spirit been grieved; how often has He brought some vision of the Master that has made demands upon devotion, that has claimed new consecration; and because the way of devotion and the way of consecration are always the way of the Altar and the Cross, the children of His love have drawn back. The Spirit has been grieved, because hindered in His purposes; the day of the saints' perfecting has been postponed, and the coming of the kingdom of God has been delayed. It is a very terrible thought that the grieving of the Spirit within the Church postpones the coming of the kingdom of God in the world. In proportion as men are obedient to the indwelling Spirit, and allow Him in the whole territory of their own lives to have His way, they are hastening the coming of the day of God, and bringing in the Kingdom of Peace.

The things which grieve the Spirit of God are spoken of by the apostle in the section of the Epistle from which this warning is taken, and should be pondered in solemn loneliness.

The third and last peril is that described in the words: *Quench not the Spirit* (1 Thess. 5:19). The word *quench* has no reference to the indwelling of the Spirit for life and development in the believer. It refers wholly to His presence as a power in service. The word itself is suggestive. To resist presupposes the coming of the Holy Spirit to storm the citadel of the soul. To grieve presupposes the residence of the Spirit as the Comforter within. The word *quench* presupposes the presence of the Spirit as a fire. This suggestion of fire carries thought back to the words: *There appeared unto them tongues parting asunder, like as of fire; and it sat upon each one of them* (Acts 2:3). Fire was the symbol of power to praise, to pray, and to prophesy. Moreover, the context of this injunction clearly indicates its meaning. In the argument of the apostle two things are linked: *Quench not the Spirit; despise not prophesyings* (1 Thess. 5:19, 20). Here, then, is the third peril. The Spirit, Who comes upon the believer for praise, prayer, and prophecy, may be quenched. It is possible that the gift of the Holy Spirit, bestowed for service, may be lost; it is possible that those upon whom there has fallen, unseen by mortal eye, the Tongue of Fire, who have been called by God to the place of actual service in the Church, may quench the Spirit, and thus lose their power of testimony.

This is done by reversing the conditions upon which the Spirit was received. The apostles first received the Spirit of Fire upon the condition of loyalty to Jesus Christ. The glorifying of Christ in the life, and the obedience of the soul to the word of the Master, were the first conditions for the falling of the Fire. That included within itself the second condition of human helplessness, confessed by their waiting until the Holy Spirit came.

There has been much quenching of the Holy Spirit by service that does not wait but rushes, and by the burning of false fires upon the altars of God. The attempt to carry on the work of the kingdom of God by worldly means, the perpetual desecration of holy things by alliance with things that are unholy, the pressing of Mammon into the service of God, have meant the quenching of the Spirit; for God will never allow the Fire of the Holy Spirit to be mingled with strange fires upon His altars. What is true of the Churches is true of the individual. God has equipped His people for service with spiritual gifts. To each one some Fire-gift of speech or of influence has been given, but it has been lost, when it has ceased to be used in loyalty to Christ. Very many men have lost their gift of power in service, and have become barren of results in their work for God, because they have prostituted a heavenly gift to sordid, selfish service, to the glorification of their own lives, instead of exercising the gift only for its true end. Men have perpetually quenched the Spirit by attempting to work in their own strength, hoping that God would step in and make up what they lacked. God will not come and help men to do their work. He asks that they should give themselves to Him, for the doing of His work. This is no mere idle play upon words; the difference is radical. If men make their plan of service and then ask God to help them, they may, by that very assertion of self, quench the Holy Spirit. If, on the other hand, they await the Divine vision and the Divine voice and the Divinely marked-out path; if they wait until they hear God saying, *I am going there, I would have you go with Me*—then the Holy Spirit can exercise His gift in their lives. The Spirit is quenched by disloyalty to Christ, or when His gift is used for any other purposes than that upon which the heart of God is set. *Resist not, grieve not, quench not the Spirit!*

The deep meaning of these solemn warnings may the Spirit Himself reveal to all the Spirit-born children of the Father.

Twelve Sermons on the Holy Spirit

by Rev. Charles H. Spurgeon

1

The Comforter

But the Comforter, which is the Holy Ghost, whom the
Father will send in my name, he shall teach you all things,
and bring all things to your remembrance, whatsoever I
have said unto you—John 14:26.

G ood old Simeon called Jesus the consolation of Israel; and
so He was. Before His actual appearance, His name was the
Day-Star; cheering the darkness, and prophetic of the rising sun. To Him they looked with the same hope which cheers the
nightly watcher, when from the lonely castle-top he sees the fairest
of the stars, and hails her as the usher of the morn. When He was
on earth, He must have been the consolation of all those who were
privileged to be his companions. We can imagine how readily the
disciples would run to Christ to tell Him of their griefs, and how
sweetly with that matchless intonation of His voice, He would speak
to them and bid their fears be gone. Like children, they would consider Him as their Father; and to Him every want, every groan, every
sorrow, every agony, would at once be carried; and he, like a wise
physician, had a balm for every wound; He had mingled a cordial
for their every care; and readily did He dispense some mighty remedy to allay all the fever of their troubles. Oh! It must have been
sweet to have lived with Christ. Surely sorrows then were but joys in

171

masks, because they gave an opportunity to go to Jesus to have them removed. Oh! Would to God, some of us may say, that we could have lain our weary heads upon the bosom of Jesus, and that our birth had been in that happy era, when we might have heard His kind voice, and seen His kind look, when He said "Let the weary ones come unto me."

But now He was about to die. Great prophecies were to be fulfilled, and great purposes were to be answered, and therefore Jesus must go. It behooved Him to suffer, that He might be made a propitiation for our sins. It behooved Him to slumber in the dust awhile, that He might perfume the chamber of the grave to make it—

> No more a charnel house to fence
> The relics of lost innocence.

It behooved Him to have a resurrection, that we who shall one day be the dead in Christ, might rise first, and in glorious bodies stand upon earth. And it behooved Him that He should ascend up on high, that He might lead captivity captive; that He might chain the fiends of hell; that He might lash them to His chariot wheels and drag them up high heaven's hill, to make them feel a second overthrow from His right arm when He should dash them from the pinnacles of heaven down to deeper depths beneath. "It is right I should go away from you," said Jesus, "for if I go not away, the Comforter will not come." Jesus must go. Weep, ye disciples. Jesus must be gone. Mourn, ye poor ones who are to be left without a Comforter. But hear how kindly Jesus speaks: "I will not leave you comfortless, I will pray the Father, and He shall send you another Comforter, who shall be with you, and shall dwell in you forever." He would not leave those few poor sheep alone in the wilderness; He would not desert His children and leave them fatherless. Before He left He gave soothing words of comfort; like the good Samaritan, He poured in oil and wine; and we see what he promised: "I will send you another Comforter—one who shall be just what I have been, yea even more; who shall console you in your sorrows, remove your doubts, comfort you in your afflictions, and stand as My vicar on earth, to do that which I would have done, had I tarried with you."

Before I discourse of the Holy Ghost as the Comforter, I must make one or two remarks on the different translations of the word rendered "Comforter." The Rhemish translation, which you are aware is adopted by Roman Catholics, has left the word untranslated, and gives it "Paraclete." "But the Paraclete which is the Holy Ghost, whom the Father will send in my name, he shall teach you all things." This is the original Greek word, and it has some other meanings besides "Comforter." Sometimes it means the monitor or instructor: "I will send you another monitor, another teacher." Frequently it means "Advocate," but the most common meaning of the word is that which we have here: "I will send you another *Comforter*." However, we cannot pass over those other two interpretations without saying something upon them.

"I will send you another *teacher*." Jesus Christ had been the official teacher of His saints while on earth. They called no man Rabbi except Christ. They sat at no men's feet to learn their doctrines, but they had them direct from the lips of Him who "spake as never man spake." "And now," says He, "when I am gone, where shall you find the great infallible teacher? Shall I set you up a Pope at Rome, to whom you shall go, and who shall be your infallible oracle? Shall I give you the councils of the church to be held to decide all knotty points?" Christ said no such thing. "I am the infallible paraclete or teacher, and when I am gone, I will send you another teacher and He shall be the person who is to explain Scripture; He shall be the authoritative oracle of God, who shall make all dark things light, who shall unravel mysteries, who shall untwist all knots of revelation, and shall make you understand what you could not discover, had it not been for His influence."

And beloved, no man ever learns anything aright, unless he is taught of the Spirit. No man can know Jesus Christ unless he is taught of God. There is no doctrine of the Bible which can be safely, thoroughly, and truly learned, except by the agency of the one authoritative teacher. Ah! Tell me not of systems of divinity; tell me not of schemes of theology; tell me not of infallible commentators, or most learned and most arrogant doctors, but tell me of the Great Teacher, who shall instruct us, the sons of God, and shall make us wise to understand all things. He is *the* Teacher; it matters not what this or that man says; I rest on no man's boasting authority, nor will you. Ye are not to be carried away with the craftiness of men, nor sleight of words, this is the authoritative oracle, the Holy Ghost resting in the hearts of His children.

The other translation is *Advocate*. Have you ever thought how the Holy Ghost can be said to be an advocate? You know Jesus Christ is called the wonderful, the counselor, and mighty God, but how can the Holy Ghost be said to be an advocate? I suppose it is thus: He is an advocate on earth to plead against the enemies of the cross. How was it that Paul could so ably plead before Felix and Agrippa? How was it that the Apostles stood unawed before the magistrates and confessed their Lord? How has it come to pass that in all times God's ministers have been made fearless as lions, and their brows have been firmer than brass, their hearts sterner than steel, and their words like the languages of God? Why, it is simply for this reason, that it was not the man who pleaded, but it was God the Holy Ghost pleading through him.

But, besides this, the Holy Ghost is the advocate in men's hearts. Ah! I have known men reject a doctrine until the Holy Ghost began to illumine them. We who are the advocates of the truth are often very poor pleaders; we spoil our cause by the words we use, but it is a mercy that the brief is in the hand of a special pleader, who will advocate successfully and overcome the sinner's opposition. Did you ever know Him to fail once? Brethren, I speak to your souls: has not God in old times convinced you of sin? Did not the Holy Ghost come and prove that you were guilty, although no minister could ever get you out of your self-righteousness? Did He not advocate Christ's righteousness? Did He not stand and tell you that your works were filthy rags? And did He not convince you of the judgment to come? He is a mighty advocate when He pleads in the soul—of sin, of righteousness, and of the judgment to come. Blessed advocate! Plead in my heart, plead with my conscience. When I sin, make conscience bold to tell me of it; when I err, make conscience speak at once; and when I turn aside to crooked ways, then advocate the cause of righteousness, and bid me sit down in confusion, knowing my guiltiness in the sight of God.

But there is yet another sense in which the Holy Ghost advocates, and that is, He advocates our cause with Jesus Christ, with groanings that cannot be uttered. O my soul, thou art ready to burst within me! O my heart, thou art swelled with grief; the hot tide of my emotion would well-nigh overflow the channels of my veins. I long to speak, but the very desire chains my tongue. I wish to pray, but the fervency of my feeling curbs my language. There is a groaning within that cannot be uttered. Do you know who can utter that groaning, who can understand it, and who can put it into heavenly language and utter it in a celestial tongue, so that Christ can hear it? Oh, yes! It is God the Holy Spirit; He advocates our cause with Christ, and then Christ advocates it with His Father. He is the advocate, who maketh intercession for us, with groanings that cannot be uttered.

Having thus explained the Spirit's office as teacher and advocate, we come now to the translation of our version—the *Comforter*; and here I shall have three divisions. First, the *comforter*; secondly, the *comfort*; and thirdly, the *comforted*.

I. First, then, the COMFORTER. Briefly let me run over in my mind and in your minds, too, the characteristics of this glorious Comforter. Let me tell you some of the attributes of His comfort, so that you may understand how well adapted He is to your case.

And first, we will remark that God the Holy Ghost is a very *loving* Comforter. I am in distress and want consolation. Some passerby hears of my sorrow, and he steps within, sits down and essays to cheer me; he speaks soothing words, but he loves me not, he is a stranger, he knows me not at all, he has only come in to try his skill; and what is the consequence? His words run o'er me like oil upon a slab of marble—they are like the pattering rain upon the rock; they do not break my grief; it stands unmoved as adamant, because he has no love for me. But let someone who loves me dearly as his own life come and plead with me, then truly his words are music; they taste like honey; he knows the password of the doors of my heart, and my ear is attentive to every word; I catch the intonation of each syllable as it falls, for it is like the harmony of the harps of heaven. Oh, there is a voice in love, it speaks a language which is its own, it is an idiom and an accent which none can mimic; wisdom cannot imitate it; oratory cannot attain unto it; it is love alone which can reach the mourning heart; love is the only handkerchief which can wipe the mourner's tears away.

And is not the Holy Ghost a loving Comforter? Dost thou know, O saint, how much the Holy Spirit loves thee? Canst thou measure the love of the Spirit? Dost thou know how great is the affection of His soul towards thee? Go, measure heaven with thy span; go, weigh the mountains in the scales; go, take the ocean's water, and tell each drop; go, count the sand upon the sea's wide shore; and when thou hast accomplished this, thou canst tell how much He loveth thee. He has loved thee long; He has loved thee well; He loved thee ever; and He still shall love thee. Surely He is the person to comfort thee, because He loves. Admit Him, then, to your heart, O Christian, that He may comfort you in your distress.

But next He is a *faithful* Comforter. Love sometimes proveth unfaithful. "Sharper than a serpent's tooth" is an unfaithful friend! Far more bitter than the gall of bitterness, to have a friend to turn from me in my distress! Woe of woes, to have one who loves me in my prosperity forsake me in the dark day of my trouble. Sad indeed: but such is not God's Spirit. He ever loves, and loves even to the end — a faithful Comforter. Child of God, you are in trouble. A little while ago you found Him a sweet and loving Comforter; you obtained relief from Him when others were but broken cisterns; He sheltered you in His bosom, and carried you in His arms. Oh, wherefore dost thou distrust Him now? Away with thy fears! For He is a faithful Comforter. "Ah, but," thou sayest, "I have sinned." So thou hast, but sin cannot sever thee from His love; He loves thee still. Think not, O poor downcast child of God, because the scars of thine old sins have marred thy beauty, that He loves thee less because of that blemish. Oh, no! He loved thee when He foreknew thy sin; He loved thee with the knowledge of what the aggregate of thy wickedness would be; and He does not love thee less now. Come to Him in all boldness of faith; tell Him thou hast grieved Him, and He will forget thy wandering, and will receive thee again; the kisses of His love shall be bestowed upon thee, and the arms of His grace shall embrace thee. He is faithful: trust Him; He will never deceive you; trust Him, He will never leave you. _TRUST HIM !_

And oh, how *wise* a Comforter is the Holy Ghost. Job had comforters, and I think he spoke the truth when he said, "Miserable comforters are ye all." But I dare say they esteemed themselves wise; and when the young man Elihu rose to speak, they thought he had a world of impudence. Were they not "grave and reverend seniors?" Did not they comprehend his grief and sorrow? If they could not comfort him, who could? But they did not find out the cause. They thought he was not really a child of God, that he was self-righteous; and they gave him the wrong physic. It is a bad case when the doctor mistakes the disease and gives a wrong prescription, and so, perhaps, kills the patient. Sometimes, when we go and visit people we mistake their disease, we want to comfort them on this point, whereas they do not require any such comfort at all, and they would be better left alone than spoiled by such unwise comforters as we are. But oh! How wise the Holy Spirit is! He takes the soul, lays it on the table, and dissects it in a moment; He finds out the root of the matter, He sees where the complaint is, and then He applies the knife where something is required to be taken away, or puts a plaster where the sore is; and He never mistakes. Oh! How wise, the blessed Holy Ghost! From every comforter I turn and leave them all, for thou art He who alone givest the wisest consolation.

Then mark how *safe* a Comforter the Holy Ghost is. All comfort is not safe; mark that. There is a young man over there very melancholy. You know how he became so. He stepped into the house of God and heard a powerful preacher, and the word was blessed and convicted him of sin. When he went home, his father and the rest found there was something different about him, "Oh," they said, "John is mad; he is crazy"; and what said his mother? "Send him into the country for a week; let him go to the ball or to the theater." John! Did you find any comfort there? "Ah, no; they made me worse, for while I was there, I thought hell might open and swallow me up." Did you find any relief in the gaieties of the world? "No," say you, "I thought it was idle waste of time." Alas! This is miserable comfort, but it is the comfort of the worldling; and when a Christian gets into distress, how many will recommend him this remedy and the other. Ah, there have been many, like infants, destroyed by elixirs given to lull them to sleep; many have been ruined by the cry of "peace, peace," when there is no peace, hearing gentle things when they ought to be stirred to the quick. Cleopatra's asp was brought in a basket of flowers; and men's ruin often lurks in fair and sweet speeches. But the Holy Ghost's comfort is safe, and you may rest on it. Let Him speak the word, and there is a reality about it; let Him give the cup of consolation, and you may drink it to the bottom, for in its depths there are no dregs, nothing to intoxicate or ruin, it is all safe.

Moreover, the Holy Ghost is an *active* Comforter: He does not comfort by words, but by deeds. Some comfort by "Be ye warmed and be ye filled," giving nothing. But the Holy Ghost gives, He intercedes with Jesus, He gives us promises, He gives us grace, and so He comforts us. Mark again, He is always a *successful* Comforter; He never attempts what He cannot accomplish.

Then to close up, He is an *ever-present* Comforter, so that you never have to send for Him. Your God is always near you, and when you need comfort in your distress, behold, the word is nigh thee, it is in thy mouth, and in thy heart; He is an ever-present help in time of trouble.

II. The second thing is the COMFORT. Now there are some persons who make a great mistake about the influence of the Holy Spirit. A foolish man, who had a fancy to preach in a certain pulpit, though in truth he was quite incapable of the duty, called upon the minister, and assured him solemnly that it had been revealed to him by the Holy Ghost, that he was to preach in his pulpit. "Very well," said the minister, "I suppose I must not doubt your assertion, but as it has not been revealed to me that I am to let you preach, you must go your way until it is." I have heard many fanatical persons say the Holy Spirit revealed this and that to them. Now that is very generally revealed nonsense. The Holy Ghost does not reveal anything fresh now. He brings old things to our remembrance. "He shall teach you all things, and bring all things to your remembrance whatsoever I have told you." The canon of revelation is closed; there is no more to be added. God does not give a fresh revelation, but He rivets the old one. When it has been forgotten, and laid in the dusty chamber of our memory, He fetches it out and cleans the picture, but does not paint a new one. There are no new doctrines, but the old ones are often revived. It is not, I say, by any new revelation that the Spirit comforts. He does so by telling us old things over again; He brings a fresh lamp to manifest the treasures hidden in Scripture; He unlocks the strong chests in which the truth had long lain, and He points to secret chambers filled with untold riches, but He coins no more, for enough is done. Believer! There is enough in the Bible for thee to live upon forever. If thou shouldst outnumber the years of Methuselah, there would be no need for a fresh revelation; if thou shouldst live till Christ should come upon the earth, there would be no necessity for the addition of a single word; if thou shouldst go down as deep as Jonah, or even descend as David said he did, into the belly of hell, still there would be enough in the Bible to comfort thee without a supplementary sentence. But Christ says, "He shall take of mine and shall show it unto you." Now let me just tell you briefly what it is the Holy Ghost tells us.

Ah! Does He not whisper to the heart, Saint, be of good cheer; there is one who died for thee; look to Calvary; behold His wounds; see the torrent gushing from His side; there is thy purchaser, and thou art secure. He loves thee with an everlasting love, and this chastisement is meant for thy good; each stroke is working thy healing; by the blueness of the wound thy soul is made better. "Whom he loveth he chasteneth, and scourgeth every son whom he receiveth." Doubt not His grace, because of thy tribulation, but believe that He loveth thee as much in seasons of trouble as in times of happiness. And then, moreover, He says, "What is all thy suffering compared with that of thy Lord's? Or what, when weighed in the scales of Jesu's agonies, is all thy distress?" And especially at times does the Holy Ghost take back the veil of heaven, and lets the soul behold the glory of the upper word! Then it is that the saint can say, "Oh, thou art a Comforter to me!"

> Let cares like a wild deluge come,
>   And storms of sorrow fall;
> May I but safely reach my home,
>   My God, my heaven, my all.

Some of you could follow, were I to tell of manifestations of heaven. You too have left sun, moon, and stars, at your feet, while in your flight, outstripping the tardy lightning, you have seemed to enter the gates of pearl, and tread the golden streets, borne aloft on wings of the Spirit. But here we much not trust ourselves, lest, lost in reverie, we forget our theme.

III. And now thirdly, who are the COMFORTED PERSONS? I like, you know, at the end of my sermon to cry out "Divide! divide!" There are two parties here—some who are the comforted, and others who are the comfortless ones—some who have received the consolation of the Holy Ghost, and some who have not. Now let us try and sift you, and see which is the chaff, and which is the wheat; and may God grant that some of the chaff may this night be transformed into His wheat.

You may say, "How am I to know whether I am a recipient of the comfort of the Holy Ghost?" You may know it by one rule. If you have received one blessing from God, you will receive all other blessings too. Let me explain myself. If I could come here as an auctioneer, and sell the gospel off in lots, I should dispose of it all. If I could say here is justification through the blood of Christ, free, given away, gratis; many a one would say, "I will have justification: give it me; I wish to be justified, I wish to be pardoned." Suppose I took sanctification, the giving up of all sin, a thorough change of heart, leaving off drunkenness and swearing, many would say, "I don't want that; I should like to go to heaven, but I do not want that holiness; I should like to be saved at last, but I should like to have my drink still; I should like to enter glory, but I should like to have an oath or two on the road." Nay, but sinner, if thou hast one blessing, thou shalt have all. God will never divide the gospel. He will not give justification to that man, and sanctification to another; pardon to one and holiness to another. No, it all goes together. Whom He calls them He justifies; whom He justifies, them He sanctifies; and whom He sanctifies, them He also glorifies.

Oh; if I could lay down nothing but the *comforts* of the gospel, ye would fly to them as flies do to honey. When ye come to be ill, ye send for the clergyman. Ah! You all want your minister then to come and give you consoling words. But if he be an honest man, he will not give some of you a particle of consolation. He will not commence pouring oil when the knife would be better. I want to make a man feel his sins before I dare tell him anything about Christ. I want to probe into his soul and make him feel that he is lost before I tell him anything about the purchased blessing. Have you had conviction of sin? Have you ever felt your guilt before God? Have your souls been humbled at Jesus' feet? And have you been made to look at Calvary alone for your refuge? If not, you have no right to consolation. Do not take an atom of it. The Spirit is a Convicter before He is a Comforter; and you must have the other operations of the Holy Spirit before you can derive anything from this.

And now I have finished. You have heard what this babbler hath said once more. What has it been? Something about the Comforter. But let me ask you, before you go, what do you know about the Comforter? Each one of you before descending the steps of this chapel, let this solemn question thrill through your souls—What do you know of the Comforter? Oh! Poor souls, if ye know not the Comforter, I will tell you what you shall know—You shall know the Judge! If ye know not the Comforter on earth, ye shall know the Condemner in the next world, who shall cry, "Depart ye cursed into everlasting fire in hell." Well might Whitfield call out, "O earth, earth, earth, hear the Word of the Lord!" If we were to live here forever, ye might slight the gospel; if ye had a lease of your lives, ye might despise the Comforter. But sirs, ye must die. Since last we met together, probably some have gone to their long last home; and ere we meet again in this sanctuary, some here will be amongst the glorified above, or amongst the damned below. Which will it be? Let your soul answer. If tonight you fell down dead in your pews, or where you are standing in the gallery, where would you be? In *heaven* or in *hell?*

Ah! Deceive not yourselves; let conscience have its perfect work; and if, in the sight of God, you are obliged to say, "I tremble and fear least my portion should be with unbelievers," listen one moment, and then I have done with thee. "He that believeth and is baptized shall be saved, and he that believeth not shall be damned." Weary sinner, thou who art the devil's castaway, reprobate, profligate, harlot, robber, thief, adulterer, fornicator, drunkard, swearer, Sabbath-breaker—list! I speak to thee as well as the rest. I exempt no man. God hath said there is no exemption here. "*Whosoever* believeth in the name of Jesus Christ shall be saved." Sin is no barrier: thy guilt is no obstacle. Whosoever—though he were as black as Satan, though he were filthy as a fiend—whosoever this night believes, shall have every sin forgiven, shall have every crime effaced, shall have every iniquity blotted out; shall be saved in the Lord Jesus Christ, and shall stand in heaven safe and secure. That is the glorious gospel. God apply it home to your hearts, and give you faith in Jesus!

> We have listened to the preacher—
>   Truth by him has now been shown;
> But we want a greater teacher,
>   From the everlasting throne:
>   APPLICATION
>   Is the work of God alone.

2
The Power of the Holy Ghost

The power of the Holy Ghost—Romans 15:13.

Power is the special and peculiar prerogative of God, and God alone. "Twice have I heard this: that power belongeth unto God." God is God: and power belongeth to him. If He delegates a portion of it to His creatures, still it is *His* power. The sun, although he is "like a bridegroom coming out of his chamber, and rejoiceth as a strong man to run his race," yet has no power to perform his motions except as God directs him. The stars, although they travel in their orbits and none could stay them, yet have neither might nor force except that which God daily infuses into them. The tall archangel, near His throne, who outshines a comet in its blaze, though he is one of those who excel in strength and hearken to the voice of the commands of God, yet has no might except that which his Maker gives to him. As for Leviathan, who so maketh the sea to boil like a pot that one would think the deep were hoary: as for Behemoth, who drinketh up Jordan at a draught, and boasteth that he can snuff up rivers; as for those majestic creatures that are found on earth, they own their strength to Him who fashioned their bones of steel and made their sinews of brass. And when we think of man, if he has might or power, it is so small and insignificant, that we can scarcely call it such; yea, when it is at its greatest—when he sways

183

his scepter, when he commands hosts, when he rules nations—still the power belongeth unto God; and it is true, "Twice have I heard this, that power belongeth unto God."

This exclusive prerogative of God is to be found in each of the three persons of the glorious Trinity. The Father hath power: for by His word were the heavens made, and all the host of them; by His strength all things stand, and through Him they fulfill their destiny. The Son hath power: for like His Father, He is the Creator of all things; "Without Him was not anything made that was made," and "by him all things consist." And the Holy Spirit hath power. It is concerning the power of the Holy Ghost that I shall speak this morning; and may you have a practical exemplification of that attribute in your own hearts, when you shall feel that the influence of the Holy Ghost is being poured out upon me, so that I am speaking the words of the living God to your souls, and bestowed upon you when you are feeling the effects of it in your own spirits.

We shall look at the power of the Holy Ghost in three ways this morning. First, *the outward and visible displays of it*; second, *the inward and spiritual manifestations of it*; and third, *the future and expected works thereof.* The power of the Spirit will thus, I trust, be made clearly present to your souls.

I. First, then, we are to view the power of the Spirit in the OUT-WARD AND VISIBLE DISPLAYS OF IT. The power of the Spirit has not been dormant; it has exerted itself. Much has been done by the Spirit of God already; more than could have been accomplished by any being except the Infinite, Eternal, Almighty Jehovah, of whom the Holy Spirit is one person. There are four works which are the outward and manifest signs of the power of the Spirit: creation works; resurrection works; works of attestation, or of witness; and works of grace. Of each of the works I shall speak very briefly.

1. First, the Spirit has manifested the omnipotence of His power in *creation works*; for though not very frequently in Scripture, yet sometimes creation is ascribed to the Holy Ghost, as well as to the Father and the Son. The creation of the heavens above us is said to be the work of God's Spirit. This you will see at once by referring

to the sacred Scriptures, Job 26:13 verse, "By his Spirit he hath garnished the heavens; his hand hath formed the crooked serpent." All the stars of heaven are said to have been placed aloft by the Spirit, and one particular constellation called the "crooked serpent" is specially pointed out as his handiwork. He looseth the bands of Orion; He bindeth the sweet influences of the Pleiades, and guides Acturus with his sons. He made all those stars that shine in heaven. The heavens were garnished by His hands, and He formed the crooked serpent by His might. So also in those continued acts of creation which are still performed in the world; as the bringing forth of man and animals, their birth and generation. These are ascribed also to the Holy Ghost. If you look at Psalm 104, the 29th verse, you will read, "Thou hidest thy face, they are troubled: thou takest away their breath, they die, and return to their dust. Thou sendest forth thy Spirit, they are created: and thou renewest the face of the earth." So that the creation of every man is the work of the Spirit: and the creation of all life and all flesh-existence in this work is as much to be ascribed to the power of the Spirit as the first garnishing of the heavens, or the fashioning of the crooked serpent.

But if you will look in the first chapter of Genesis, you will there see more particularly set forth that peculiar operation of power upon the universe which was put forth by the Holy Spirit; you will then discover what was His special work. In Genesis 1:2 we read, "And the earth was without form, and void; and darkness was upon the face of the deep. And the spirit of God moved upon the face of the waters." We know not how remote the period of the creation of this globe may be—certainly many millions of years before the time of Adam. Our planet has passed through various stages of existence, and different kinds of creatures have lived on its surface, all of which have been fashioned by God. But before that era came, wherein man should be its principal tenant and monarch, the Creator gave up the world to confusion. He allowed the inward fires to burst up from beneath and melt all the solid matter, so that all kinds of substances were commingled in one vast mass of disorder; the only name you could give to the world then was, that it was a chaotic mass of matter; what it should be, you could not guess or define. It was entirely without form, and void; and darkness was upon the face of the deep. The Spirit came, and stretching His broad wings, bade the darkness disperse, and as He moved over it, all the different portions of matter came into their places, and it was no longer "without form, and void," but became round like its sister planets, and moved, singing the high praises of God—not discordantly as it had done before, but as one great note in the vast scale of creation.

But there was one particular instance of creation in which the Holy Spirit was more especially concerned; viz., the formation of the body of our Lord Jesus Christ. Though our Lord Jesus Christ was born of a woman and made in the likeness of sinful flesh, yet the power that begat Him was entirely in God the Holy Spirit—as the Scriptures express it, "The power of the Highest shall overshadow thee." He was begotten as the Apostles' Creed says, begotten of the Holy Ghost. "That holy thing which is born of thee shall be called the Son of the Highest." The corporeal frame of the Lord Jesus Christ was a masterpiece of the Holy Spirit. I suppose His body to have excelled all others in beauty; to have been like that of the first man, the very pattern of what the body is to be in heaven, when it shall shine forth in all its glory. That fabric, in all its beauty and perfection, was modeled by the Spirit. In His book were all the members written when as yet there were none of them. He fashioned and formed Him; and here again we have another instance of the creative energy of the Spirit.

2. A second manifestation of the Holy Spirit's power is to be found in the *resurrection of the Lord Jesus Christ.* If ye have ever studied this subject, ye have perhaps been rather perplexed to find that sometimes the resurrection of Christ is ascribed to Himself. By His own power and Godhead He could not be held by the bond of death, but as He willingly gave up His life He had power to take it again. In another portion of Scripture you find it ascribed to God the Father: "He raised him up from the dead": "Him hath God the Father exalted." And many other passages of similar import. But, again, it is said in Scripture that Jesus Christ was raised by the Holy Spirit. Now all these things were true. He was raised by the Father

because the Father said, "Loose the prisoner—let him go. Justice is satisfied. My law requires no more satisfaction—vengeance has had its due—let him go." Here He gave an official message which delivered Jesus from the grave. He was raised by His own majesty and power because He had a right to come out; and He felt He had, and therefore "burst the bonds of death: he could be no longer holden of them." But, He was raised by the Spirit as to that energy which His mortal frame received, by the which it rose again from the grave after having lain there for three days and nights. If you want proofs of this you must open your Bibles again, 1 Peter 3:18 "For Christ also hath once suffered for sins, the just for the unjust, that he might bring us to God, being put to death in the flesh but quickened by the Spirit." And a further proof you may find in Romans 8:11 "But if the Spirit of him that raised up Jesus from the dead dwell in you, he that raised up Christ from the dead shall also quicken your mortal bodies by his Spirit that dwelleth in you."

The resurrection of Christ, then, was effected by the agency of the Spirit; and here we have a noble illustration of His omnipotence. Could you have stepped, as angels did, into the grave of Jesus, and seen His sleeping body, you would have found it cold as any other corpse. Lift up the hand; it falls by the side. Look at the eye: it is glazed. And there is a death-thrust which must have annihilated life. See His hands: the blood distills not from them. They are cold and motionless. Can that body live? Can it start up? Yes; and be an illustration of the might of the Spirit. For when the power of the Spirit came on Him, as it was when it fell upon the dry bones of the valley: "he arose in the majesty of his divinity, and bright and shining, astonished the watchmen so that they fled away; yea, he rose no more to die, but to live forever, King of kings and Prince of the kings of the earth."

3. The third of the works of the Holy Spirit which have so wonderfully demonstrated His power, are *attestation works*. I mean by this, works of witnessing. When Jesus Christ went into the stream of baptism in the river Jordan, the Holy Spirit descended upon Him like a dove, and proclaimed Him God's beloved son. That was what I style an attestation work. And when afterwards Jesus Christ raised

the dead, when He healed the leper, when He spoke to diseases and they fled apace, when demons rushed in thousands from those who were possessed of them, it was done by the power of the Spirit. The Spirit dwelt in Jesus without measure, and by that power all those miracles were worked. These were attestation works. And when Jesus Christ was gone, you will remember that master attestation of the Spirit when He came like a rushing mighty wind upon the assembled apostles, and cloven tongues sat upon them; and you will remember how He attested their ministry by giving them to speak with tongues as He gave them utterance; and how, also, miraculous deeds were wrought by them, how they taught, how Peter raised Dorcas, how He breathed life into Eutycus, how great deeds were wrought by the apostles as well as their Master—so that "mighty signs and wonders were done by the Holy Ghost, and many believed thereby." Who will doubt the power of the Holy Spirit after that? Ah! Those Socinians who deny the existence of the Holy Ghost and His absolute personality, what will they do when we get them on creation, resurrection, and attestation? They must rush in the very teeth of Scripture. But mark! It is a stone upon which if any man fall he shall be bruised, but if it fall upon him, as it will do if he resists it, it shall grind him to powder. The Holy Spirit has power omnipotent, even the power of God.

4. Once more, if we want another outward and visible sign of the power of the Spirit, we may look at the *works of grace*. Behold a city where a soothsayer hath the power—who has given out himself to be some great one, a Philip enters it and preaches the Word of God, straightway a Simon Magus loses his power and himself seeks for the power of the Spirit to be given to him, fancying it might be purchased with money. See, in modern times, a country where the inhabitants live in miserable wigwams, feeding on reptiles and the meanest creatures; observe them bowing down before their idols and worshiping their false gods, and so plunged in superstition, so degraded and debased, that it became a question whether they had souls or not; behold a Moffat go with the Word of God in his hand, hear him preach as the Spirit gives him utterance, and accompanies that Word with power. They cast aside their idols

—they hate and abhor their former lusts; they build houses, wherein they dwell; they become clothed, and in their right mind. They break the bow, and cut the spear in sunder; the uncivilized become civilized; the savage becomes polite; he who knew nothing begins to read the Scripture; thus out of the mouths of savages God attests the power of His mighty Spirit.

Take a household in this city—and we could guide you to many such—the father is a drunkard; he has been the most desperate of characters; see him in his madness, and you might just as well meet an unchained tiger as meet such a man. He seems as if he could rend a man to pieces who should offend him. Mark his wife. She, too, has a spirit in her, and when he treats her ill she can resist him; many broils have been seen in that house, and often has the neighborhood been disturbed by the noise created there. As for the poor little children—see them in their rags and nakedness, poor untaught things. Untaught, did I say? They are taught and well taught in the devil's school, and are growing up to be the heirs of damnation. But someone whom God has blessed by His Spirit is guided to the house. He may be but a humble city missionary perhaps, but he speaks to such a one: O, says he, come and listen to the voice of God. Whether it is by His own agency, or a minister's preaching, the Word, which is quick and powerful, cuts to the sinner's heart. The tears run down his cheeks—such as had never been seen before. He shakes and quivers. The strong man bows down—the mighty man trembles—and those knees that never shook begin to knock together. That heart which never quailed before, now begins to shake before the power of the Spirit. He sits down on a humble bench by the penitent; he lets his knees bend, whilst his lips utter a child's prayer, but, whilst a child's prayer, a prayer of a child of God. He becomes a changed character. Mark the reformation in his house! That wife of his becomes the decent matron. Those children are the credit of the house, and in due time they grow up like olive branches round his table, adorning his house like polished stones. Pass by the house—no noise or broils, but songs of Zion. See him—no drunken revelry; he has drained his last cup; and, now forswearing it, he comes to God and is His servant. Now, you will not hear at midnight the bacchanalian shout, but should there be a noise, it will be the sound of the solemn hymn of praise to God. And, now, is there not such a thing as the power of the Spirit? Yes! And these must have witnessed it, and seen it.

I know a village, once, perhaps, the most profane in England — a village inundated by drunkenness and debauchery of the worst kind, where it was impossible almost for an honest traveler to stop in the public house without being annoyed by blasphemy; a place noted for incendiaries and robbers. One man, the ringleader of all, listened to the voice of God. That man's heart was broken. The whole gang came to hear the gospel preached, and they sat and seemed to reverence the preacher as if he were a God, and not a man. These men became changed and reformed; and everyone who knows the place affirms that such a change had never been wrought but by the power of the Holy Ghost. Let the gospel be preached and the Spirit poured out, and you will see that it has such power to change the conscience, to ameliorate the conduct, to raise the debased, to chastise and to curb the wickedness of the race, that you must glory in it. I say, there is naught like the power of the Spirit. Only let that come, and, indeed, everything can be accomplished.

II. Now, for the second point, THE INWARD AND SPIRITUAL POWER OF THE HOLY SPIRIT. What I have already spoken of may be seen; what I am about to speak of must be felt, and no man will apprehend what I say with truth unless he has felt it.

1. First, in that the Holy Ghost has *a power over men's hearts.* Now, men's hearts are very hard to affect. If you want to get them for any worldly object you can do it. A cheating world can win man's heart; a little gold can win man's heart; a trump of fame and a little clamor of applause can win man's heart. But there is not a minister breathing that can win man's heart himself. He can win his ears and make them listen; he can win his eyes and fix those eyes upon him; he can win the attention, but the heart is very slippery. Yes, the heart is a fish that troubles all gospel fisherman to hold. You may sometimes pull it almost all out of the water, but

slimy as an eel, it slippeth between your fingers, and you have not captured it after all. Many a man has fancied that he has caught the heart but has been disappointed. It would need a strong hunter to overtake the hart on the mountains. It is too fleet for human foot to approach.

The Spirit alone has power over man's heart. Do you ever try your power on a heart? If any man thinks that a minister can convert the soul, I wish he would try. Let him go and be a Sabbath-school teacher. He shall take his class, he shall have the best books that can be obtained, he shall have the best rules, he shall draw his lines of circumvolution about his spiritual Sebastopol, he shall take the best boy in his class, and if he is not tired in a week I shall be very much mistaken. Let him spend four or five Sabbaths in trying, but he will say, "The young fellow is incorrigible." Let him try another. And he will have to try another, and another, and another, before he will manage to convert one. He will soon find "It is not by might nor by power, but by my Spirit, saith the Lord." We cannot reach the soul, but the Holy Spirit can. "My beloved can put in his hand by the hole in the door and my bowels will move for sin." He can give a sense of blood-bought pardon that shall dissolve a heart of stone. He can

> Speak with that voice which wake the dead,
>   And bids the sinner rise:
> And makes the guilty conscience dread
>   The death that never dies.

He can make Sinai's thunders audible; yea, and He can make the sweet whisperings of Calvary enter into the soul. He has power over the heart of man. And here is a glorious proof of the omnipotence of the Spirit that He has rule over the heart.

2. But if there is one thing more stubborn than the heart it is *the will.* "My lord Will-be-will," as Bunyan calls him in his "Holy War," is a fellow who will not easily be bent. The will, especially in some men, is a very stubborn thing, and in all men, if the will is once stirred up to opposition, there is nothing can be done with them. *Freewill* somebody believes in. *Freewill* many dream of. Freewill!

Wherever is that to be found? Once there was freewill in Paradise, and a terrible mess freewill made there, for it all spoiled all Paradise and turned Adam out of the garden. Freewill was once in heaven, but it turned the glorious archangel out, and a third part of the stars of heaven fell into the abyss. Yet some boast of freewill. I wonder whether those who believe in it have any more power over persons' wills than I have. I know I have not any. I find the old proverb very true, "One man can bring a horse to the water, but a hundred cannot make him drink." I do not think any man has power over his fellow-creature's will, but the Spirit of God has. "I will make them willing in the day of my power." He maketh the unwilling sinner so willing that he is impetuous after the gospel; he who was obstinate, now hurries to the cross. He who laughed at Jesus, now hands on His mercy; and he who would not believe, is now made by the Holy Spirit to do it, not only willingly, but eagerly; he is happy, is glad to do it, rejoices in the sound of Jesus' name, and delights to run in the way of God's commandments. The Holy Spirit has power over the will.

3. And yet there is one thing more which I think is rather worse than the will. You will guess what I mean. The will is somewhat worse than the heart to bend, but there is one thing that excels the will in its naughtiness, and that is the *imagination*. I hope that my will is managed by Divine Grace. But I am afraid my imagination is not at times. Those who have a fair share of imagination know what a difficult thing it is to control. You cannot restrain it. It will break the reins. You will never be able to manage it. The imagination will sometimes fly up to God with such a power that eagles' wings cannot match it. It sometimes has such might that it can almost see the King in His beauty, and the land which is very far off. With regard to myself, my imagination will sometimes take me over the gates of iron, across that infinite unknown, to the very gates of pearl, and discover the blessed glorified.

But if it is potent one way it is another; for my imagination has taken me down to the vilest kennels and sewers of earth. It has given me thoughts so dreadful, that while I could not avoid them, yet I was thoroughly horrified at them. These thoughts will come;

and when I feel in the holiest frame, the most devoted to God, and the most earnest in prayer, it often happens that that is the very time when the plagues break out the worst. But I rejoice and think of one thing, that I can cry out when this imagination comes upon me. I know it is said in the Book of Leviticus, when an act of evil was committed, if the maiden cried out against it, then her life was to be spared. So it is with the Christian. If he cries out, there is hope. Can you chain your imagination? No, but the power of the Holy Ghost can. Ah, it shall do it, and it does do it at last; it does it even on earth.

III. But the last thing was, THE FUTURE AND DESIRED EFFECTS; for after all, though the Holy Spirit has done so much, He cannot say, "It is finished." Jesus Christ could exclaim concerning His own labor—"It is finished." But the Holy Spirit cannot say that. He has more to do yet: and until the consummation of all things, when the Son Himself becomes subject to the Father, it shall not be said by the Holy Spirit, "It is finished." What, then, has the Holy Spirit to do?

1. First, He has to *perfect us in holiness*. There are two kinds of perfection which a Christian needs—one is the perfection of justification in the person of Jesus; and the other is, the perfection of sanctification worked in him by the Holy Spirit. At present corruption still rests even in the breasts of the regenerate. At present the heart is partially impure. At present there are still lusts and evil imaginations. But, oh! My soul rejoices to know that the day is coming when God shall finish the work which He has begun; and He shall present my soul, not only perfect in Christ, but, perfect in the Spirit, without spot or blemish, or any such thing. And it is true that this poor depraved heart is to become as holy as that of God? And is it true that this poor spirit, which often cries, "O wretched man that I am, who shall deliver me from the body of this sin and death!" shall get rid of sin and death—I shall have no evil things to vex my ears, and no unholy thoughts to disturb my peace? Oh! Happy hour! Oh! To be washed white, clean, pure, perfect! Not an angel more pure than I shall be—yea, not God Himself more holy! And I

shall be able to say, in a double sense, "Great God, I am clean — through Jesus' blood I am clean, through the Spirit's work I am clean too!" Must we not extol the power of the Holy Ghost in thus making us fit to stand before our Father in heaven?

2. Another great work of the Holy Spirit which is not accomplished is *the bringing on of the latter-day glory*. In a few more years — I know not when, I know not how — the Holy Spirit will be poured out in a far different style from the present. There are diversities of operations; and during the last few years it has been the case that the diversified operations have consisted in very little pouring out of the Spirit. Ministers have gone on in dull routine, continually preaching — preaching — preaching, and little good has been done. But the hour is coming when the Holy Ghost shall be poured out again in such a wonderful manner that many shall run to and fro, and knowledge shall be increased — the knowledge of the Lord shall cover the earth as the waters cover the surface of the great deep; when His kingdom shall come, and His will shall be done on earth even as it is in heaven. We are not going to be dragging on forever like Pharaoh with the wheels off his chariot. Perhaps there shall be no miraculous gifts — for they will not be required, but yet there shall be such a miraculous amount of holiness, such an extraordinary fervor of prayer, such a real communion with God and so much vital religion, and such a spread of the doctrines of the cross, that everyone will see that verily the Spirit is poured out like water, and the rains are descending from above. For that let us pray: let us continually labor for it, and seek it of God.

3. One more work of the Spirit which will especially manifest His power — *the general resurrection*. We have reason to believe from Scripture that the resurrection of the dead, while it will be effected by the voice of God and of His Word (the Son) shall also be brought about by the Spirit. That same power which raised Jesus Christ from the dead, shall also quicken your mortal bodies. The power of the resurrection is perhaps one of the finest proofs of the works of the Spirit. Ah! My friends, if this earth could but have its mantle torn away for a little while, if the green sod could be cut from it, and we could look about six feet deep into its bowels, what

a world it would seem! What should we see? Bones, carcasses, rottenness, worms, corruption. And you would say, "Can these dry bones live? Can they start up?" "Yes! In a moment! In the twinkling of an eye, at the last trump, the dead shall be raised." He speaks: they are alive! See them scattered: bone comes to his bone! See them naked: flesh comes upon them! See them still lifeless: "Come from the four winds, O breath, and breathe upon these slain!" When the wind of the Holy Spirit comes, they live, and they stand upon their feet an exceeding great army.

I have thus attempted to speak of the power of the Spirit, and I trust I have shown it to you. We must now have a moment or two for practical inference. The Spirit is very powerful, Christian! What do you infer from that fact? Why, that you never need distrust the power of God to carry you to heaven. O how that sweet verse was laid to my soul yesterday!

> His tried Almighty arm
> Is raised for your defense;
> Where is the power can reach you there?
> Or what can pluck you thence?

The power of the Holy Spirit is your bulwark, and all His omnipotence defends you. Can your enemies overcome omnipotence? Then they can conquer you. Can they wrestle with Deity, and hurl Him to the ground? Then they might conquer you. For the power of the Spirit is our power; the power of the Spirit is our might.

Once again, Christian, if this is the power of the Spirit, *why should you doubt anything?* There is your son. There is that wife of yours for whom you have supplicated so frequently: do not doubt the Spirit's power. "Though he tarry, wait for him." There is thy husband, O holy woman! And thou hast wrestled for his soul. And though he is ever so hardened and desperate a wretch, and treats thee ill, there is power in the Spirit. And, O ye who have come from barren churches with scarcely a leaf upon the tree. Do not doubt the power of the Spirit to raise you up. For it shall be a "pasture for flocks, a den of wild asses," open, but deserted, until the Spirit is poured out from on high. And then the parched ground shall be made a pool, and the thirsty land springs of water, and in the habitations of dragons, where each day shall be grass with reeds and rushes. And, O ye who remember what your God has done for you especially, never distrust the power of the Spirit. Ye have seen the wilderness blossom like Carmel, ye have seen the desert blossom like the rose; trust Him for the future. Then go out and labor with this conviction, that the power of the Holy Ghost is able to do anything. Go to your Sunday school; go to your tract distribution; go to your missionary enterprise! Go to your preaching in your rooms, with the conviction that the power of the Spirit is our great help.

And now, lastly, to you sinners: What is there to be said to you about this power of the Spirit? Why, to me, there is some hope for some of you. I cannot save you: I cannot get at you. I make you cry sometimes—you wipe your eyes, and it is all over. But I know my Master can. That is my consolation. Chief of sinners, there is hope for thee! This power can save you as well as anybody else. It is able to break your heart, though it is an iron one; to make your eyes run with tears though they have been like rocks before. His power is able this morning, if He will, to change your heart, to turn the current of all your ideas; to make you at once a child of God, to justify you in Christ. There is power enough in the Holy Spirit. Ye are not straightened in Him, but in your own bowels. He is able to bring sinners to Jesus: He is able to make you willing in the day of His power. Are you willing this morning? Has He gone so far as to make you desire His name, to make you wish for Jesus? Then, O sinner! While He draws you, say, "Draw me, I am wretched without thee." Follow Him, follow Him; and, while He leads, tread you in His footsteps, and rejoice that He has begun a good work in you, for there is an evidence that He will continue it even unto the end. And, O desponding one! Put thy trust in the power of the Spirit. Rest on the blood of Jesus, and thy soul is safe, not only now, but throughout eternity. God bless you, my hearers. Amen.

3

The Holy Ghost —
The Great Teacher

*Howbeit when he, the Spirit of truth, is come, he will
guide you into all truth: for he shall not speak of himself,
but whatsoever he shall hear, that shall he speak: and he
will show you things to come — John 16:13.*

This generation hath gradually, and almost imperceptibly, become to a great extent a godless generation. One of the diseases of the present generation of mankind, is their secret but deep-seated godlessness, by which they have so far departed from the knowledge of God. Science has discovered to us second causes; and hence, many have too much forgotten the first Great Cause, the Author of all: they have been able so far to pry into secrets, that the great axiom of the existence of a God, has been too much neglected. Even among professing Christians, while there is a great amount of religion, there is too little godliness: there is much external formalism, but too little inward acknowledgment of God, too little living on God, living with God, and relying upon God. Hence arises the sad fact, that when you enter many of our places of worship you will certainly hear the name of God mentioned, but except in the benediction, you would scarcely know there was

197

a Trinity. In many places dedicated to Jehovah, the name of Jesus is too often kept in the background; the Holy Spirit is almost entirely neglected; and very little is said concerning His sacred influence.

Even religious men have become to a large degree godless in this age. We sadly require more preaching regarding God; more preaching of those things which look not so much at the creature to be saved, as at God the Great One to be extolled. My firm conviction is, that in proportion as we have more regard for the sacred godhead, the wondrous Trinity in Unity, shall we see a greater display of God's power, and a more glorious manifestation of His might in our churches. May God send us a Christ-exalting, Spirit-loving ministry—men who shall proclaim God the Holy Ghost in all His offices, and shall extol God the Savior as the author and finisher of our faith; not neglecting that Great God, the Father of His people, who before all worlds, elected us in Christ His Son, justified us through His righteousness, and will inevitably preserve us and gather us together in one, in the consummation of all things at the last great day.

Our text has regard to God the Holy Spirit; of Him we shall speak and Him only, if His sweet influence shall rest upon us.

The disciples had been instructed by Christ concerning certain elementary doctrines, but Jesus did not teach His disciples more than what we should call the A B C of religion. He gives His reasons for this in the 12th verse: "I have yet many things to say unto you, but you cannot bear them now." His disciples were not possessors of the Spirit. They had the Spirit so far as the work of conversion was concerned, but not as to the matters of bright illumination, profound instruction, prophecy, and inspiration. He says, "I am now about to depart, and when I go from you I will send the Comforter unto you. Ye cannot bear these things now, howbeit, when he, the Spirit of truth is come, he will guide you into all truth." The same promise that He made to His apostles, stands good to all His children; and in reviewing it, we shall take it as *our* portion and heritage, and shall not consider ourselves intruders upon the manor of the apostles, or upon their exclusive rights and prerogatives; for we conceive that Jesus says even to us, "When he, the Spirit of truth is come, he will guide you into all truth."

Dwelling exclusively upon our text, we have five things. First of all, here is *an attainment mentioned*—a knowledge of all truth; secondly, here is *a difficulty suggested*—which is, that we need guidance into all truth: thirdly, here is *a person provided*—"when he, the Spirit shall come, he shall guide you into all truth"; fourthly, here is *a manner hinted at*—"he shall guide you into all truth"; fifthly here is *a sign given as to the working of the Spirit*—we may know whether He works, by His "guiding us into *all* truth,"—into all of one thing; not *truths*, but *truth*.

I. Here is AN ATTAINMENT MENTIONED, which is a knowledge of all truth. We know that some conceive doctrinal knowledge to be of very little importance, and of no practical use. We do not think so. We believe the science of Christ crucified and a judgment of the teachings of Scripture to be exceedingly valuable; we think it is right, that the Christian ministry should not only be arousing but instructing; not merely awakening, but enlightening; that it should appeal not only to the passions but to the understanding. We are far from thinking doctrinal knowledge to be of secondary importance; we believe it to be one of the first things in the Christian life, to know the truth, and then to practice it. We scarcely need this morning tell you how desirable it is for us to be well taught in things of the kingdom.

First of all, *nature itself* (when it has been sanctified by grace) *gives us a strong desire to know all truth.* The natural man separateth himself and intermeddleth with all knowledge. God has put an instinct in him by which he is rendered unsatisfied if he cannot probe mystery to its bottom; he can never be content until he can unriddle secrets. What we call curiosity is something given us of God impelling us to search into the knowledge of natural things; that curiosity, sanctified by the Spirit, is also brought to bear in matters of heavenly science and celestial wisdom. "Bless the Lord," said David, "O my soul, and *all that is within me* bless his holy name!" If there is a curiosity within us, it ought to be employed and developed in a search after truth. "All that is within me," sanctified by the Spirit should be developed. And, verily, the Christian man feels an intense longing to bury his ignorance and receive wisdom. If he, when in his natural estate panted for terrestrial knowledge, how much more ardent is the wish to unravel, if possible, the sacred mysteries of God's Word! A true Christian is always intently reading and searching the Scripture that he may be able to certify himself as to its main and cardinal truths.

Not only is this attainment to be desired because nature teaches us so, but a knowledge of all truth is *very essential for our comfort.* I do believe that many persons have been distressed half their lives from the fact that they had not clear views of truth. Many poor souls, for instance, under conviction, abide three or four times as long in sorrow of mind as they would require to do if they had someone to instruct them in the great matter of justification. So there are believers who are often troubling themselves about falling away, but if they knew in their soul the great consolation that we are kept by the grace of God through faith unto salvation, they would be no more troubled about it. So have I found some distressed about the unpardonable sin, but if God instructs us in that doctrine, and shows us that no conscience that is really awakened ever can commit that sin, but that when it is committed God gives us up to a seared conscience, so that we never fear or tremble afterwards, all that distress would be alleviated. Depend on this, the more you know of God's truth — all things else being equal — the more comfortable you will be as a Christian. Nothing can give a greater light on your path than a clear understanding of divine things. It is a mingle-mangled gospel too commonly preached which causes the downcast faces of Christians. Give me the congregation whose faces are bright with joy, let their eyes glisten at the sound of the gospel, then will I believe that it is God's own words they are receiving. Instead thereof you will often see melancholy congregations whose visages are not much different from the bitter countenance of poor creatures swallowing medicine, because the word spoken terrifies them by its legality, instead of comforting them by its grace. We love a cheerful gospel, and we think "all the truth" will tend to comfort the Christian.

Again, I hold also that this attainment to the knowledge of all truth is very desirable for *the usefulness which it will give us in the world at large*. We should not be selfish: we should always consider whether a thing will be beneficial to others. A knowledge of all truth will make us very serviceable in this world. We shall be skillful physicians who know how to take the poor distressed soul aside, to put the finger on his eye, and take the scale off for him, that heaven's light may comfort him. There will be no character, however perplexing may be its peculiar phase, but we shall be able to speak to it and comfort it. He who holds the truth is usually the most useful man. As a good Presbyterian brother said to me the other day: "I know God has blessed you exceedingly in gathering in souls, but it is an extraordinary fact that nearly all the men I know—with scarcely an exception—who have been made useful in gathering in souls, have held the great doctrines of the grace of God." Almost every man whom God has blessed to the building up of the church in prosperity, and around whom the people have rallied, has been a man who has held firmly free grace from first to last, through the finished salvation of Christ.

II. Now, again, here is a DIFFICULTY SUGGESTED, and that is—that we require a guide to conduct us into all truth. The difficulty is that truth is not so easy to discover. There is no man born in this world by nature who has the truth in his heart. There is no creature that ever was fashioned, since the fall, who has a knowledge of truth innate and natural. It has been disputed by many philosophers whether there are such things as innate ideas at all. But is of no use disputing as to whether there are any innate ideas of truth. There are none such. There are ideas of everything that is wrong and evil, but in us—that is our flesh—there dwelleth no *good* thing; we are born in sin, and shapened in iniquity; in sin did our mother conceive us. There is nothing in us good, and no tendency to righteousness. Then, since we are not born with the truth, we have the

task of searching for it. If we are to be blest by being eminently useful as Christian men, we must be well instructed in matters of revelation, but here is the difficulty—that we cannot follow without a
guide the winding paths of truth. Why this?

First, because of *the very great intricacy of truth itself.* Truth itself
is no easy thing to discover. Those who fancy they know everything
and constantly dogmatize with the spirit of "We are the men, and
wisdom will die with us," of course see no difficulties whatever in
the system they hold, but I believe the most earnest student of
Scripture will find things in the Bible which puzzle him; however
earnestly he reads it, he will see some mysteries too deep for him to
understand. He will cry out "Truth! I cannot find thee; I know not
where thou art, thou art beyond me; I cannot fully view thee."
Truth is a path so narrow that two can scarce walk together in it;
we usually tread the narrow way in single file; two men can seldom
walk arm in arm in the truth. We believe the same truth in the
main but we cannot walk together in the path, it is too narrow. The
way of truth is very difficult. If you step an inch aside on the right
you are in a dangerous error, and if you swerve a little to the left
you are equally in the mire. On the one hand there is a huge
precipice, and on the other a deep morass; and unless you keep to
the true line, to the breadth of a hair, you will go astray. Truth is a
narrow path indeed. It is a path the eagle's eye hath not seen, and a
depth the diver hath not visited. It is like the veins of metal in a
mine, it is often of excessive thinness, and moreover it runneth not
in one continued layer. Lose it once, and you may dig for miles and
not discover it again; the eye must watch perpetually the direction
of the lode. Grains of truth are like the grains of gold in the rivers of
Australia—they must be shaken by the hand of patience, and
washed in the stream of honesty, or the fine gold will be mingled
with sand. Truth is often mingled with error, and it is hard to distinguish it, but we bless God it is said, "When the Spirit of truth is
come, he will guide you into all truth."

Another reason why we need a guide is, *the invidiousness of
error.* It easily steals upon us, and, if I may so describe our position,
we are often like we were on Thursday night in that tremendous

fog. Most of us were feeling for ourselves, and wondering where on earth we were. We could scarcely see an inch before us. We came to a place where there were three turnings. We thought we knew the old spot. There was the lamp-post, and now we must take a sharp turn to the left. But not so. We ought to have gone a little to the right. We have been so often to the same place, that we think we know every flagstone: and there's our friend's shop over the way. It is dark, but we think we must be quite right, and all the while we are quite wrong, and find ourselves half-a-mile out of the way. So it is with matters of truth. We think, surely this is the right path; and the voice of the evil one whispers, "that is the way, walk ye in it." You do so, and you find to your great dismay, that instead of the path of truth, you have been walking in the paths of unrighteousness and erroneous doctrines. The way of life is a labyrinth; the grassiest paths and the most bewitching, are the farthest away from right; the most enticing, are those which are garnished with wrested truths. I believe there is not a counterfeit coin in the world so much like a genuine one, as some errors are like the truth. One is base metal, the other is true gold; still in externals they differ very little.

We also need a guide, because *we are so prone to go astray*. Why, if the path of heaven were as straight as Bunyan pictures it, with no turning to the right hand or left—and no doubt it is, we are so prone to go astray, that we should go to the right hand to the Mountains of Destruction, or to the left in the dark Wood of Desolation. David says, "I have gone astray like a lost sheep." That means very often: for if a sheep is put into a field twenty times, if it does not get out twenty-one times, it will be because it cannot, because the place is hurdled up, and it cannot find a hole in the hedge. If grace did not guide a man, he would go astray, though there were hand-posts all the way to heaven. Let it be written, "Miklat, Miklat, the way to refuge," he would turn aside, and the avenger of blood would overtake him, if some guide did not, like the angels in Sodom, put his hand on his shoulders, and cry, "Escape, escape, for thy life! Look not behind thee; stay not in all the plain." These, then, are the reasons why we need a guide.

III. In the third place, here is A PERSON PROVIDED. This is none other than God, and this God is none other than a person. This person is "he, the Spirit," the "Spirit of truth"; not an influence or an emanation, but actually a person. "When the Spirit of truth is come, he shall guide you into all truth." Now, we wish you to look at this guide, to consider how adapted He is to us.

In the first place, He is *infallible*; He knows everything and cannot lead us astray. If I pin my sleeve to another man's coat, he may lead me part of the way rightly, but by-and-bye he will go wrong himself, and I shall be led astray with him. But if I give myself to the Holy Ghost and ask His guidance, there is no fear of my wandering.

Again, we rejoice in this Spirit because He is *ever-present*. We fall into difficulty sometimes; we say, "Oh, if I could take this to my minister, he would explain it, but I live so far off, and am no able to see him." That perplexes us, and we turn the text round and round and cannot make anything of it. We look at the commentators. We take down pious Thomas Scott, and, as usual, he says nothing about it if it be a dark passage. Then we go to holy Matthew Henry, and if it is an easy Scripture, he is sure to explain it, but if it is a text hard to be understood, it is likely enough, of course, left in his own gloom. And even Dr. Gill himself, the most consistent of commentators, when he comes to a hard passage, manifestly avoids it in some degree. But when we have no commentator or minister, we have still the Holy Spirit. And let me tell you a little secret: whenever you cannot understand a text, open your Bible, bend your knee, and pray over that text; and if it does not split into atoms and open itself, try again. If prayer does not explain it, it is one of the things God did not intend you to know, and you may be content to be ignorant of it. Prayer is the key that openeth the cabinets of mystery. Prayer and faith are sacred picklocks that can open secrets, and obtain great treasures. There is no college for holy education like that of the blessed Spirit, for He is an ever-present tutor, to Whom we have only to bend the knee, and He is at our side, the great expositor of truth.

But there is one thing about the suitability of this guide which is remarkable. I do not know whether it has struck you — the Holy

Spirit can "guide us *into* a truth." Now, man can guide us *to* a truth, but it is only the Holy Spirit who can "guide us *into* a truth." "When he, the Spirit of truth, shall come, he shall guide you *into*"—mark that word—"all truth." Now, for instance, it is a long while before you can lead some people to election, but when you have made them see its correctness, you have not led them "into" it. You may show then that it is plainly stated in Scripture, but they will turn away and hate it. You take them to another great truth, but they have been brought up in a different fashion, and though they cannot answer your arguments, they say, "The man is right, perhaps," and they whisper—but so low that conscience itself cannot hear—"but it is so contrary to my prejudices, that I cannot receive it." After you have led them *to* the truth, and they see it is true, how hard it is to lead them *into* it! There are many of my hearers who are brought *to* the truth of their depravity, but they are not brought *into* it, and made to feel it. Some of you are brought to know the truth that God keeps us from day to day, but you rarely get into it, so as to live in continual dependence upon God the Holy Ghost, and draw fresh supplies from Him. The thing is—to get inside it. A Christian should do with truth as a snail does with his shell—live inside it, as well as carry it on his back, and bear it perpetually about with him. The Holy Ghost, it is said, shall lead us into all truth. You may be brought to a chamber where there is an abundance of gold and silver, but you will be no richer unless you effect an entrance. It is the Spirit's work to unbar the two-leaved gates, and bring us into a truth, so that we may get inside it, and, as dear old Rowland Hill said, "Not only hold the truth, but have the truth hold us."

IV. Fourthly, here is A METHOD SUGGESTED: "He shall guide you into all truth." Now I must have an illustration. I must compare truth to some cave or grotto that you have heard of, with wondrous stalactites hanging from the roof, and others starting from the floor; a cavern, glittering with spar and abounding in marvels. Before entering the cavern you inquire for a guide, who comes with his lighted flambeau. He conducts you down to a considerable depth, and you find yourself in the midst of the cave. He leads you through different chambers. Here he points to a little stream rushing from amid the rocks, and indicates its rise and progress; there he points to some peculiar rocks and tells you its name; then takes you into a large natural hall, tells you how many persons once feasted in it; and so on. Truth is a grand series of caverns, it is our glory to have so great and wise a conductor. Imagine that we are coming to the darkness of it. He is a light shining in the midst of us to guide us. And by the light he shows us wondrous things. In three ways the Holy Ghost teaches us: by suggestion, direction, and illumination.

First, He guides us into all truth *by suggesting it*. There are thoughts that dwell in our minds that were not born there, but which were exotics brought from heaven and put there by the spirit. It is not a fancy that angels whisper into our ears, and that devils do the same: both good and evil spirits hold converse with men; and some of us have known it. We have had strange thoughts which were not the offspring of our souls, but which came from angelic visitants; and direct temptations and evil insinuations have we had which were not brewed in our own souls, but which came from the pestilential cauldron of hell. So the Spirit doth speak in men's ears, sometimes in the darkness of the night. In ages gone by He spoke in dreams and visions, but now He speaketh by His Word. Have you not at times had unaccountably in the middle of your business a thought concerning God and heavenly things, and could not tell whence it came? Have you not been reading or studying the Scripture, but a text came across your mind, and you could not help it; though you even put it down it was like cork in water, and would swim up again to the top of your mind. Well, that good thought was put there by the Spirit; He often guides His people into all truth by suggesting just as the guide in the grotto does with his flambeau. He does not say a word, perhaps, but he walks into a passage himself, and you follow him; so the Spirit suggests a thought, and your heart follows it up.

Well can I remember the manner in which I learned the doctrines of grace in a single instant. Born, as all of us are by nature, an Arminian, I still believed the old things I had heard continually from the pulpit, and did not see the grace of God. I remember sitting one day in the house of God and hearing a sermon as dry as possible, and as worthless as all such sermons are, when a thought struck my mind—how came I to be converted? I prayed, thought I. Then I thought how came I to pray? I was induced to pray by reading the Scriptures. How came I to read the Scriptures? Why—I did read them; and what led me to that? And then, in a moment, I saw that God was at the bottom of all, and that He was the author of faith. And then the whole doctrine opened up to me, from which I have not departed.

But sometimes He leads us *by direction*. The guide points and says—"There, gentlemen, go along that particular path; that is the way." So the Spirit gives a direction and tendency to our thoughts; not suggesting a new one but letting a particular thought when it starts take such-and-such a direction; not so much putting a boat on the stream as steering it when it is there. When our thoughts are considering sacred things He leads us into a more excellent channel from that in which we started. Time after time have you commenced a meditation on a certain doctrine and, unaccountably, you were gradually led away into another, and you saw how one doctrine leaned on another, as is the case with the stones in the arch of a bridge, all hanging on the keystone of Jesus Christ crucified. You were brought to see these things not by a new idea suggested, but by direction given to your thoughts.

But perhaps the best way in which the Holy Ghost leads us into all truth is by *illumination*. He illuminates the Bible. Now, have any of you an illuminated Bible at home? "No," says one, "I have a morocco Bible; I have a marginal reference Bible." Ah! That is all very well, but have you an illuminated Bible? "Yes; I have a large family Bible with pictures in it." There is a picture of John the Baptist baptizing Christ by pouring water on His head and many other nonsensical things, but that is not what I mean; have you an illuminated Bible? "Yes; I have a Bible with splendid engravings in it." Yes; I know you may have, but have you an illuminated Bible? "I don't understand what you mean by an illuminated Bible." Well, it is the Christian man who has an illuminated Bible. He does not buy it illuminated originally, but when he reads it

> A glory gilds the sacred page,
> Majestic like the sun;
> Which gives a light to every age—
> It gives, but borrows none.

There is nothing like reading an illuminated Bible, beloved. You may read to all eternity, and never learn anything by it, unless it is illuminated by the Spirit; and then the words shine forth like stars. The book seems made of gold leaf; every single letter glitters like a diamond. Oh! It is a blessed thing to read an illuminated Bible lit up by the radiance of the Holy Ghost. Hast thou read the Bible and studied it, my brother, and yet have thine eyes been unenlightened? Go and say, "O Lord, gild the Bible for me. I want an expounded Bible. Illuminate it; shine upon it; for I cannot read it to profit, unless you enlightenest me." Blind men may read the Bible with their fingers, but blind souls cannot. We want a light to read the Bible by; there is no reading it in the dark. Thus the Holy Spirit leads us into all truth, by suggesting ideas, by directing our thoughts, and by illuminating the Scriptures when we read them.

V. The last thing is AN EVIDENCE. The question arises, How may I know whether I am enlightened by the Spirit's influence, and led into all truth? First, you may know the Spirit's influence by its *unity*—He guides us into all *truth:* secondly, by its *universality*—He guides us into *all* truth.

First, if you are judging a minister, whether he has the Holy Ghost in him or not, you may know him in the first place, by *the constant unity of his testimony.* A man cannot be enlightened by the Holy Spirit, who preaches yea and nay. The Spirit never says one thing at one time and another thing at another time. There are indeed many good men who say both yea and nay, but still their contrary testimonies are not both from God the Spirit, for God the Spirit cannot witness to black and white, to a falsehood and truth. But some persons say, "I find one thing in one part of the Bible and another thing in another, and though it contradicts itself I must believe it." All quite right, brother, if it did contradict itself, but the fault is not in the wood but in the carpenter. Many carpenters do not understand dove-tailing; so there are many preachers who do not understand dove-tailing. It is very nice work, and it is not easily learned; it takes some apprenticeship to make all doctrines square together.

And you may know it by its *universality*. The true child of God will not be led into some truth but into all truth. When first he starts he will not know half the truth, he will believe it but not understand it; he will have the germ of it but not the sum total in all its breadth and length. There is nothing like learning by experience. A man cannot set up for a theologian in a week. Certain doctrines take years to develop themselves. Like the aloe that taketh a hundred years to be dressed, there be some truths that must lie long in the heart before they really come out and make themselves appear so that we can speak of them as that we do know, and testify of that which we have seen. The Spirit will gradually lead us into all truth. For instance, if it be true that Jesus Christ is to reign upon the earth personally for a thousand years, as I am inclined to believe it is, if I be under the Spirit, that will be more and more opened to me, until I with confidence declare it. Some men begin very timidly. A man says, at first, "I know we are justified by faith, and have peace with God, but so many have cried out against eternal justification, that I am afraid of it." But he is gradually enlightened, and led to see that in the same hour when all his debts were paid, a full discharge was given; that in the moment when its sin was canceled, every elect soul was justified in God's mind, though they were not justified in their own minds till afterwards. The Spirit shall lead you into all truth.

Now, what are the practical inferences from this great doctrine? The first is with reference to the Christian who is afraid of his own ignorance. How many are there who are just enlightened and have tasted of heavenly things, who are afraid they are too ignorant to be saved! Beloved, God the Holy Spirit can teach anyone, however illiterate, however uninstructed. I have known some men who were almost idiots before conversion, but they afterwards had their faculties wonderfully developed. Some time ago there was a man who was so ignorant that he could not read, and he never spoke anything like grammar in his life, unless by mistake; and moreover, he was considered to be what the people in his neighborhood called "daft." But when he was converted, the first thing he did was to pray. He stammered out a few words, and in a little time his powers of speaking began to develop themselves. Then he thought he would like to read the Scriptures, and after long, long months of labor, he learned to read. And what was the next thing? He thought he could preach; and he did preach a little in his own homely way, in his house. Then he thought "I must read a few more books." And so his mind expanded, until, I believe he is at the present day, a useful minister, settled in a country village, laboring for God. It needs but little intellect to be taught of God. If you feel your ignorance, do not despair. Go to the Spirit—the great Teacher—and ask his sacred influence; and it shall come to pass that He "shall guide you into all truth."

Another inference is this: whenever any of our brethren do not understand the truth let us take a hint as to the best way of dealing with them. Do not let us controvert with them. I have heard many controversies, but never heard of any good from one of them. Few men are taught by controversy, for

A man convinced against his will, is of the same opinion still.

Pray for them that the Spirit of truth may lead them "into all truth." Do not be angry with your brother, but pray for him; cry, "Lord! open thou his eyes that he may behold wondrous things out of thy law."

Lastly, we speak to some of you who know nothing about the Spirit of truth, nor about the truth itself. It may be that some of you are saying, "We care not much which of you are right, we are happily indifferent to it." Ah! But, poor sinner, if thou knewest the gift of God, and who it was that spake the truth, thou wouldst not say, "I care not for it"; if thou didst know how essential the truth is to thy salvation, thou wouldst not take so; if thou didst know that the truth of God is—that thou art a worthless sinner, but if thou believest, then God from all eternity, apart from all thy merits, loved thee, and bought thee with the Redeemer's blood, and justified thee in the forum of heaven, and will by-and-bye justify thee in the forum of thy conscience through the Holy Ghost by faith; if thou didst know that here is a heaven for thee beyond the chance of a failure, a crown for thee, the luster of which can never be dimmed; then thou wouldst say, "Indeed the truth is precious to my soul!" Why, my ungodly hearers, these men of error want to take away the truth, which alone can save you, the only gospel that can deliver you from hell; they deny the great truths of free-grace, those fundamental doctrines which alone can snatch a sinner from hell; and even though you do not feel interest in them now, I still would say, you ought to desire to see them promoted. May God give you to know the truth in your hearts! May the Spirit "guide you into all truth!" For if you do not know the truth here, recollect there will be a sorrowful learning of it in the dark chambers of the pit, where the only light shall be the flames of hell! May you here know the truth! And the truth shall make you free: and if the Son shall make you free, you shall be free indeed, for He says, "I am the way, the truth, and the life." Believe on Jesus thou chief of sinners; trust His love and mercy, and thou art saved, for God the Spirit giveth faith and eternal life.

4

The Outpouring
of the Holy Spirit

*While Peter yet spake these words, the Holy Ghost fell
on all them which heard the Word—Acts 10:44.*

The Bible is a book of the Revelation of God. The God after
whom the heathen blindly searched, and for whom reason
gropes in darkness, is here plainly revealed to us in the pages
of divine authorship, so that he who is willing to understand as
much of Godhead as man can know, may here learn it if he be not
willingly ignorant and willfully obstinate. The doctrine of the Trinity
is specially taught in Holy Scripture. The word certainly does not
occur, but the three divine persons of the One God are frequently
and constantly mentioned, and Holy Scripture is exceedingly careful
that we should all receive and believe that great truth of the Christian religion, that the Father is God, that the Son is God, that the
Spirit is God, and yet there are not three Gods but one God: though
they be each of them very God of very God, yet three in one and
one in three is the Jehovah whom we worship.

You will notice in the works of *Creation* how carefully the Scriptures assure us that all the three divine persons took their share. "In
the beginning Jehovah created the heavens and the earth"; and in

another place we are told that God said "Let *us* make man"—not one person, but all three taking counsel with each other with regard to the making of mankind. We know that the Father hath laid the foundations and fixed those solid beams of light on which the blue arches of the sky are sustained, but we know with equal certainty that Jesus Christ, the eternal *Logos*, was with the Father in the beginning, and "without him was not anything made that was made": moreover we have equal certainty that the Holy Spirit had a hand in Creation, for we are told that "the earth was without form and void, and darkness was upon the face of the earth; and the spirit of the Lord moved upon the face of the waters"; and brooding with His dove-like wing, He brought out of the egg of chaos this mighty thing, the fair round world.

We have the like proof of the three persons in the Godhead in the matter of *Salvation*. We know that God the Father gave His Son; we have abundant proof that God the Father chose His people from before the foundation of the world, that He did invent the plan of salvation, and hath always given His free, willing, and joyous consent to the salvation of His people. With regard to the share that the Son had in salvation, that is apparent enough to all. For us men and for our salvation He came down from heaven; He was incarnate in a mortal body; He was crucified, dead, and buried; He descended into hades; the third day He rose again from the dead; He ascended into heaven; He sitteth at the right hand of God, where also He maketh intercession for us. As to the Holy Spirit, we have equally sure proof that the Spirit of God worketh in conversion; for everywhere we are said to be begotten of the Holy Spirit; continually it is declared, that unless a man be born again from above, he cannot see the kingdom of God; while all the virtues and the graces of Christianity are described as being the fruits of the Spirit, because the Holy Spirit doth from first to last work in us and carry out that which Jesus Christ hath beforehand worked for us in His great redemption, which also God the Father hath designed for us in His great predestinating scheme of salvation.

Now, it is to the work of the Holy Spirit that I shall this morning specially direct your attention; and I may as well mention the rea-

son why I do so. It is this. In the United States of America there has
been a great awakening.* Two hundred and fifty thousand persons—that is a quarter of a million—profess to have been regenerated, and have united themselves with different sections of God's
church. And that which makes me believe the work to be genuine
is just this—that the enemies of Christ's holy gospel are exceedingly
wroth at it. When the devil roars at anything, you may rest assured
there is some good in it. The devil is not like some dogs we know of;
he never barks unless there is something to bark at. When Satan
howls, we may rest assured he is afraid his kingdom is in danger.
Now this great work in America has been manifestly caused by the
outpouring of the Spirit, for no one minister has been a leader in it.
All the ministers of the gospel have cooperated in it, but none of
them have stood in the van. God Himself has been the leader of
His own hosts. It began with a desire for prayer. God's people began
to pray; the prayer meetings were better attended than before; it was
then proposed to hold meetings at times that had never been set
apart for prayer; these also were well attended. And there has been
real prayer. Sinners beyond all count, have risen up in the prayer
meeting, and have requested the people of God to pray for them;
thus making public to the world that they had a desire after Christ;
they have been prayed for, and the church has seen that God verily
doth hear and answer prayer.

Now, if we have the like effect produced in this land, the one
thing we must seek is the outpouring of the Holy Spirit, and I
thought, perhaps, this morning in preaching upon the work of the
Holy Spirit, that text might be fulfilled—"Him that honoreth me I
will honor." My sincere desire is to honor the Holy Spirit this morning, and if He will be pleased to honor His church in return, unto
Him shall be the glory forever.

"While Peter yet spake these words, the Holy Ghost fell on all
them which heard the word."

In the first place, I shall endeavor to describe *the method of the
Spirit's operation*; secondly, *the absolute necessity of the Holy Spirit's*

---

* The great revival of 1858, afterwards experienced in Britain.

influence, if we could see men converted; and then, in the third place, I shall suggest the ways and means by which under divine grace we may obtain a like falling down of the Spirit upon our churches.

I. In the first place, then, I will endeavor to explain THE METHOD OF THE HOLY SPIRIT'S OPERATIONS. But let me guard myself against being misunderstood. We can explain what the Spirit does, but how He does it, no man must pretend to know. The work of the Holy Spirit is the peculiar mystery of the Christian religion. Almost any other thing is plain, but this must remain an inscrutable secret into which it were wrong for us to attempt to pry. Who knoweth where the winds are begotten? Who knoweth, therefore, how the Spirit worketh, for He is like the wind? "The wind bloweth where it listeth, and thou hearest the sound thereof, but canst not tell whence it cometh, and whither it goeth: so is everyone that is born of the Spirit." I take it that the Holy Spirit's work in conversion is two-fold. First, it is an awakening of the powers that man already has, and secondly, it is an implantation of powers which he never had at all.

In the great work of the new birth, the Holy Spirit first of all *awakens the mental powers*; for be it remembered that, the Holy Spirit never gives any man new *mental* powers. Take for instance reason—the Holy Spirit does not give men reason, for they have reason prior to their conversion. What the Holy Spirit does is to teach our reason, right reason—to set our reason in the right track, so that we can use it for the high purpose of discerning between good and evil; between the precious and vile. The Holy Spirit does not give man a will, for man has a will before, but He makes the will that was in bondage to Satan free to the service of God. The Holy Spirit gives no man the power to think, or the organ of belief—for man has power to believe or think as far as the mental act is concerned, but He gives that belief which is already there a tendency to believe the right thing, and He gives to the power of thought the propensity to think in the right way, so that instead of thinking irregularly, we begin to think as God would have us think, and our mind desireth to walk in the steps of God's revealed truth.

There may be here, this morning, a man of enlarged understanding in things political—but his understanding is darkened with regard to spiritual things—he sees no beauty in the person of Christ—he sees nothing desirable in the way of holiness—he chooses the evil and forsakes the good. Now the Holy Spirit will not give him a new understanding, but He will cleanse his old understanding so that he will discern between things that differ, and shall discover that it is but a poor thing to enjoy "the pleasures of sin for a season," and let go an "eternal weight of glory." There shall be a man here too who is desperately set against religion, and willeth not to come to God, and do what we will, we are not able to persuade him to change his mind and turn to God. The Holy Spirit will not make a new will in that man, but He will turn his old will, and instead of willing to do evil He will make him will to do right—He will make him will to be saved by Christ—He will make him "willing in the day of his power."

Remember, there is no power in man so fallen but that the Holy Spirit can raise it up. However debased a man may be, in one instant, by the miraculous power of the Spirit, all his faculties may be cleansed and purged. Ill-judging reason may be made to judge rightly; stout, obstinate will may be made to run willingly in the ways of God's commandments; evil and depraved affections may in an instant be turned to Christ, and old desires that are tainted with vice, may be replaced by heavenly aspirations. The work of the Spirit on the mind is the remodeling of it; the new forming of it. He doth not bring new materials to the mind—it is in another part of the man that He puts up a new structure—but He puts the mind that had fallen out of order into its proper shape. He builds up pillars that had fallen down, and erects the palaces that had crumbled to the earth. This is the first work of the Holy Spirit upon the mind of man.

Besides this, the Holy Spirit gives to men *powers which they never had before.* According to Scripture, I believe man is constituted in a three-fold manner. He has a body; by the Holy Spirit that body is made the temple of the Lord. He has a mind; by the Holy Spirit that mind is made like an altar in the temple. But man by nature is nothing higher than that, he is mere body and soul. When the Spirit comes, He breathes into him a third higher principle which we call the spirit. The apostle describes man as man, "body, soul and spirit." Now if you search all the mental writers through, you will find they all declare there are only two parts—body and mind; and they are quite right, for they deal with unregenerate man, but in regenerate man there is a third principle as much superior to mere mind as mind is superior to dead animal matter—that third principle is that with which a man prays; it is that with which he savingly believes; or rather it is that which compels the mind to perform their acts. It is that which, operating upon the mind, makes the same use of the mind as the mind does of the body. When, after desiring to walk I make my legs move, it is my mind that compels them; and so my Spirit, when I desire to pray, compels my mind to think the thought of prayer and compels my soul also, if I desire to praise, to think the thought of praise, and lift itself upward towards God. As the body without the soul is dead, so the soul without the Spirit is dead, and one work of the Spirit is to quicken the dead soul by breathing into it the living Spirit; as it is written, "The first man, Adam, was made a living *soul*, but the second Adam was made a quickening *Spirit*"—and, "as we have borne the image of the earthy, so must we bear the image of the heavenly"; that is, we must have in us, if we would be converted, the quickening Spirit, which is put into us by God the Holy Ghost.

I say again, the spirit has powers which the mind never has. It has the power of communion with Christ, which to a degree is a mental act, but it can no more be performed by man without the Spirit, than the act of walking could be performed by man, if he were destitute of a soul to suggest the idea of walking. The Spirit suggests the thoughts of communion which the mind obeys and carries out. Nay, there are times, I think, when the spirit leaves the mind altogether; times when we forget everything of earth, and one almost ceases to think, to reason, to judge, to weigh, or to will. Our souls are like the chariots of Amminadib, drawn swiftly onwards without any powers of volition. We lean upon the breast of Jesus, and in rhapsody divine, and in ecstasy celestial, we enjoy the fruits of the land of the blessed, and pluck the clusters of Eschol before entering into the land of promise.

I think I have clearly put these two points before you. The work of the Spirit consists, first in awakening powers already possessed by man, but which were asleep and out of order; and in the next place in putting into man powers which he had not before. And to make this simple to the humblest mind, let me suppose man to be something like a machine; the wheels are out of order, the cogs do not strike upon each other, the wheels do not turn regularly, the rods will not act, the order is gone. Now, the first work of the Spirit is to put these wheels in the right place, to fit the wheels upon the axles, to put the right axle to the right wheel, then to put wheel to wheel, so that they may act upon each other. But that is not all His work. The next thing is to put fire and steam so that these things shall go to work. He does not put fresh wheels, He puts old wheels into order, and then He puts the motive power which is to move the whole. First He puts our mental powers into their proper order and condition, and then He puts a living quickening spirit, so that all these shall move according to the holy will and law of God.

And I must say, before I leave this point, that all the former part of what I have mentioned is done instantaneously. When a man is converted to God, it is done in a moment. Regeneration is an instantaneous work. Conversion to God, the fruit of regeneration, occupies all our life, but regeneration itself is effected in an instant. A man hates God; the Holy Spirit makes him love God. A man is opposed to Christ, he hates His gospel, does not understand it and will not receive it: the Holy Spirit comes, puts light into his darkened understanding, takes the chain from his bondaged will, gives liberty to his conscience, gives life to his dead soul, so that the voice of conscience is heard, and the man becomes a new creature in Christ Jesus. And all this is done, mark you, by the instantaneous supernatural influence of God the Holy Ghost working as He willeth among the sons of men.

II. Having thus dwelt upon the method of the Holy Spirit's work, I shall now turn to the second point, the absolute necessity of the

Spirit's work in order to conversion. In our text we are told that "while Peter spake these words, the Holy Ghost fell on all them which heard the word." Beloved, the Holy Ghost fell on Peter first, or else it would not have fallen on his hearers. There is a necessity that the preacher himself, if we are to have souls saved, should be under the influence of the Spirit. I have constantly made it my prayer that I might be guided by the Spirit even in the smallest and least important parts of the service; for you cannot tell but that the salvation of a soul may depend upon the reading of a hymn, or upon the selection of a chapter. Two persons have joined our church and made a profession of being converted simply through my reading a hymn—

Jesus, lover of my soul.

They did not remember anything else in the hymn, but those words made such a deep impression upon their mind, that they could not help repeating them for days afterwards, and then the thought arose, "Do I love Jesus?" And then they considered what strange ingratitude it was that He should be the lover of their souls, and yet they should not love Him. Now I believe the Holy Spirit led me to read that hymn. And many persons have been converted by some striking saying of the preacher. But why was it the preacher uttered that saying? Simply because he was led thereunto by the Holy Spirit.

Rest assured, beloved, that when any part of the sermon is blessed to your heart, the minister said it because he was ordered to say it by his Master. I might preach today a sermon which I preached on Friday, and which was useful then, and there might be no good whatever come from it now, because it might not be the sermon which the Holy Ghost would have delivered today. But if with sincerity of heart I have sought God's guidance in selecting the topic, and He rests upon me in the preaching of the Word, there is no fear but that it shall be found adapted to your immediate wants. The Holy Spirit must rest upon your preachers. Let them have all the learning of the wisest men, and all the eloquence of such men as Demosthenes and

Cicero, still the Word cannot be blessed to you, unless first of all the Spirit of God hath guided the minister's mind in the selection of his subject, and in the discussion of it.

But if Peter himself were under the hand of the Spirit, that would fail unless the Spirit of God, then, did fall upon our hearers; and I shall endeavor now to show the absolute necessity of the Spirit's work in the conversion of men.

Let us remember what kind of thing the work is, and we shall see that other means are altogether out of the question. It is quite certain that men cannot be converted by physical means. The Church of Rome thought that she could convert men by means of armies; so she invaded countries, and threatened them with war and bloodshed unless they would repent and embrace her religion. However, it availed but little, and men were prepared to die rather than leave their faith; she therefore tried those beautiful things—stakes, racks, dungeons, axes, swords, fire; and by these things she hoped to convert men. You have heard of the man who tried to wind up his watch with a pickax. That man was extremely wise, compared with the man who thought to touch mind through matter. All the machines you like to invent cannot touch the mind. Talk about tying angels' wings with green withes, or manacling the cherubim with iron chains, and then talk about meddling with the minds of men through physical means. Why, the things don't act; they cannot act. All the king's armies that ever were, and all the warriors clothed with mail, with all their ammunition, could never touch the mind of man. That is an impregnable castle which is not to be reached by physical agency.

Nor, again, can man be converted by moral argument. "Well," says one, "I think he may. Let a minister preach earnestly, and he may persuade men to be converted." Ah! Beloved, it is for want of knowing better that you say so. Melancthon thought so, but you know what he said after he tried it—"Old Adam is too strong for young Melancthon." So will every preacher find it, if he thinks his arguments can ever convert man. Let me give you a parallel case. Where is the logic that can persuade an Ethiopian to change his skin? By what argument can you induce a leopard to renounce his spots? Even so may he that is accustomed to do evil learn to do well. But if the Ethiopian's skin be changed it must be by supernatural process; and if the leopard's spots be removed, he that made the leopard must do it. Even so is it with the heart of man. If sin were a thing *ab extra*, and external, we could induce man to change it. For instance, you may induce a man to leave off drunkenness or swearing, because those things are not a part of his nature—he has added that vice to his original depravity. But the hidden evil of the heart is beyond all moral suasion. I dare say a man might have enough argument to induce him to hang himself, but I am certain no argument will ever induce him to hang his sins, to hand his self-righteousness, and to come and humble himself at the foot of the cross; for the religion of Christ is so contrary to all the propensities of man, that it is like swimming against the stream to approach it, for the stream of man's will and man's desire is exactly the opposite of the religion of Jesus Christ.

I have seen the tears run down a man's cheeks when he has come to me in order to be united to the church of Christ, and he has said, "Sir, I wonder how it is I am here today; if anyone had told me a year ago that I should think as I now think, and feel as I now feel, I should have called him a born fool for his pains; I liked to spend my Sunday in pleasure, and I did not see why I was to be cooping myself up in the house of God listening to a man talk. *I* pray, sir? No, not I. I said the best providence in all the world was a good strong pair of hands, and to take care of what you got. If any man talked to me about religion, why, I would slam the door in his face, and pretty soon put him out, but the things that I loved then, I now hate, and the things that then I hated now I love, I cannot do or say enough to show how total is the change that has been wrought in me. It must have been the work of God; it could not have been wrought by me, I feel assured; it must be someone greater than myself, who could thus turn my heart." I think these two things are proofs that we want something more than nature, and since physical agency will not do, and mere moral suasion will never accomplish it, that there must be an absolute necessity for the Holy Spirit.

But again, if you will just think a minute what the work is, you will soon see that none but God can accomplish it. In the Holy Scripture, conversion is often spoken of as being a new creation. If you talk about creating yourselves, I should feel obliged if you would create a fly first. Create a gnat, create a grain of sand, and when you have created that, you may talk about creating a new heart. Both are alike, impossible, for creation is the work of God. But still, if you could create a grain of dust, or create even a world, it would not be half the miracle, for you must first find a thing which has created itself. Could that be? Suppose you had no existence, how could you create yourself? Nothing cannot produce anything. Now, how can man recreate himself? A man cannot create himself into a new condition, when he has no being in that condition, but is, as yet, a thing that is not.

Then, again, the work of creation is said to be like the resurrection. "We are alive from the dead." Now, can the dead in the grave raise themselves? Let any minister who thinks he can convert souls, go and raise a corpse; let him go and stand in one of the cemeteries, and bid the tombs open wide their mouths, and make room for those once buried there to awaken, and he will have to preach in vain. But if he could do it, that is not the miracle: it is for the dead to raise themselves, for an inanimate corpse to kindle in its own breast the spark of like anew. If the work be a resurrection, a creation, does it not strike you that it must be beyond the power of man? It must be wrought in him by no one less than God Himself.

And there is yet one more consideration, and I shall have concluded this point. Beloved, even if man could save himself, I would have you recollect how averse he is to it? If we could make our hearers all willing, the battle would be accomplished. "Well," says one, "if I am willing to be saved, can I not be saved?" Assuredly you can, but the difficulty is, we cannot bring men to be willing. That shows, therefore, that there must be a constraint put upon their will. There must be an influence exerted upon them, which they have not in themselves, in order to make them willing in the day of God's power. And this is the glory of the Christian religion. The Christian religion has within its own bowels power to spread itself.

We do not ask you to be willing first. We come and tell you the news, and we believe that the Spirit of God working with us, will make you willing. If the progress of the Christian religion depended upon the voluntary assent of mankind, it would never go an inch further, but because the Christian religion has with it an omnipotent influence, constraining men to believe it, it is therefore that it is and must be triumphant, "till like a sea of glory it spreads from shore to shore."

III. Now I shall conclude by bringing one or two thoughts forward, with regard to WHAT MUST BE DONE AT THIS TIME IN ORDER TO BRING DOWN THE HOLY SPIRIT. It is quite certain, beloved, if the Holy Spirit willed to do it, that every man, woman, and child in this place might be converted now. If God, the Sovereign Judge of all, would be pleased now to send out his Spirit, every inhabitant of this million-peopled city might be brought at once to turn unto the living God. Without instrumentality, with the preacher, without books, without anything, God has it in His power to convert men. We have known persons about their business, not thinking about religion at all, who have had a thought injected into their heart, and that thought has been the prolific mother of a thousand meditations; and through these meditations they have been brought to Christ. Without the aid of the minister, the Holy Spirit has thus worked, and today He is not restrained. There may be some men, great in infidelity, staunch in opposition to the Cross of Christ, but, without asking their consent, the Holy Spirit can pull down the strong man, and make the mighty man bow himself. For when we talk of the Omnipotent God, there is nothing too great for Him to do.

But, beloved, God has been pleased to put great honor upon instrumentality; He could work without it if He pleased, but He does not do so. However, this is the first thought I want to give you; if you would have the Holy Spirit exert Himself in our midst, you must first of all look to Him and not to instrumentality. When Jesus Christ preached, there were very few converted under Him, and the reason was, because the Holy Spirit was not abundantly poured forth. He had the Holy Spirit without measure Himself, but on others the Holy Spirit was not as yet poured out. Jesus Christ said, "Greater works than these shall ye do because I go to my Father, in order to send the Holy Spirit"; and recollect that those few who were converted under Christ's ministry, were not converted by Him, but by the Holy Spirit that rested upon Him at that time. Jesus of Nazareth was anointed of the Holy Spirit. Now then, if Jesus Christ, the great founder of our religion, needed to be anointed of the Holy Spirit, how much more our ministers?

And now another thought. If we would have the Spirit, beloved, we must each of us try to honor Him. There are some chapels into which if you were to enter, you would never know there was a Holy Spirit. Mary Magdalen said of old, "They have taken away my Lord, and I know not where they have laid him," and the Christian might often say so, for there is nothing said about the Lord until they come to the end, and then there is just the benediction, or else you would not know that there were three persons in one God at all. Until our churches honor the Holy Spirit, we shall never see it abundantly manifested in our midst. Let the preacher always confess before he preaches that he relies upon the Holy Spirit. Let him burn his manuscript and depend upon the Holy Spirit. If the Spirit does not come to help him, let him be still and let the people go home and pray that the Spirit will help him next Sunday.

And do you also, in the use of all your agencies, always honor the Spirit? We often begin our religious meetings without prayer; it is all wrong. We must honor the Spirit; unless we put Him first, He will never make crowns for us to wear. He will get victories, but He will have the honor of them, and if we do not give to Him the honor, He will never give to us the privilege and success. And best of all, if you would have the Holy Spirit, let us meet together earnestly to pray for Him. Remember, the Holy Spirit will not come to us as a church, unless we seek Him. "For this thing will I be inquired of by the house of Israel to do it for them." "Prove me now here, saith the Lord of hosts, and see if I do not pour you out a blessing so that there shall not be room enough to receive it." Let us meet and pray, and if God doth not hear us, it will be the first time He has broken His promise. Come, let us go up to the sanctuary; let us meet together in the house of the Lord, and offer solemn supplication; and I say again, if the Lord doth not make bare His arm in the sight of all the people, it will be the reverse of all His previous actions, it will be the contrary of all His promises, and contradictory to Himself. We have only to try Him, and the result is certain. In dependence on His Spirit, if we only meet for prayer, the Lord shall bless us, and all the ends of the earth shall fear Him. O Lord, lift up Thyself because of Thine enemies; pluck Thy right hand out of Thy bosom, O Lord our God, for Christ's sake, Amen.

5

The Holy Spirit
Compared to the Wind

The wind bloweth where it listeth, and thou hearest the sound thereof, but canst not tell whence it cometh, and whither it goeth: so is everyone that is born of the Spirit—John 3:8.

I am not proposing to enter fully into the subject of the new birth, but to bring before you the parallel which our Savior here draws, between the wind and the Holy Spirit. It is a remarkable fact, known I dare say to most of you, that both in the Hebrew and Greek languages the same word is used for spirit and for wind, so that our Savior as it were rode upon the wings of the wind, while he was instructing the seeking Rabbi in the deep things of God; He caught at the very name of the wind, as a means of fastening a spiritual truth upon the memory of the inquirer, hinting to us that language should be watched by the teacher, that he may find out suitable words, and employ those which will best assist the disciple to comprehend and to retain his teaching. "The wind," said He, "bloweth," and the very same word would have been employed if He has meant to say, "The Spirit bloweth where he listeth." There was intended, doubtless, to be a very close and intimate parallel between

227

the Spirit of God and the wind, or otherwise the great ruler of providence, who invisibly controlled the confusion of Babel, would not have fashioned human language so that the same word should stand for both. Language, as well as nature, illustrates the wisdom of God.

It is only in *His light* that we see light: may the Holy Spirit be graciously pleased to reveal Himself in His divine operations to all our waiting minds. We are taught in God's Word that the Holy Spirit comes upon the sons of men, and makes them new creatures. Until He enters them they are "dead in trespasses and sins." They cannot discern the things of God, because divine truths are spiritual and spiritually discerned, and unrenewed men are carnal, and possess not the power to search out the deep things of God. The Spirit of God new-creates the children of God, and then in their new-born spirituality, they discover and come to understand spiritual things, but not before; and, therefore, my beloved hearers, unless you *possess* the Spirit, no metaphors however simple can reveal Him to you. Let us not mention the name of the Holy Spirit without due honor. Forever blessed be Thou, most glorious Spirit, co-equal and coeternal with the Father and with the Son; let all the angels of God worship Thee! Be Thou had in honor, world without end!

I. We will consider IN WHAT SENSE THE HOLY GHOST MAY BE COMPARED TO THE WIND.

The Spirit of God, to help the spiritually minded in their study of His character and nature, condescends to compare Himself to dew, fire, oil, water, and other suggestive types; and among the rest, our Savior uses the metaphor of wind. What was the first thought here but that of *mystery*? It was the objection on the score of mystery which our Lord was trying to remove from the mind of Nicodemus. Nicodemus in effect said, "I cannot understand it; how can it be? A man born again when he is old, created over again, and that from an invisible agency from above? How can these things be?" Jesus at once directed his attention to the wind, which is none the less real and operative because of its mysterious origin and operation. You cannot tell whence the wind cometh: you know it blows from the north or from the west, but at what particular place does that wind start on its career? Where will it pause in its onward flight? You see that it is blowing to the east or to the west, but where is its halting-place? Whence came these particles of air which rush so rapidly past? Whither are they going? By what law are they guided in their course, and where will their journey end? The gale may be blowing due east here, but it may be driving west a hundred miles away. In one district the wind may be rushing from the north, and yet not far from it there may be a strong current from the south. If you have watched the skies, you must occasionally have noticed a stream of clouds hurrying to the right, while higher up, another company is sailing to the left.

The philosopher may scheme some conjecture to prove that the "trade winds" blow at certain intervals because of the sun crossing the equator at those periods, and that there must necessarily be a current of air going towards the equator because of the rarefaction, but he cannot tell you why the weathercock on yonder church steeple turned this morning from south-west to due east. He cannot tell me why it is that the sailor finds that his sails are at one time filled with wind, and in a few minutes they fall loosely about, so that he must steer upon another tack if he would make headway. The various motions of the air remain a mystery to all but the infinite Jehovah.

My brethren, the like mystery is observed in the work of the Spirit of God. His person and work are not to be comprehended by the mind of man. He may be here tonight, but you cannot see Him: He speaks to one heart, but others cannot hear His voice. He is not recognizable by the unrefined senses of the unregenerate. The spiritual man discerns Him, feels Him, hears Him, and delights in Him, but neither wit nor learning can lead a man into the secret. The believer is often bowed down with the weight of the Spirit's glory, or lifted up upon the wings of His majesty, but even he knows not how these feelings are wrought in him. The fire of holy life is at seasons gently fanned with the soft breath of divine comfort, or the deep sea of spiritual existence stirred with the mighty blast of the Spirit's rebuke, but still it is evermore a mystery how the eternal God

comes into contact with the finite mind of His creature man, filling
all heaven meanwhile, and yet dwelling in a human body as in a
temple—occupying all space, and yet operating upon the will, the
judgment, the mind of the poor insignificant creature called man.
We may inquire, but who can answer us? We may search, but who
shall lead us into the hidden things of the Most High? He brooded
over chaos and produced order, but who shall tell us after what
fashion He wrought? He overshadowed the Virgin and prepared a
body for the Son of God, but into this secret who shall dare to pry?
His is the anointing, sealing, comforting, and sanctifying of the
saints, but how worketh He all these things? He maketh intercession for us according to the will of God, He dwelleth in us and lead-
eth us into all truth, but who among us can explain to his fellow
the order of the divine working? Though veiled from human eye
like the glory which shone between the cherubim, we believe in
the Holy Ghost, and therefore see Him, but if our faith needed
sight to sustain it, we should never believe at all.

Mystery is far from being all which the Savior would teach by
this simile. Surely He meant to show us that the operations of the
Spirit are like the wind for *divinity*. Who can create a wind? The
most ambitious of human princes would scarcely attempt to turn,
much less to send forth the wind. These steeds of the storm know
no bit nor bridle, neither will they come at any man's bidding. Let
our senators do what they will, they will scarcely have the madness
to legislate for winds. Old Boreas, as the heathens called him, is not
to be bound with chains and welded on earthly anvil, or in vulcan-
ian forge. "The wind bloweth where it listeth"; and it does so because God directeth it and suffereth it not to stay for man, nor to
tarry for the sons of men. So with the Spirit of God. All the true operations of the Spirit are due in no sense whatever to man, but always to God and to His sovereign will. Revivalists may get up
excitement with the best intentions, and may warm peoples' hearts
till they begin to cry out, but all this ends in nothing unless it is divine work. Have I not said scores of times in this pulpit, "All that is
of nature's spinning, must be unraveled?" Every particle which nature puts upon the foundation will turn out to be but "wood, hay,

and stubble," and will be consumed. It is only "the gold, the silver, and the precious stones" of God's building that will stand the fiery test. "Ye must be born again from above," for human regenerations are a lie. Thou mayest blow with thy mouth and produce some trifling effects upon trifles as light as air; man in his zeal may set the windmills of silly minds in motion, but, truly, to stir men's hearts with substantial and eternal verities, needs a celestial breeze, such as the Lord alone can send.

Did not our Lord also intend to hint at the *sovereignty* of the Spirit's work? For what other reason did He say, "The wind bloweth where it listeth?" There is an arbitrariness about the wind, it does just as it pleases, and the laws which regulate its changes are to man unknown. "Free as the wind," we say—"the wild winds." So is the mighty working of God. It is a very solemn thought, and one which should tend to make us humble before the Lord—that we are, as to the matter of salvation, entirely in His hand! If I have a moth in my hand tonight, I can bruise its wings, or I can crush it at my will, and by no attempts of its own can it escape from me. And every sinner is absolutely in the hand of God, and, let him recollect, he is in the hand of an angry God, too. The only comfort is that he is in the hand of a God Who, for Jesus' sake, delights to have mercy upon even the vilest of the vile.

Sinner, God can give thee the Holy Spirit if He wills, but if He should say, "Let him alone," thy fate is sealed; thy damnation is sure. Dost thou tremble at this? Dost thou cry, "O God! Have pity upon me?" He will hear thy cry, sinner, for there never yet was a sincere cry that went up to heaven, though it were never so feeble, but what it had an answer of peace. When one of the old saints lay dying, he could only say, "O Lord, I trust thee *languida fide*," with a languid faith. It is poor work that, but, oh! It is safe work. You can only trust Christ with a feeble faith; if it is such a poor trembling faith that it does not grip Him, but only touches the hem of His garment, it nevertheless saves you. If you can look at Him, though it be only a great way off, yet it saves you. And, oh what a comfort this is, that you are still on pleading terms with Him and in a place of hope. "Whosoever believeth is not condemned." But, oh, do not trifle with the day of grace, lest having frequently heard the warning, and hardened thy neck just as often, thou shouldest "suddenly be destroyed, and that without remedy"; for if He shut out, none can bid thee come in; if He do but put to the iron bar, thou art shut out in the darkness of obstinacy, obduracy, and despair forever, the victim of thine own delusions. Sinner, if God save thee; He shall have all the glory, for He hath a right to do as He will, for He says, "I will have mercy on whom I will have mercy, and I will have compassion on whom I will have compassion."

But still I think I have not yet brought out what is in the text. Do you not think that the text was intended to show the *varied methods* in which the Spirit of God works in the conversion and regeneration of men? "The wind bloweth where it listeth." Now, observe the different *force* of the wind. This afternoon the wind seemed as if it would tear up every tree, and doubtless, had they been in leaf, many of those noble princes of the forest must have stretched themselves prone upon the earth, but God takes care that in these times of boisterous gales there should be no leaf, and therefore the wind gets but little purchase with which to drag up a tree. But the wind does not always blow as it did this afternoon. On a summer's evening there is such a gentle zephyr that even the gnats who have been arranging a dance among themselves are not disturbed, but keep to their proper places. Yea, the aspen seems as if it could be quiet, though you know it keeps forever quivering, according to the old legend, that it was the tree on which the Savior hung, and therefore trembles still as though through fear of the sin which came upon it. 'Tis but a legend. There are times when all is still and calm, when everything is quiet, and you can scarcely detect the wind at all.

Now, just so it is with the Spirit of God. To some of us He came like a "rushing mighty wind." Oh, what tearings of soul there were then! My spirit was like a sea tossed up into tremendous waves; made, as Job says, "To boil like a pot," till one would think the deep were hoary. Oh, how that wind came crashing through my soul, and every hope I had was bowed as the trees of the wood in the tempest. Read the story of John Bunyan's conversion: it was just the same. Turn to Martin Luther: you find his conversion of the same sort. So might I mention hundreds of biographies in which the Spirit of God came like a tornado sweeping everything before it, and the men could but feel that God was in the whirlwind.

To others He comes so gently, they cannot tell when first the Spirit of God came. They recollect that night when mother prayed so with brothers and sisters, and when they could not sleep for hours, because the big tears stood in their eyes on account of sin. They recollect the Sunday school and the teacher there. They remember that earnest minister. They cannot say exactly when they gave their hearts to God, and they cannot tell about any violent convictions. They are often comforted by that text, "One thing I know, whereas I was blind, now I see," but they cannot get any farther: they sometimes wish they could. Well, they need not wish it, for the Spirit of God, as a sovereign, will always choose His own way of operation; and if it be but the wind of the Holy Spirit, recollect it is as saving in its gentleness as in its terror, and is as efficient to make us new creatures when it comes with the zephyr's breath as when it comes with the hurricane's force. Do not quarrel with God's way of saving you. If you are brought to the Cross be thankful for it, Christ will not mind how you got there. If you can say "He is all my salvation, and all my desire," you never came to that without the Spirit of God bringing you to it. Do not therefore think you came the wrong way, for that is impossible.

Again, the wind not only differs in force, but it differs in *direction*. We have been saying several times the wind is always shifting. Perhaps there never were two winds that did blow exactly in the same direction. I mean that if we had power to detect the minute points of the compass, there would be found some deviation in every current, although, of course, for all practical purposes, it blows from certain distinct points which the mariner marks out. Now, the Spirit of God comes from different directions. You know very well, dear friends, that sometimes the Spirit of God will blow with mighty force from one denomination of Christians; then suddenly they seem to be left, and another body of Christians God will raise up, fill with Himself, and qualify for usefulness. In the days of

Wesley and Whitefield, there was very little of the divine Spirit any-where, except among the Methodists. I am sure they have not a monopoly of Him now. The divine Spirit blows also from other quarters. Sometimes He uses one man, sometimes another. We hear of a revival in the North of Ireland, by-and-by it is in the South of Scotland. It comes just as God wills, for direction; and you know, too, dear friends, it comes through different instrumentalities in the same Church. Sometimes the wind blows from this pulpit: God blesses me to your conversion. Another time it is from my good sister, Mrs. Bartlett's class; on a third occasion it is the Sunday school; again, it may be another class, or the preaching of the young men, or from the individual exertion of private believers. God causes that wind to blow just which way He wills.

He works also through different texts of Scripture. *You* were con-verted and blessed under one text: it was quite another that was made useful to *me*. Some of you were brought to Christ by terrors, others of you by love, by sweet wooing words. The wind blows as God directs. Now, dear friends, whenever you take up a religious biography, do not sit down and say, "Now I will see whether I am just like this person." Nonsense! God never repeats Himself. Men make steel pens—thousands of grosses of them—all alike, but I will be bound to say that in quills from the common, there are no two of them precisely the same. If you look, you will soon discover that they differ in a variety of ways.

Certain gardeners cut their trees into the shape of cheeses and a number of other unnatural forms, but God's trees do not grow that way, they grow just anyhow—gnarl their roots and twist their branches. Great painters do not continually paint the same picture again, and again, and again, and my Divine Master never puts His pencil on the canvas to produce the same picture twice. Every Christian is a distinct work of grace on God's part, which has in it some originality, some portion distinct from all others. I do not be-lieve in trying to make all history uniform. It is said that Richard III had a hump-back. Whether he really was deformed, or whether his-tory gave him the hump-back, I cannot tell, but it is said, that all his courtiers thought it the most beautiful hump-back that ever was seen, and they all began to grow hump-backs too; and I have known ministers who had some peculiar idiosyncrasy of experience which was nothing better than a spiritual hump-back, but their people all began to have hump-backs too—to think and talk all in the same way, and to have the same doubts and fears. Now that will not do. It is not the way in which the Most High acts with regard to the wind, and if he chooses to take all the points of the compass, and make use of them all, let us bless and glorify His Name.

Are not the different winds *various in their qualities?* Few of us like an east wind. Most of us are very glad when the wind blows from the south. Vegetation seems to love much the southwest. A stiff northeaster is enough to make us perish; and long continuance of the north, may well freeze the whole earth; while from the west, the wind seems to come laden with health from the deep blue sea; and though sometimes too strong for the sick, yet it is never a bad time when the west wind blows. The ancients all had their different opinions about wind; some were dry, some were rainy, some affected this disease, some touched this part of men, some the other. Certain it is that God's Holy Spirit has different qualities. In the Canticles He blows softly with the sweet breath of love: turn on farther, and you get that same Spirit blowing fiercely with threatening and denunciation; sometimes you find Him convincing the world "of sin, of righteousness, of judgment," that is the north wind; at other times opening up Christ to the sinner, and giving him joy and comfort; that is the south wind, that blows softly, and gives a balminess in which poor troubled hearts rejoice; and yet "all these worketh the self-same Spirit."

Indeed, my subject is all but endless, and therefore I must stay. But in the matter of *duration* you know how the wind will sometimes blow six weeks in this direction, and, again, continue in another direction. And the Spirit of God does not always work with us: He does as He pleases; He comes, and He goes. We may be in a happy hallowed frame at one time, and at another we may have to cry, "Come from the four winds, O breath!"

II. We will consider, in the second place, THE PARALLEL BE-
TWEEN THE HOLY SPIRIT AND THE EFFECTS OF THE WIND. "Thou
hearest the sound thereof." Ah, that we do! The wind sometimes
wails as if you could hear the cry of mariners far out at sea, or the
moanings of the widows that must weep for them. And, oh! The
Spirit of God sets men wailing with an exceeding bitter cry for sin,
as one that is in sorrow for his firstborn, "Thou hearest the sound
thereof." Oh, it is a blessed sound, that wailing! Angels rejoice over
"one sinner that repenteth." Then comes the wind at another time
with a triumphant sound, and if there be an aeolian harp in the
window, how it swells, sweeps, descends, then rises again, gives all
the tones of music, and makes glad the air with its jubilant notes. So
with the Holy Spirit; sometimes He gives us faith, makes us bold,
full of assurance, confidence, joy and peace in believing. "Thou
hearest the sound" of a full diapason of the Holy Spirit's mighty
melody within the soul of man, filling him with peace and joy, and
rest, and love. Sometimes the wind comes, too, with another sound
as though it were contending. You heard it, perhaps, this afternoon.
We who are a little in the country hear it more than you do: it is as
though giants were struggling in the sky together. It seems as if two
seas of air, both lashed to fury, met, and dashed against some unseen cliffs with terrible uproar. The Spirit of God comes into the
soul sometimes, and makes great contention with the flesh. Oh,
what a stern striving there is against unbelief, against lust, against
pride, against every evil thing.

"Thou hearest the sound thereof." Thou that knowest what divine experience means, thou knowest when to go forth to fight thy
sins. When thou canst hear "the sound of a going in the tops of the
mulberry trees," then thou dost bestir thyself to smite thy sins.
Sometimes the wind comes with a sweep as though it were going
on forever. It came past, and dashed through the trees, sweeping
away the rotten branches, then away across the Alps, dashing down
an avalanche in its course, still onward; and as it flew, it bore away
everything that was frail and weak, and on, on, on it sped its way to
some unknown goal. And thus it is sometimes the Spirit of God will
come right through us, as if He were bearing us away to that spiri-

tual heritage which is our sure future destiny—bearing away coldness, barrenness, everything before it. We do not lament then that we do not pray, we do not believe that we cannot pray, but "I can do everything," is our joyful shout as we are carried on the wings of the wind. "Thou hearest the sound thereof." I hope you have heard it sometimes in all its powerful, overwhelming, mighty influence, till your soul has been blown away. "Thou hearest the sound thereof."

But then the wind does something more than make a sound; and so does the Holy Spirit. It WORKS and produces manifest results. Just think what the wind is doing tonight. I cannot tell at what pitch it may be now. It is just possible that in some part of the ocean a vessel scuds along almost under bare poles; the mariners do their best to reef the sails: away she goes: now the mast has gone: they do their best to bear up, but they find that in the teeth of the gale they cannot stand; the ship dashes on the rocks, and she is wrecked.

And, oh! The Spirit of God is *a great wrecker* of false hopes and carnal confidences. I have seen the Spirit of God come to a sinner like a storm to a ship at sea. He had to take down the top-gallants of his pride, and then every thread of carnal confidence had to be reefed, and then his hope itself had to be cut away; and on, on the vessel went, until she struck a rock, and down she went. The man from that time never dared trust in his merits, for he had seen his merits wrecked and broken in pieces by the wind.

The wind, too, recollect, is *a great leveler*. It always aims at everything that is high. If you are down low in the street, you escape its fury, but climb to the top of the Monument, or St. Paul's, and try whether you do not feel it. Get into the valley, it is all right. The lower branches of the trees are scarcely moved, but the top branches are rocked to and fro by it. It is a great leveler; so is the Holy Spirit. He never sees a man high but He brings him down. He makes every high thought bow before the majesty of His might; and if you have any high thought tonight, rest assured that when the Spirit of God comes, He will lay it low, even with the ground.

Now, do not let this make you fear the Holy Spirit. It is a blessed thing to be rocked so as to have our hopes tested, and it is a precious thing to have our carnal confidences shaken. And how blessedly the wind *purifies* the atmosphere! In the Swiss valleys there is a heaviness in the air which makes the inhabitants unhealthy. They take quinine, and you see them going about with big swellings in their necks. From Martigny to Bretagne, there is a great valley in which you will see hundreds of persons diseased. The reason is that the air does not circulate. They are breathing the same air, or some of it, that their fathers breathed before them. There seems to be no ventilation between the two parts of the giant Alps, and the air never circulates, but if they have a great storm which sweeps through the valleys, it is a great blessing to the people. And so the Spirit of God comes and cleanses out our evil thoughts and vain imaginations, and though we do not like the hurricane, it brings spiritual health to our soul. .

Again the wind is a great *trier of the nature of things*. Here comes a great rushing up the street, it sweeps over the heaps of rubbish lying in the road, away goes all the light chaff, paper, and other things which have no weight in them; they cannot stand the brunt of its whirling power, but see, the pieces of iron, the stones, and all weighty things are left unmoved. In the country the farmer severed the chaff from the wheat by throwing it up into a current of air, and the light husks all blew away, while the heavy wheat sank on the heap, cleansed and purified.

So is the Holy Ghost the great testing power, and the result of His operations will be to show men what they are. Here is a hypocrite, he has passed muster hitherto, and reckons himself to be a true and genuine man, but there comes a blast from heaven's mighty spirit, and he finds himself to be lighter than vanity: he has no weight in him, he is driven on and has no rest, can find no peace, he hurries from one refuge of lies to another. "There is no peace, saith my God, to the wicked." Thus also we try the doctrines of men, we bring the breath of inspiration to bear upon them: do they abide the test, or are they driven away? Can you hold that truth in the presence of God? Can you cling to it and find it stable in the hour of trial? Is it a nice pleasant speculation for a sunny day when all is calm and bright, or will it bear the rough rude blast of adversity, when God's Holy Spirit is purifying you with His healthful influence? True Christians and sound doctrines have ballast and weight in them, they are not moved nor driven away, but empty professors and hollow dogmas are scattered like chaff before the wind when the Lord shall blow upon them with the breath of His Spirit. Examine yourselves therefore, try the doctrines and see if they be of God. "What is the chaff to the wheat? saith the Lord." Have root in yourselves, then will you not wither in the hot blast, nor be driven away in the tempestuous day.

Is not the Spirit moreover like unto the wind in its *developing of character?* Men get all covered with dust in the hot dusty roadside of life till they are nearly the color of the earth itself, but they come to the hill-top of Calvary, and here they stand till the wind of heaven has cleansed them from all the dust that has gathered around their garments. Oh, there is nothing like communion with the Spirit of God to counteract the earthly tendencies of a business life. There are some men that get covered with a yellow dust, till they are almost hidden by it; they can talk of nothing else but money. Gold, gold, gold, is getting to occupy nearly every thought now. I have no quarrel with money in its right place, but I do not like to see men live in it. I always try to drive away that mean and groveling spirit which lives for nothing else but to accumulate money, but I cannot always succeed. Now the Spirit of God will make a man see his folly and put his money into its right position, and place the graces of the Christian character where men can see them and glorify God in them. Never let your business character or professional skill dim and hide your Christianity. If you do, God's Spirit will come to brighten you up, and He will have no mercy on these, but will, in love to your soul, cleanse and give luster to God's work which is wrought in you.

I see also here a thought as to the cooperation of man and the Spirit in all Christian work. It has pleased God to make us coworkers with Him, fellow laborers, both in the matter of our own salvation, and also in the effort to benefit others. Look for a moment at yon stately bark, she moves not because of her sails, but she would not reach the desired haven without them. It is the wind which propels her forward, but the wind would not act upon her as it does, unless she had the rigging all fixed, her masts standing, and her sails all bent, so as to catch the passing breeze. But now that human seamanship has done its best, see how she flies! She will soon reach her haven with such a favoring gale as that. You have only to stand still and see how the wind bears her on like a thing of life.

And so it is with the human heart. When the Spirit comes to the soul that is ready to receive such influences, then He helps you on to Christian grace and Christian work, and makes you bear up through all opposition, till you come to the port of peace, and can anchor safely there. Without Him we can do nothing: without us He will not work. We are to preach the gospel to every creature, and while one plants, and another waters, God adds the increase. We are to work out our own salvation, but He worketh in us to will and to do of His own good pleasure. We must go up to possess the goodly land with our own spear and sword, but the hornet goes before us to drive out the foe. Jericho shall be captured by a divine and miraculous interference, but even there rams' horns shall find a work to do, and must be employed. The host of Midian shall be slain, but our cry is, "The sword of the Lord and of Gideon." We give God all the glory, nevertheless we use the means. The water of Jordan must be sought out, and used by all who desire a cleansing like Naaman the Syrian. A lump of figs must be used if other Hezekiahs are to be healed, but the Spirit is, after all, the great Cleanser and Healer of His people Israel. The lesson is clear to all: the wind turns mills that men make; fills sails that human hands have spread; and the Spirit blesses human effort, crowns with success our labors, establishes the work of our hands upon us, and teaches us all through, that "the hand of the diligent maketh rich," but "if a man will not work, neither shall he eat."

Another thought suggests itself to my mind in connection with the wind and human effort; it is this: How completely dependent men are upon the wind as to what it shall do for them. They are entirely at its mercy as to its time of blowing, its strength, and the direction it will take. I have already dwelt upon this thought of the sovereignty of the wind, but it comes up here in a more practical form. The steamer now can steer almost anywhere it please, and at all times it will proceed on its voyage, but the sailing-ship must tack according to the wind, and when becalmed must wait for the breeze to spring up. The sailor who is depending on the wind, anxiously looks up to the masthead to see how the breeze is shifting and turning round the vane; and he scans the heavens to see what weather he is likely to have. He would not need to care nearly so much as he does now that he is absolutely dependent on the wind if he had steam-power, so as to sail in the very teeth of the storm is he so willed. God, then, keeps us looking up to heaven by making us to be completely at His mercy as to the times and ways of giving us His helping-power. It is a blessed thing to wait on God, watching for His hand and in quiet contentment leaving all to Him. Brethren, let us do our part faithfully, spread every sail, make all as perfect as human skill and wisdom can direct, and then in patient continuance in well-doing, wait the Spirit's propitious gales, neither murmuring because He tarries, nor be taken unawares when He comes upon us in His sovereign pleasure to do that which seemeth good in His sight.

And now, my dear hearer, whether you listen often to my voice, or have now stepped in for the first time, I would like to ring this in your ear, Dost thou know the Spirit of God? If ye have not the Spirit, ye are none of His. "Ye must be born again." "What, Lord—'must?' Dost Thou not mean 'may?' " No, ye *must*. "Does it not mean, 'Ye can be?' " No, ye *must*. When a man says, "must," it all depends upon who he is. When God says "must," there it stands, and it cannot be questioned. There are the flames of hell: would you escape from them? You must be born again. There are heaven's glories sparkling in their own light, would you enjoy them? You must be born again. There is the peace and joy of a believer; would you have it? You must be born again. What, not a crumb from off the table with this? No, not one. Not a drop of water to cool your burning tongues except you are born again. This is the one condition that never moves. God never alters it, and never will. You must, *must*, MUST. Which shall it be? Shall your will stand, or God's will? O, let God's "must" ride right over you, and bow yourselves down, and say, "Lord, I must, then I will; ah! And it has come to this—I must tonight.

Give me Christ, or else I die.

I have hold of the knocker of the door of Thy mercy, and I *must*, I WILL get that door open. I will never let Thee go except Thou bless me. Thou sayest *must*, Lord, and I say *must* too."

"Ye must, ye must be born again." God fulfill the "must" in each of your cases, for Jesus Christ's sake. Amen.

6
The Withering Work
of the Spirit

> *The voice said, Cry. And he said What shall I cry? All flesh is grass, and all the goodliness thereof is as the flower of the field: the grass withereth, the flower fadeth: because the Spirit of the Lord bloweth upon it: surely the people is grass. The grass withereth, the flower fadeth: but the word of our God shall stand forever—Isaiah 40:6–8.*
>
> *Being born again, not of corruptible seed, but of incorruptible, by the word of God, which liveth and abideth forever. For all flesh is as grass, and all the glory of man as the flower of grass. The grass withereth, and the flower thereof falleth away: but the word of the Lord endureth forever. And this is the word which by the gospel is preached unto you—1 Peter 1:23–25.*

The passage in Isaiah which I have just read in your hearing may be used as a very eloquent description of our mortality, and if a sermon should be preached from it upon the frailty of human nature, the brevity of life, and the certainty of death, no one could dispute the appropriateness of the text. Yet I venture to question whether such a discourse would strike the central teaching of the prophet. Something more than the decay of our material flesh is intended here; the carnal mind, the flesh in another sense, was intended by the Holy Ghost when He bade His messenger proclaim

243

those words. It does not seem to me that a mere expression of the morality of our race was needed in this place by the context; it would hardly keep pace with the sublime revelations which surround it, and would in some measure be a digression from the subject in hand. The notion that we are here simply and alone reminded of our morality does not square with the New Testament exposition of it in Peter, which I have also placed before you as a text. There is another and more spiritual meaning here beside and beyond that which would be contained in the great and very obvious truth, that all of us must die.

Look at the chapter in Isaiah with care. What is the subject of it? It is the divine consolation of Zion. Zion had been tossed to and fro with conflicts; she had been smarting under the result of sin. The Lord, to remove her sorrow, bids His prophets announce the coming of the long-expected Deliverer, the end and accomplishment of all her warfare and the pardon of her iniquity. There is no doubt that this is the theme of the prophecy; and further, there is no sort of question about the next point, that the prophet goes on to foretell the coming of John the Baptist as the harbinger of the Messiah. We have no difficulty in the explanation of the passage, "Prepare ye the way of the Lord, make straight in the desert a highway for our God"; for the New Testament again and again refers this to the Baptist and his ministry. The object of the coming of the Baptist and the mission of the Messiah, whom he heralded, was the manifestation of divine glory.

Observe the fifth verse: "The glory of the Lord shall be revealed, and all flesh shall see it together: for the mouth of the Lord hath spoken it." Well, what next? Was it needful to mention man's mortality in this connection? We think not. But there is much more appropriateness in the succeeding verses, if we see their deeper meaning. Do they not mean this? In order to make room for the display of the divine glory in Christ Jesus and His salvation, there would come a withering of all the glory wherein man boasts himself; the flesh should be seen in its true nature as corrupt and dying, and the grace of God alone should be exalted. This would be seen under the ministry of John the Baptist first, and should be the preparatory work of the Holy Ghost in men's hearts, in all time, in order that the glory of the Lord should be revealed and human pride be forever confounded.

The Spirit blows upon the flesh, and that which seemed vigorous becomes weak, that which was fair to look upon is smitten with decay; the true nature of the flesh is thus discovered, its deceit is laid bare, its power is destroyed, and there is space for the dispensation of the ever-abiding word, and for the rule of the Great Shepherd, whose words are spirit and life. There is a withering wrought by the Spirit which is the preparation for the sowing and implanting by which salvation is wrought.

The withering before the sowing was very marvelously fulfilled in the preaching of John the Baptist. Most appropriately he carried on his ministry in the desert, for a spiritual desert was all around him; he was the voice of one crying in the wilderness. It was not his work to plant, but to hew down. The fleshly religion of the Jews was then in its prime. Phariseeism stalked through the streets in all its pomp; men complacently rested in outward ceremonies only, and spiritual religion was at the lowest conceivable ebb. Here and there might be found a Simeon and an Anna, but for the most part men knew nothing of spiritual religion, but said in their hearts: "We have Abraham to our father," and this is enough. What a stir he made when he called the lordly Pharisees a generation of vipers! How he shook the nation with the declaration, "Now also the ax is laid unto the root of the trees!" Stern as Elias, his work was to level the mountains, and lay low every lofty imagination. That word, "Repent," was as a scorching wind to the verdure of self-righteousness, a killing blast for the confidence of ceremonialism. His food and his dress called for fasting and mourning. The outward token of his ministry declared the death amid which he preached, as he buried in the waters of Jordan those who came to him. "Ye must die and be buried, even as He who is to come will save by death and burial." This was the meaning of the emblem which he set before the crowd. His typical act was as thorough in its teaching as were his words; and as if that were not enough, he warned them of a yet more searching and trying baptism with the Holy Ghost and with fire, and of the coming of One whose fan was in His hand, thoroughly to purge His floor. The Spirit in John blew as the rough north wind, searching and withering, and made him to be a destroyer of the vain gloryings of a fleshly religion, that the spiritual faith might be established.

When our Lord Himself actually appeared, He came into a withered land, whose glories had all departed. Old Jesse's stem was bare, and our Lord was the branch which grew out of his root. The scepter had departed from Judah, and the lawgiver from between his feet, when Shiloh came. An alien sat on David's throne, and the Roman called the covenant-land his own. The lamp of prophecy burned but dimly, even if it had not utterly gone out. No Isaiah had arisen of late to console them, nor even a Jeremiah to lament their apostasy. The whole economy of Judaism was as a worn-out vesture; it had waxed old, and was ready to vanish away. The priesthood was disarranged. Luke tells us that Annas and Caiaphas were high priests that year—two in a year or at once, a strange setting aside of the laws of Moses. All the dispensation which gathered around the visible, or as Paul calls it, the "worldly" sanctuary, was coming to a close; and when our Lord has finished His work, the veil of the temple was rent in twain, the sacrifices were abolished, the priesthood of Aaron was set aside, and carnal ordinances were abrogated, for the Spirit revealed spiritual things. When He came who was made a priest, "not after the law of a carnal commandment, but after the power of an endless life," there was "a disannulling of the commandment going before for the weakness and unprofitableness thereof."

Such are the facts of history, but I am not about to dilate upon them; I am coming to your own personal histories—to the experience of every child of God. In every one of us it must be fulfilled that all that is of the flesh in us, seeing it is but as grass, must be withered, and the comeliness thereof must be destroyed. The Spirit of God, like the wind, must pass over the field of our souls, and cause our beauty to be as a fading flower. He must so convince us of sin, and so reveal ourselves to ourselves, that we shall see that the flesh profiteth nothing; that our fallen nature is corruption itself, and that "they who are in the flesh cannot please God." There must be brought home to us the sentence of death upon our former legal and carnal life, that the incorruptible seed of the Word of God, implanted by the Holy Ghost, may be in us, and abide in us forever.

The subject of this morning is the withering work of the Spirit upon the souls of men, and when we have spoken upon it, we shall conclude with a few words upon the implanting work, which always follows where this withering work has been performed.

I. Turning then to THE WORK OF THE SPIRIT IN CAUSING THE GODLINESS OF THE FLESH TO FADE, let us first observe that the work of the Holy Spirit upon the soul of man in withering up that which is of the flesh, is *very unexpected.* You will observe in our text, that even the speaker himself, though doubtless one taught of God, when he was bidden to cry, said, "What shall I cry?" Even he did not know that in order to the comforting of God's people, there must first be experienced a preliminary visitation. Many preachers of God's gospel have forgotten that the law is the schoolmaster to bring men to Christ. They have sown on the unbroken fallow ground, and forgotten that the plow must break the clods. We have seen too much of trying to sew without the sharp needle of the Spirit's convincing power. Preachers have labored to make Christ precious to those who think themselves rich and increased in goods; and it has been labor in vain. It is our duty to preach Jesus Christ even to self-righteous sinners, but it is certain that Jesus Christ will never be accepted by them while they hold themselves in high esteem. Only the sick will welcome the physician. It is the work of the Spirit of God to convince men of sin, and until they are convinced of sin, they will never be led to seek the righteousness which is of God by Jesus Christ.

I am persuaded, that wherever there is a real work of grace in any soul, it begins with a pulling down: the Holy Ghost does not build on the old foundation. Wood, hay, and stubble will not do for Him to build upon. He will come as the fire, and cause a conflagration of all proud nature's Babels. He will break our bow and cut our spear in sunder, and burn our chariot in the fire. When every sandy foundation is gone, then, but not till then, behold He will lay in our souls the great foundation-stone, chosen of God, and precious.

Dost thou not see that it is divinely wise that before thou art clothed thou shouldest be stripped! What, wouldst thou have Christ's lustrouˢ righteousness outside whiter than any fuller can make it, and thine own filthy rags concealed within? Nay, man; they must be put away; not a single thread of thine own must be left upon thee. It cannot be that God should cleanse thee until He has made thee see somewhat of thy defilement; for thou wouldst never value the precious blood which cleanses us from all sin if thou hadst not first of all been made to mourn that thou art altogether an unclean thing.

The convincing work of the Spirit, wherever it comes, is unexpected, and even to the child of God in whom this process has still to go on, it is often startling. We begin again to build that which the Spirit of God had destroyed. Having begun in the spirit, we act as if we would be made perfect in the flesh; and then when our mistaken up-building has to be leveled with the earth, we are almost as astonished as we were when first the scales fell from our eyes. In some such condition as this was Newton when he wrote:

> I asked the Lord that I might grow
>   In faith and love and every grace,
> Might more of his salvation know,
>   And seek more earnestly his face.
>
> 'Twas he who taught me thus to pray,
>   And he, I trust, has answered prayer;
> But it has been in such a way
>   As almost drove me to despair.
>
> I hop'd that in some favor'd hour,
>   At once he'd answer my request,
> And by his love's constraining power.
>   Subdue my sins, and give me rest.
>
> Instead of this, he made me feel
>   The hidden evils of my heart;

And let the angry powers of hell
Assault my soul in ev'ry part.

Ah, marvel not, for thus the Lord is wont to answer His people. The voice which saith, "Comfort ye, comfort ye my people," achieves its purpose by first making them hear the cry, "All flesh is grass, and all the goodliness thereof is as the flower of the field." .

2. Furthermore, *this withering is after the usual order of the divine operation.* If we consider well the way of God, we shall not be astonished that He beginneth with His people by terrible things in righteousness. Observe the method of creation. I will not venture upon any dogmatic theory of geology, but there seems to be every probability that this world has been fitted up and destroyed, refitted and then destroyed again, many times before the last arranging of it for the habitation of men. "In the beginning God created the heaven and the earth"; then came a long interval, and at length, at the appointed time, during seven days, the Lord prepared the earth for the human race. Consider then the state of matters when the great architect began His work. What was there in the beginning? Originally, nothing. When He commanded the ordering of the earth how was it? "The earth was without form and void; and darkness was upon the face of the deep." There was no trace of another's plan to interfere with the Great Architect. "With whom took he counsel, and who instructed him, and taught him in the path of judgment, and taught him knowledge, and showed to him the way of understanding." He received no contribution of column or pillar towards the temple which He intended to build. The earth was, as the Hebrew puts it, Tohu and Bohu, disorder and confusion—in a word, chaos. So it is in the new creation. When the Lord new creates us, He borrows nothing from the old man, but makes all things new. He does not repair and add a new wing to the old house of our depraved nature, but He builds a new temple for His own praise. We are spiritually without form and empty, and darkness is upon the face of our heart, and His word comes to us, saying, "Light be," and there is light, and ere long life and every precious thing.

To take another instance from the ways of God. When man has fallen, when did the Lord bring him to the gospel? The first whisper of the gospel, as you know, was, "I will put enmity between thee and the woman, between thy seed and her seed. He shall bruise thy head." That whisper came to man shivering in the presence of his Maker, having nothing more to say by way of excuse, but standing guilty before the Lord. When did the Lord God clothe our parents? Not until first of all He had put the question, "Who told thee that thou wast naked?" Not until the fig-leaves had utterly failed did the Lord bring in the covering skin of the sacrifice, and wrap them in it. If you will pursue the meditation upon the acts of God with men, you will constantly see the same thing. God has given us a wonderful type of salvation in Noah's ark, but Noah was saved in that ark in connection with death; he himself, as it were, immured alive in a tomb, and all the world besides left to destruction. All other hope for Noah was gone, and then the ark rose upon the waters.

Remember the redemption of the children of Israel out of Egypt: it occurred when they were in the saddest plight, and their cry went up to heaven by reason of their bondage. When no arm brought salvation, then with a high hand and an outstretched arm the Lord brought forth His people. Everywhere before the salvation there comes the humbling of the creature, the overthrow of human hope. As in the back woods of America before there can be tillage, the planting of cities, the arts of civilization, and the transactions of commerce, the woodman's ax must hack and hew: the stately trees of centuries must fall: the roots must be burned, the old reign of nature disturbed. The old must go before the new can come. Even thus the Lord takes away the first, that he may establish the second. The first heaven and the first earth must pass away, or there cannot be a new heaven and a new earth. Now, as it has been outwardly, we ought to expect that it would be the same within us; and when these witherings and fadings occur in our souls, we should only say, "It is the Lord, let him do as seemeth him good."

3. I would have you notice, thirdly, that we are taught in our text *how universally this process is in its range* over the hearts of all those upon whom the Spirit works. The withering is a withering of what?

Of part of the flesh and some portion of its tendencies? Nay, observe, "All flesh is grass; and *all* the goodliness thereof"—the very choice and pick of it—"is as the flower of the field," and what happens to the grass? Does any of it live? "The grass withereth," all of it. The flower, will not that abide? So fair a thing, has not that an immortality? No, it fades: it utterly falls away. So wherever the Spirit of God breathes on the soul of man, there is a withering of everything that is of the flesh, and it is seen that to be carnally minded is death. Of course, we all know and confess that where there is a work of grace, there must be a destruction of our delight in the pleasures of the flesh. When the Spirit of God breathes on us, that which was sweet becomes bitter; that which was bright becomes dim. A man cannot love sin and yet possess the life of God. If he takes pleasure in fleshly joys wherein he once delighted, he is still what he was: he minds the things of the flesh, and therefore he is after the flesh, and he shall die. The world and the lusts thereof are to the unregenerate as beautiful as the meadows in spring, when they are bedecked with flowers, but to the regenerate soul they are a wilderness, a salt land, and not inhabited. Of those very things wherein we once took delight we say, "Vanity of vanities; all is vanity." We cry to be delivered from the poisonous joys of earth, we loathe them, and wonder that we could once riot in them. Beloved hearers, do you know what this kind of withering means? Have you seen the lusts of the flesh, and the pomps and the pleasures thereof all fade away before your eyes? It must be so, or the Spirit of God has not visited your soul.

But mark, wherever the Spirit of God comes, He destroys the goodliness and flower of the flesh; that is to say, our righteousness withers as our sinfulness. Before the Spirit comes we think ourselves as good as the best. We say, "All these commandments have I kept from my youth up," and we superciliously ask, "What lack I yet?" Have we not been moral? Nay, have we not even been religious? We confess that we may have committed faults, but we think them very venial, and we venture, in our wicked pride, to imagine that, after all, we are not so vile as the word of God would lead us to think. Ah, my dear hearer, when the Spirit of God blows on the comeliness of thy flesh, its beauty will fade as a leaf, and thou wilt have quite another idea of thyself; thou wilt then find no language too severe in which to describe thy past character. Searching deep into thy motives, and investigating that which moved thee to thine actions, thou wilt see so much of evil, that thou wilt cry with the publican, "God be merciful to me, a sinner!"

Where the Holy Ghost has withered up in us our self-righteousness, He has not half completed His work; there is much more to be destroyed yet, and among the rest, away must go our boasted power of resolution. Most people conceive that they can turn to God whenever they resolve to do so. "I am a man of such strength of mind," says one, "that if I made up my mind to be religious, I should be without difficulty." "Ah," saith another volatile spirit, "I believe that one of these days I can correct the errors of the past, and commence a new life." Ah, dear hearers, the resolutions of the flesh are goodly flowers, but they must all fade. When visited by the Spirit of God, we find that even when the will is present with us, how to perform that which we would we find not; yea, and we discover that our will is averse to all that is good, and that naturally we will not come unto Christ that we may have life. What poor frail things resolutions are when seen in the light of God's Spirit!

Still the man will say, "I believe I have, after all, within myself an enlightened conscience and an intelligence that will guide me aright. The light of nature I will use, and I do not doubt that if I wander somewhat I shall find my way back again." Ah, man! Thy wisdom, which is the very flower of thy nature, what is it but folly, though thou knowest it not? Unconverted and unrenewed, thou art in God's sight no wiser than the wild ass's colt. I wish thou were in thine own esteem humbled as a little child at Jesus' feet, and made to cry, "Teach thou me."

When the withering wind of the Spirit moves over the carnal mind, it reveals the death of the flesh in all respects, especially in the matter of power towards that which is good. We then learn that word of our Lord: "Without me ye can do nothing." When I was seeking the Lord, I not only believed that I could not pray without divine help, but I felt in my very soul that I could not. Then I could not even feel aright, or mourn as I would, or groan as I would. I longed to long more after Christ, but, alas! I could not even feel that I needed Him as I ought to feel it. This heart was then as hard, as adamant, as dead as those that rot in their graves. Oh, what would I at times have given for a tear! I wanted to repent, but could not; longed to believe, but could not; I felt bound, hampered, and paralyzed.

This is a humbling revelation of God's Holy Spirit, but a needful one; for the faith of the flesh is not the faith of God's elect. The faith which justifies the soul is the gift of God and not of ourselves. That repentance which is the work of the flesh will need to be repented of. The flower of the flesh must wither; only the seed of the Spirit will produce fruit unto perfection. The heirs of heaven are born not of blood, nor of the will of the flesh, nor of man, but of God. If the work in us be not the Spirit's working, but our own, it will droop and die when most we require its protection; and its end will be as the grass which today is, and tomorrow is cast into the oven.

4. You see, then, the universality of this withering work within us, but I beg you also to notice *the completeness of it*. The grass, what does it do? Droop? Nay, wither. The flower of the field: what of that? Does it hang its head a little? No, according to Isaiah it fades; and according to Peter it falleth away. There is no reviving it with showers, it has come to its end. Even thus are the awakened led to see that in their flesh there dwelleth no good thing. What dying and withering work some of God's servants have had in their souls! Look at John Bunyan, as he describes himself in his "Grace Abounding!" For how many months and even years was the Spirit engaged in writing death upon all that was the old Bunyan, in order that he might become by grace a new man fitted to track the pilgrims along their heavenly way. We have not all endured the ordeal so long, but in every child of God there must be a death to sin, to the law, and to self, which must be fully accomplished ere he is perfected in Christ and taken to heaven. Corruption cannot inherit incorruption; it is through the Spirit that we mortify the deeds of the body and therefore live.

But cannot the fleshly mind be improved? By no means; for "the carnal mind is enmity against God: for it is not subject to the law of

God, neither indeed can be." Cannot you improve the old nature? No; "ye must be born again." Can it not be taught heavenly things? No. "The natural man receiveth not the things of the Spirit of God: for they are foolishness unto him: neither can he know them, because they are spiritually discerned." There is nothing to be done with the old nature but to let it be laid in the grave; it must be dead, and buried, and when it is so, then the incorruptible seed that liveth and abideth forever will develop gloriously, the fruit of the new birth will come to maturity, and grace shall be exalted in glory. The old nature never does improve, it is as earthly, and sensual, and devilish in the saint of eighty years of age as it was when first he came to Christ; it is unimproved and unimprovable; towards God it is enmity itself: every imagination of the thoughts of the heart is evil, and that continually. The old nature called "the flesh lusteth against the Spirit, and the Spirit against the flesh: and these are contrary the one to the other," neither can there be peace between them.

5. Let us further notice that all *this withering work in the soul is very painful.* As you read these verses do they not strike you as having a very funereal tone? "All flesh is grass, and all the goodliness thereof is as the flower of the field: the grass withereth, the flower fadeth." This is mournful work, but it must be done. I think those who experience much of it when they first come to Christ have great reason to be thankful. Their course in life will, in all probability, be much brighter and happier, for I have noticed that persons who are converted very easily, and come to Christ with but comparatively little knowledge of their own depravity, have to learn it afterwards, and they remain for a long time babes in Christ, and are perplexed with matters that would not have troubled them if they had experienced a deeper work at first. No, sir; if grace has begun to build in your soul and left any of the old walls of self-trust standing, they will have to come down sooner or later. You may congratulate yourself upon their remaining, but it is a false congratulation, your glorying is not good. I am sure of this, that Christ will never put a new piece upon an old garment, or new wine in old bottles: he knows the rent would be worse in the long run, and

the bottles would burst. All that is of nature's spinning must be unraveled. The natural building must come down, lath and plaster, roof and foundation, and we must have a house not made with hands.

It was a great mercy for our city of London that the great fire cleared away all the old buildings which were the lair of the plague, a far healthier city was then built; and it is a great mercy for a man when God sweeps right away all his own righteousness and strength, when He makes him feel that he is nothing and can be nothing, and drives him to confess that Christ must be all in all, and that his only strength lies in the eternal might of the ever-blessed Spirit.

Observe, brethren, that although this is painful *it is inevitable.* I have already entrenched upon this, and shown you how necessary it is that all of the old should be taken away, but let me further remark that it is inevitable that the old should go, because it is in itself corruptible. Why does the grass wither? Because it is a withering thing. "Its root is ever in its grave, and it must die." How could it spring out of the earth, and be immortal? It is no amaranth: it blooms not in Paradise: it grows in a soil on which the curse has fallen. Every supposed good thing that grows out of your own self, is like yourself, mortal, and it must die. The seeds of corruption are in all the fruits of manhood's tree; let them be as fair to look upon as Eden's clusters, they must decay.

Moreover, it would never do, my brother, that there should be something of the flesh in our salvation and something of the Spirit; for if it were so there would be a division of the honor. Hitherto the praises of God; beyond this my own praises. If I were to win heaven partly through what I had done, and partly through what Christ had done, and if the energy which sanctified me was in a measure my own, and in a measure divine, they that divide the work shall divide the reward, and the songs of heaven while they would be partly to Jehovah must also be partly to the creature. But it shall not be. Down, proud flesh! Down! I say. Though thou cleanse and purge thyself as thou mayst, thou art to the core corrupt; though thou labor unto weariness, thou buildest wood that will be burned, and stubble that will be turned to ashes. Give up thine own self-confidence, and let the work be, and the merit be where the honor shall be, namely, with God alone. It is inevitable, then, that there should be all this withering.

II. Now, let us close with a few sentences concerning THE IMPLANTATION.

According to Peter, although the flesh withers, and the flower thereof falls away, yet in the children of God there is an unwithering something of another kind. "Being born again, not of corruptible seed, but of incorruptible, by the word of God, which liveth and abideth forever." "The word of the Lord endureth forever. And this is the word which by the gospel is preached unto you." Now, the gospel is of use to us because it is not of human origin. If it were of the flesh, all it could do for us would not land us beyond the flesh, but the gospel of Jesus Christ is super-human, divine, and spiritual. In its conception it was of God; its great gift, even the Savior, is a divine gift; and all its teachings are full of Deity. If you, my hearer, believe a gospel which you have thought out for yourself, or a philosophical gospel which comes from the brain of man, it is of the flesh, and will wither, and you will die, and be lost through trusting in it. The only word that can bless you and be a seed in your soul must be the living and incorruptible word of the eternal Spirit.

Now this is the incorruptible word, that "God was made flesh and dwelt among us"; that "God was in Christ, reconciling the world unto Himself, not imputing their trespasses unto them." This is the incorruptible word, that "Whosoever believeth that Jesus is the Christ is born of God." "He that believeth on Him is not condemned: but he that believeth not is condemned already because he hath not believed in the name of the only begotten Son of God." "God hath given to us eternal life, and this life is in His Son." Now, brethren, this is the seed, but before it can grow in your soul, it must be planted there by the Spirit. Do you receive it this morning? Then the Holy Spirit implants it in your soul. Do you leap up to it, and say, "I believe it! I grasp it! On the incarnate God I fix my hope; the substitutionary sacrifice, the complete atonement of Christ is all my confidence; I am reconciled to God by the blood of Jesus." Then you possess the living seed within your soul.

And what is the result of it? Why, then there comes, according to the text, a new life into us, as the result of the indwelling of the living word, and our being born again by it. A new life it is; it is not the old nature putting out its better parts; not the old Adam refining and purifying itself, and rising to something better. No; have we not said aforetime that the flesh withers and the flower thereof fades? It is an entirely new life. Ye are as much new creatures at your regeneration, as if you had never existed, and had been for the first time created. "Old things are passed away; behold, all things are become new." The child of God is beyond and above other men. Other men do not possess the life which he has received. They are but duplex —body and soul have they. He is of triple nature—he is spirit, soul, and body. A fresh principle, a spark of the divine life has dropped into his soul; he is no longer a natural or carnal man, but he has become a spiritual man, understanding spiritual things and possessing a life far superior to anything that belongs to the rest of mankind. O that God, who has withered in the souls of any of you that which is of the flesh, may speedily grant you the new birth through the Word.

Now observe, to close, wherever this new life comes through the word, it is incorruptible, it lives and abides forever. To get the good seed out of a true believer's heart and to destroy the new nature in him, is a thing attempted by earth and hell, but never yet achieved. Pluck the sun out of the firmament, and you shall not even then be able to pluck grace out of a regenerate heart. It "liveth and abideth forever," saith the text; it neither can corrupt of itself nor be corrupted. "It sinneth not, because it is born of God." "I give unto them eternal life, and they shall never perish, neither shall any man pluck them out of my hand." "The water that I shall give him shall be in him a well of water springing up into everlasting life." You have a natural life—that will die, it is of the flesh. You have a spiritual life—of that it is written: "Whosoever liveth and believeth in me shall never die." You have now within you the noblest and truest immortality: you must live as God liveth, in peace and joy, and happiness.

But oh, remember, dear hearer, if you have not this "you shall not see life." What then—shall you be annihilated? Ah! No, but "the wrath of the Lord is upon you." You shall exist, though you shall not live. Of life you shall know nothing, for that is the gift of God in Christ Jesus, but of an everlasting death, full of torment and anguish, you shall be the wretched heritor—"the wrath of God abideth on him." You shall be cast into "the lake of fire, which is the second death." You shall be one of those whose "worm dieth not, and whose fire is not quenched." May God, the ever-blessed Spirit, visit you! If He be now striving with you, O quench not His divine flame! Trifle not with any holy thought you have. If this morning you must confess that you are not born again, be humbled by it. Go and seek mercy of the Lord, entreat Him to deal graciously with you and save you. Many who have had nothing but moonlight have prized it, and ere long they have had sunlight.

Above all, remember what the quickening seed is, and reverence it when you hear it preached, "for this is the word which by the gospel is preached unto you." Respect it and receive it. Remember that the quickening seed is all wrapped up in this sentence: "Believe in the Lord Jesus Christ, and thou shalt be saved," "He that believeth and is baptized shall be saved, but he that believeth not shall be damned."

The Lord bless you, for Jesus' sake. Amen.

7

The Heavenly Wind

The wind bloweth where it listeth, and thou hearest the sound thereof, but canst not tell whence it cometh, and whither it goeth: so is everyone that is born of the Spirit—
John 3:8.

The Holy Spirit is to be admired, not only for the great truths which He teaches us in Holy Scripture, but also for the wonderful manner in which those truths are balanced. The word of God never gives us too much of one thing or too little of another: it never carries a doctrine to an extreme, but tempers it with its corresponding doctrine. Truth seems to run at least in two parallel lines, if not in three, and when the Holy Spirit sets before us one line He wisely points out to us the other. The truth of divine sovereignty is qualified by human responsibility, and the teaching of abounding grace is seasoned by a remembrance of unflinching justice. Scripture gives us as it were the acid and the alkali; the rock and the oil which flows from it; the sword which cuts and the balm which heals. As our Lord sent forth His evangelists two and two so doth He seem to send out His truths two and two, that each may help the other, for the blessing of those who hear them.

Now in this most notable third of John you have two truths taught as plainly as if they were written with a sunbeam, and taught side by

259

side. The one is the necessity of faith in the Lord Jesus Christ, and the fact that whosoever believeth in Him is not condemned. This is a vital doctrine, but the Holy Ghost in this chapter lays equal stress upon the necessity of the new birth or the work of the Holy Spirit, and He states it quite as plainly as the other grand truth. See how they blend — "Ye must be born again," but "whosoever believeth in him shall not perish, but have everlasting life"; "Except a man be born of water and of the Spirit, he cannot enter into the kingdom of God," but "he that believeth on him is not condemned." Two great truths are written in letters of light over the gate of heaven, as the requisites of all who enter there — *Reconciliation by the blood of Jesus Christ*; and *Regeneration by the work of the Holy Ghost*. We must not put one of these truths before the other, nor allow one to obliterate or hide the other: they are of equal importance, for they are revealed by the same divine Spirit, and are alike needful to eternal salvation. Faith gives us the rights of the children of God, but the new birth must be experienced that we may have the nature of children; of what use would rights be if we had not the capacity to exercise them?

I. Take the text in reference to THE HOLY SPIRIT HIMSELF. The figure is the wind, and, as most of you know, the Hebrew word for "wind" and for "spirit" is the same; and it is interesting to note that the same is true with the Greek word *"pneuma,"* which signifieth both "breath" and "spirit," so that the figure which the Savior used might very naturally grow out of the word which he employed. The wind is air in motion, and is, of course, material, but air is apparently more spiritual than any of the other elements, except fire, since it is not to be grasped by the hand nor seen with the eye. It is certain that wind really exists, for we hear the sound thereof and observe its various effects, but it is not to be touched, handled or gazed upon; men cannot traffic in it, or measure it in scales, or weigh it in balances. We may watch for hours as we will the clouds as they hasten along like winged fowl, but the wind which driveth them is out of our sight; we observe the waves roused to fury in the tempest, but the breath which so excites them we cannot see. Hence the word becomes all the more excellent a figure of that mighty power, the Holy Ghost, of whose existence no man ever doubts who has come under His influence, but who, nevertheless, is not to be tracked in His movements, nor to be seen as to His divine person; for He is mysterious, incomprehensible, and divine.

First, the wind is a figure of the Holy Ghost in *its freeness*—"The wind bloweth where it listeth." We speak of the wind as the very image of freedom: we say to those who would enthrall us, "go bind the winds," as for ourselves we claim to be "free as the winds which roam at their own will." No one can fetter the wind. Xerxes threw chains into the Hellespont to bind the sea, but even he was not fool enough to talk of forging fetters for the winds. The breezes are not to be dictated to. Caesar may decree what he pleases, but the wind will blow in his face if he looks that way. The Pope may command the gale to change its course, but it will blow around the Vatican neither less nor more for the holy father and the cardinals. A conference of plenipotentiaries from all the powers of Europe may sit for a week and resolve unanimously that the east wind shall not blow for the next six months, but it will take no heed of the arrangement, and will cast dust into the counselor's eyes, and whistle at their wisdom. No proclamation nor purpose under heaven will be able to affect the wind by so much as half a point of the compass. It will blow according to its own sweet will, where it pleases, when it pleases, how it pleases, and as it pleases, for "the wind bloweth where it listeth."

So is it, only in a far higher and more emphatic sense, with the Holy Spirit, for He is most free and absolute. Ye know that the wind is in the hand of God, and that He ordaineth every zephyr and each tornado: winds arise and tempests blow by order from the throne supreme, but as for the Holy Spirit, He is God Himself, and absolutely free, and worketh according to His own will and pleasure amongst the sons of men. One nation has been visited by the Holy Spirit and not another—who shall tell me why? Why lie yon heathen lands in the dense darkness while on Britain in England and among the northern nations of Europe, while in Spain and Italy it has left scarce a trace? Why blows the Holy Spirit here and not there? Is it not that He doeth as He wills? "I will have mercy on whom I will have mercy, and I will have compassion on whom I will have compassion" is the declaration of the divine sovereignty, and the Spirit of God in His movements confirmeth it.

Among the nations where the Spirit of God is at work, how is it that He blesseth one man and not another? How is it that of two men hearing the same sermon, and subject to the same influences at home, one is taken and the other left? Two children nursed at the same breast, and trained by the same parents, grow up to different ends. He who perishes in sin has no one to blame but himself, but he who is saved ascribes it all to grace—why came that grace to him? We never dare to lay the fault of man's not repenting and believing upon God—that resteth with the evil will which refused to obey the gospel, but we dare not ascribe the saving difference in the case of the one who believes to any natural goodness in himself, but we attribute it all to the grace of God, and believe that the Holy Spirit worketh in such to will and to do according to His own good pleasure. But why works He in us? Why in any of the chosen? Ah, why? "The wind bloweth where it listeth."

So, too, is it with the blessing which rests upon ministries. One man winneth souls to God, and as a joyous reaper returneth with full sheaves, but another who goeth forth with strong desires, and seems at least to be as earnest as his fellow, comes home with a scanty handful of ears, which he has painfully gleaned. Why is one man's net full of fish and another's utterly empty? One servant of the Lord seems, whenever he stands up to preach the gospel, to attract men to Jesus as though he had golden chains in his mouth which he did cast about men's hearts to draw them in joyful captivity to his Lord, while another cries in bitterness of soul, "Who hath believed our report?" Truly, "the wind bloweth where it listeth."

Ay, and these changes happen to each man severally: one day the preacher shall be all alive, his spirit shall be stirred within him, and he shall speak evidently with the Holy Ghost sent down from heaven; and tomorrow he shall find himself dull and heavy, even to his own consciousness, and even more so to his people's experience, for the power rests not upon him. One day he speaketh like the voice of God, and another day he is but as a reed shaken of the wind. His fat kine of years gone by are devoured by the lean cattle of the present. He has his famine as well as his plenty. You shall see him come forth today with the unction of the Lord upon him, and his face shining with the glory of fellowship with the Most High, and tomorrow he shall say, "Look not upon me, for I am black," for the glory shall have departed. We know what it is to come forth like Samson when his locks were shorn; and to shake ourselves as at other times and discover that the Lord is not with us. Why all this? Is it not because "the wind bloweth where it listeth?" The Holy Spirit, for His own wise reasons, puts not forth an equal power upon any man at all times. We cannot control nor command the Spirit of the living God: He is in the highest sense a free agent. "Thy free Spirit" is a name which David gave Him, and a most appropriate name it is.

The wind too hath at least in some lands its times and seasons. We know that at certain times of the year we may expect winds, and if they come not to a day or two, yet, as a rule, the month is stormy; and there are also trade winds, monsoons which blow with remarkable regularity and are counted upon by mariners. And so with the Spirit of God. We know that at certain times He visits the churches, and under certain conditions puts forth His power. If, for instance, there is mighty prayer, you may be sure the Spirit of God is at work; if the people of God meet together and besiege the throne of grace with cries and tears, the spiritual barometer indicates that the blessed wind is rising. Besides, the Holy Spirit has graciously connected Himself with two things, truth and prayer. Preach the truth, publish the gospel of Jesus Christ, and it is the habit of the Holy Spirit to make the word quick and powerful to the hearts of men. If we falsify His word if we keep back part of the truth, if we become unfaithful, we cannot expect the Holy Spirit to bless us, but if our teaching be Christ crucified, lovingly set forth, and if the grace of God in its fullness be really declared, the Holy Spirit will attend the truth and make it the great power of God. I will not say that it is always, and without exception so, but I think exceptions must be rare; almost invariably the Spirit beareth witness with the truth in the conversion of men.

So too with prayer, the Holy Spirit is pleased to connect Himself with that also, if it be believing prayer. Here the connection is exceedingly intimate, because it is the Spirit of God who Himself gives the believing prayer, and it is not only true that the Spirit will be given in answer to prayer, but the Spirit is already given or the believing prayer would never have been offered. The spirit of prayerfulness, the spirit of anxiety for the conversion of men is one of the surest indications that the Holy Spirit is already at work in the minds of His people. ,

Coming back, however, to the great fact that we cannot command the Holy Spirit, what influence ought that truth to have upon us? Should it not be just this? It should lead us to be very tender and jealous in our conduct towards the Holy Ghost, so that we do not grieve Him and cause Him to depart from us. Vex not the Spirit. When you enjoy His gracious operations be devoutly grateful, and walk humbly before God, that you may retain them; and when He is at work let not negligence on your part cause you to receive the grace of God in vain. The wind blew, but the sailor was asleep; it was a favorable breeze, but he had cast anchor and his bark moved not. If he had but known it all through the night he would have spread his sail and have made good headway towards his port, but he slumbered, and the blessed wind whistled through the cordage and the ship lay idle at its moorings. Let it not be so with us. Never suffer the Spirit of God to be with us and find us regardless of His presence.

In the olden times, when country people depended more than they do now on the use of the windmill to grind their corn, some parishes would be half-starved, when week after week there had been no wind. The miller would look up anxiously, and everybody in the parish would become a watchman for his sails, hoping that they would soon be set in motion. If the breeze stirred at the dead of night, and the miller was sound asleep, somebody or other would run and knock him up. "The wind is blowing, the wind is blowing, grind our corn." So it ought to be whenever the Spirit of God is vigorously working in His church, we should eagerly avail ourselves of His power. We should be so anxious for His divine operations that all should be on the watch, so that if some did not discover it others would, and observant ones would cry, "The Holy Ghost is working with us; let us arise and labor more abundantly." Hoist sail when the wind favors; you cannot command it, therefore carefully value it.

But we must pass on. The Holy Spirit is described as being like the wind as to *His manifestations.* "Thou hearest," says Jesus, "the sound thereof." It has been suggested, and some have enlarged upon it, that there are many other manifestations of the presence of wind: you can feel it, you can see its results upon the trees and the waves, and sometimes you can be sure that the wind has been at work by the devastation which it has caused: but in this place our Savior was not so much alluding to a great wind as to the gentler breezes. The Greek word "*pneuma*" is translated "breath," and can hardly be made to mean a tempest. It was a gentle wind like a zephyr of which the Lord was here speaking. The great winds, as I have already said, can be somewhat calculated upon, but if you sit in the garden in the cool of the evening it is utterly impossible for you to tell whence the zephyrs come and where they go; they are so volatile in their movements and untrackable in their course; here, there, everywhere the soft breezes of evening steal among the flowers. Our Lord tells us that such gentle zephyrs are heard: Nicodemus in the stillness of the night could hear them. "Thou hearest the sound thereof." The leaves rustle, and that is all; you hear a gentle movement of branch and stem, and as it were the tinkling of flower-bells, and so you discover that the wind is flitting among the beds and borders.

Now, beloved, this shows us that the hearing ear is intended by God to be the discerner of the Spirit to men, to the most of men the only discerner that they have. "Thou hearest the sound thereof." What a wonderful dignity the Lord has been pleased to put upon this little organ, the ear. The Romish church gives the preference always to the eye; her priests are always for astonishing men into grace with their wonderful performances, but God's way is "Faith

cometh by hearing," and the first detector of the Holy Ghost is the
ear. To some men this is the only revealer of His mysterious presence, as I have already said: they hear the sound thereof, that is to
say, they hear the gospel preached, they hear the word of God read.
Truth when it is couched in words is the rustling of the holy wind,
it is the footstep of the Eternal Spirit as mysteriously He passes
along a congregation. Oh, what grief it is that some never get any
further than this, but abide where Nicodemus was at the first: they
hear the sound thereof and nothing more. Some of you are now
daily hearing truth which has saved thousands, but it does not save
you; you are hearing the very truth which peoples heaven, but yet it
leaves you without a hope of eternal life; yet be ye sure of this, the
kingdom of God has come nigh unto you. "Thou hearest the sound
thereof," and that wind whose whispers you hear is not far off thine
own cheek. When thou hearest the rustling amongst the boughs of
the trees the breezes are not far to seek, nor is the Spirit of God far
away when His sound is heard.

Some hearers, however, go further, for they hear the sound of the
Spirit in their consciences and it disturbs them; they would sleep as
do others, but as the wind sometimes comes whistling through the
keyhole or howls down the chimney and wakes the sluggard, or if
the man be lying in a garden asleep the breezes play around his ears
and face and startle him, so is it with many unconverted people;
they cannot be quiet, for they hear the sound of the Holy Spirit in
their consciences, and are troubled and perplexed. There is a revival
and they are not saved, but they are startled and alarmed by it; their
sister is converted, they are not, but still it comes very near them,
and they feel as if an arrow had gone whizzing by their own ear. It is
hard living in a careless state in the midst of revival. "Thou hearest
the sound thereof." But some of you in your conscience are hearing
the sound now in your family circle, from the fact that one after another of your relatives have been brought to know the Lord; you cannot avoid feeling that there is something powerful abroad, though it
has not yet exerted its regenerating power upon you.

As for the man who is saved, he hears the Holy Spirit in the most
emphatic sense, and with what variety that sound comes to him. At

first he heard it as a threatening wind, which bowed him in sadness and seemed to sweep all his hopes to the ground, as the sere leaves of the forest are carried in the autumn's wind. When the Spirit's voice sounded in mine ears at the first it was as a wail of woe, as a wind among the tombs, as a sigh among faded lilies. It seemed as if all my hopes were puffed away like smoke, or as the night mists in the morning breeze; nothing was left me but to mourn my nothingness. Then I heard a sound as of the hot sirocco of the East, as if it issued from a burning oven. You know the text, "The grass withereth and the flower thereof fadeth away because the Spirit of the Lord bloweth upon it: surely the people is grass." In my soul there had bloomed a fair meadow of golden kingcups and fair flowers of many dainty colors, but the Spirit of God blew thereon and withered it all, and left it as a dry, brown, rusty plain, whereon was neither life nor comeliness. So far the sacred wind destroys that which is evil, but it ends not there, for we thank God we have heard the sound of the Spirit as a quickening wind. The prophet cried, "Come from the four winds, O breath, and breathe upon these slain that they may live"; the wind came and the dead arose an exceeding great army.

The like miracle has been wrought on us. The sere bones of our own death have crept together, bone unto His bone, and flesh has come upon them, and now because of the divine breath we have begun to live. Now, also, when the Holy Spirit visits us He renews our life and energy, and we have life more abundantly. The Holy Spirit has since then been to us full often a melting wind, "He causeth His wind to blow and the waters flow." Locked up in the chains of ice all through the winter the waters are still as a stone, but the spring-winds come, the brooklets find liberty and leap away to the rivers, and the rivers flow in all their free force to add their volume to the sea. So hath the Spirit of God oftentimes broken up our frost, and given our spirits joyous liberty. He melts the rocky heart and dissolves the iron spirit, at the sound of His goings men are moved to feeling.

We know the sound of this wind as a diffusive breath, drawing forth and diffusing our slumbering graces. "Awake, O north wind;

and come, thou south; blow upon my garden, that the spices thereof may flow out." Oh, what a sweet unloosing of holy gratitude, and love, and hope, and joy has there been in our heart when the Spirit of God has visited us. As sweet essences lie hidden in the flowers, and come not forth until the loving wind doth entice them to fly abroad, so do sweet graces lie within renewed spirits until the Holy Ghost cometh and speaketh to them, and they know his voice and come forth to meet him, and so sweet fragrances are shed abroad.

Yes, my brethren, all this we know, and we have heard the sound of the Holy Spirit in another sense, namely, as going forth with us to the battle of the Lord. We have heard that sound of a going in the tops of the mulberry trees which David heard, and we have bestirred ourselves, and victory has been ours. If we have not heard that rushing mighty wind which came at Pentecost, yet have we felt its divine effect, which ceaseth not, but still bringeth life, power, energy, and all that is wanted for the conversion of the sons of men to us who are bidden to go forth and preach the gospel amongst the nations. In all these respects the Holy Ghost has manifested Himself, as wind does, by His sound. "Thou hearest the sound thereof." "Their sound went into all the earth and their words unto the ends of the world."

A third likeness of the Spirit to the wind is set before us in the point of *mystery*. "Thou canst not tell whence it cometh nor whither it goeth." Of the wind we may tell that it comes from such and such a quarter or point, but you cannot put your finger on the map and say, "The north wind began in this region," or "here the west wind was born." Indeed, we know very little about the winds, their origin, or their laws. One of the best and most accurate observers of the wind during thirty years recorded every wind in his region, until at the end of the term he abandoned the few rules which he had laid down during the first two or three years, for he found that no rule held good. No man can say whence the wind leapeth forth. The heathen dreamed of a certain cave wherein the winds were enclosed as in a prison, and suffered to go abroad one by one: it was but a fable; we know not where the winds first spread their wings, or where they sleep when all is still. So is it with the Holy Spirit in the mind of man, His first movements are hidden in mystery.

You know that you are converted, my dear friend, and you know somewhere about the time, and probably you remember somewhat as to the means which the Lord used for your salvation. Those outward circumstances you do know, but how the Holy Spirit operated upon you, you do not and cannot tell anymore than you can tell how swells the life within the seed until it springs up and becomes the full corn in the ear, or how the sap in the trees first descendeth in the winter and afterwards climbeth again in the spring. There are secrets which nature doth not reveal, and the work of the Spirit is even more a secret, and assuredly no man can explain it to his fellow or to himself. Why is it, my friend, that you obtained a blessing under one sermon but not under another, and yet when you spoke to your sister she had been more blessed under the second than the first? The power does not come from the preacher, then, it is clear, and "thou canst not tell whence it cometh."

There are times in which you feel not only that you can pray but that you must pray; how come you to be in that state? I know what it is to feel in a very ecstasy of delight in the Lord, for which I can scarcely account, for at another time when I have been engaged in the same work, and I think with the same earnestness, I have not been conscious of any such exceeding delight in God. At one time the heart will be full of penitence as if it would break for sin, and at another season it will overflow with such delight in Christ that the sin seems almost forgotten in the pardoning sacrifice. Why these diverse operations?

We know what it is at times to feel such a sense of death upon us as to be earnestly preparing for our last hours; and at another time to be altogether forgetful of death, and to be living, as it were, the immortal life already, raised up together and made to sit together with Christ. But how these various modes and forms and workings of the Spirit come who among us shall tell? Go trace the dewdrops, if ye can, to the womb of the morning, and discover which way went the lightning's flash, or how the thunder rolled along the mountain tops, but ye cannot tell nor can you guess whence cometh the Spirit of God into your souls.

Nor can we tell whither it goeth. Here, again, is another mystery. Oh, it charms me to think that when we let loose the truth in the power of the Spirit we never know where it will fly. A child takes a seed, one of those downy seeds which has its own parachute to bear it through the air; the little one blows it into the air, but who knows where that downy seed shall settle, and in whose garden it shall grow? Such is truth, even from the mouths of babes and sucklings. Whole continents have been covered with strange flowers simply by the wind wafting foreign seeds thither, and mariners have discovered sunny islets out there in the Southern Sea, where foot of man has never trodden, covered with abundance of vegetation which the wind has by degrees wafted thither. Scatter the truth on all sides, for you cannot tell where the Spirit will carry it. Fling it to the winds, and you shall find it after many days. Scatter the living seed with both hands, send it north, south, east and west, and God will give it wings,

> Waft, waft ye winds the story,
>   And you, ye waters roll,
> Till like a sea of glory
>   It spreads from pole to pole.

I had a letter but the other day when I was sore sick: it was written by a sister in Christ in the very heart of the empire of Brazil. She said that she had met with a copy of my "Morning Readings," and had found thereby the way of peace, and, therefore, she wrote me such a loving, touching letter, that, as I read it, it brought tears to my eyes. There was something more affecting yet, for at the end was written in another hand, some words to the effect that his dear wife who had written the above letter had died soon after finishing it, and with a bleeding heart the lone husband sent it on to me, rejoicing that ever the word came to his wife's soul in the far-off land.

Brethren, you do not know where the word will go and the Spirit with it. In Bohemia the papists thought they had stamped out the gospel, and with cruel edicts they kept down all thought of Protestanism, but just lately, since the toleration, the gospel has been preached in that country, and to the surprise of everybody there have come forward men and women from lone cottages in the woods and from different corners of the great cities of Bohemia, bringing with them ancient copies of the word of God, themselves being eager to know the precious truth for which they remember that their fathers died. A truth will go adown the centuries: like the river, it sings

> Men may come and men may go,
> But I go on forever.

"Thou canst not tell whither it goeth," it will travel on till the millennium. Send that saying abroad that the truth cannot die. The persecutor cannot kill it, it is immortal, like the God who sent it forth; the persecutor cannot even stay its course, it is divine. Popery will always be in danger so long as there is one leaf of the Bible upon earth, or one man living who knows the Savior. Antichrist cannot triumph; the Holy Spirit wars against it with the sword of the word, and thou canst not tell how far into the heart of error any truth may be driven. To the overthrow of falsehood and the death of sin the Spirit speeds on, but thou knowest not how.

"Thou canst not tell whither it goeth" either in any one heart. If you have received the Holy Spirit into your heart, you cannot tell whither He will carry you. I am sure that William Carey, when he gave his young heart to Christ never thought the Spirit of God would carry him to Serampore to preach the gospel to the Hindus; and when George Whitefield first drank of the life-giving spirit it never occurred to him that the pot-boy at the Bell Inn at Gloucester would thunder the gospel over two continents and turn thousands to Christ. No! You know not to what blessed end this wind will waft you. Commit yourselves to it: be not disobedient to the heavenly vision; be ready to be borne along as the Spirit of God shall help you, even as the dust in the summer's breeze. And O child of God, you do not yourself know to what heights of holiness and degrees of knowledge and ecstasies of enjoyment the Spirit of God will bear you. "Eye hath not seen nor ear heard the things which God hath prepared for them that love Him," and though He hath revealed them by His Spirit (for the Spirit searcheth all things, even the deep things of God), yet even to the best taught child of God it is not yet know to the full whither the Spirit of God goeth. "Trust ye in the Lord forever, for in the Lord Jehovah there is everlasting strength," and He will bear you onward and upward, even to perfection itself, and you shall be with Jesus, where He is, and behold His glory.

II. I have but a few minutes left for my second head, but I do not need many, since I do not wish to say much upon it. The text relates to THOSE WHO ARE BORN OF THE SPIRIT. "The wind bloweth where it listeth, and thou hearest the sound thereof, but canst not tell whence it cometh, and whither it goeth: so is everyone that is born of the Spirit." The birth partakes of the natures of the parent. That which is born of the Spirit is like unto the Spirit of which it is born, even as that which is born of the flesh is flesh, and is similar to the flesh by which it is begotten. The twice-born man is like the Holy Ghost who produced him, and he is like Him in each of the points which we have already dwelt upon.

As to *freedom*, you may say of Him, "He bloweth where He listeth." The Spirit of God makes the believer a free man, bestows on him the freedom of His will which he never had before, and gives him a delightful consciousness of liberty. "If the Son make you free ye shall be free indeed." I do not affirm that every spiritual man does as he lists, because, alas, I see another law in our members warring against the law of our mind, and bringing us into captivity to the law of sin and death: but still, "where the Spirit of the Lord is, there is liberty."

Now you can pray, which you could not do before; now you can praise, though you could not extract a note of praise from your ungrateful heart before; now you can cry, "Abba, Father"; now you can draw near to God. You are no longer under man's control, you blow where you list; you are not now ruled by priestcraft, nor domineered over by the opinion of your fellow man. The Lord has set you free, and you list to go where God's word bids you go, and you find the utmost liberty in going that way. Oh, brethren, I cannot tell you the change which is felt by a regenerate man in the matter of spiritual liberty. When you were under the bondage of the law, of custom and of sin, and of fear of death and dread of hell, you were like a man shut up in one of those cells in Venice which lie below the level of the water mark, where the air is foul, and the poor prisoner can only stir half-a-dozen feet and then walk back again in the darkness, but when the Spirit of God comes He brings the soul from darkness into light, from clammy damp into the open air; He sets before you an open door, He helps you to run in the way of God's commands, and as if that were not enough, He even lends you wings, and bids you mount as the eagle, for He has set you free.

Again, the man who is born of the Spirit is somewhat *manifested*; and is known by his sound. "Thou hearest the sound thereof." The most ungodly man if he lives near a Christian will hear the sound of him. The secret life within will speak; words there will be, for Christians are not dumb, but actions will speak more loudly still; and even apart from actions the very spirit and tone of the man who is really regenerated will speak, and the ungodly man will be compelled to hear it. "Thou hearest the sound thereof."

And now notice *the mystery* there is about a Christian. Thou knowest nothing, if thou art unregenerate, about the life the believer leads, for he is dead, and his life is hid with Christ in God. Thou knowest not whence he cometh forth in the morning; those beds of spices which have made his garments fragrant thou hast not seen; that weeping in prayer or that rejoicing in fellowship with which he opened the morning thou knowest nothing of, and thou canst not know until thou art thyself born of the Spirit. Neither canst thou tell whither the spiritual man goeth. In the midst of his trouble thou seest him calm; dost thou know where he went to win that rare quietude? In the hour of death thou seest him triumphant; dost thou know where he has been to learn to die so joyously? No, the unregenerate man knows not whither the believer goes. There is a secret place of the Most High, and they shall abide under the shadow of the Almighty who have once learned to enter there, but carnal men come not into this secret chamber.

The Christian life is a mystery all through, from its beginning to its end: to the worldling all a mystery; and to the Christian himself a puzzle. He cannot read his own riddle, nor understand himself. This one thing he knoweth, "Whereas I was once blind, now I see"; this also he knoweth, "O Lord, I am thy servant, I am thy servant, and the son of thine handmaid: thou hast loosed my bonds"; this also he knoweth, that when his Lord shall be revealed then will he also shine forth as the sun. The life within him in its coming and going is all a mystery to him, but he blesses God that he has fellowship therein. He goes on his way feeling that though men know not whence he is, nor whither he is going, yet the Lord knows him, and he himself is sure that he is going to his Father and his God. O that every one of you had so delightful a hope. The Lord grant it to you, for Jesus' sake.

8

The Pentecostal Wind and Fire

*And suddenly there came a sound from heaven as of a
rushing mighty wind, and it filled all the house where they
were sitting. And there appeared unto them cloven tongues
like as of fire, and it sat upon each of them. And they were
filled with the Holy Ghost, and began to speak with other
tongues, as the Spirit gave them utterance—Acts 2:2–4.*

From the descent of the Holy Ghost at the beginning we may
learn something concerning His operations at the present
time. Remember at the outset that whatever the Holy Spirit
was at the first that He is now, for as God He remaineth forever the
same: whatsoever He then did He is able to do still, for His power is
by no means diminished. As saith the prophet Micah, "O thou that
art named the house of Jacob, is the spirit of the Lord straitened?"
We should greatly grieve the Holy Spirit if we supposed that His
might was less today than in the beginning. Although we may not
expect, and need not desire, the miracles which came with the gift
of the Holy Spirit, so far as they were physical, yet we may both desire and expect that which was intended and symbolized by them,
and we may reckon to see the like spiritual wonders performed
among us at this day.

Pentecost, according to the belief of the Jews, was the time of
the giving of the law; and if when the law was given there was a

marvelous display of power on Sinai, it was to be expected that when the gospel was given, whose ministration is far more glorious, there should be some special unveiling of the divine presence. If at the commencement of the gospel we behold the Holy Spirit working great signs and wonders may we not expect a continuance—nay, if anything, an increased display—of His power as the ages roll on? The law vanished away, but the gospel will never vanish; it shineth more and more to the perfect millennial day; therefore, I reckon that, with the sole exception of physical miracles, whatever was wrought by the Holy Ghost at the first we may look to be wrought continually while the dispensation lasts. It ought not to be forgotten that Pentecost was the feast of first fruits; it was the time when the first ears of ripe corn were offered unto God. If, then, at the commencement of the gospel harvest we see so plainly the power of the Holy Spirit, may we not most properly expect infinitely more as the harvest advances and most of all when the most numerous sheaves shall be ingathered? May we not conclude that if the Pentecost was thus marvelous the actual harvest will be more wonderful still?

This morning my object is not to talk of the descent of the Holy Spirit as a piece of history, but to view it as a fact bearing upon us at this hour, even upon us who are called in these latter days to bear our testimony for the truth. The Father hath sent us the Comforter that He may dwell in us till the coming of the Lord. The Holy Ghost has never returned, for He came in accordance with the Savior's prayer, to abide with us forever. The gift of the Comforter was not temporary, and the display of His power was not to be once seen and no more. The Holy Ghost is here, and we ought to respect His divine working among us: and if He does not so work we should search ourselves to see what it is that hindereth, and whether there may not be somewhat in ourselves which vexes Him, so that He restrains His sacred energy, and doth not work among us as He did aforetime. May God grant that the meditation of this morning may increase our faith in the Holy Ghost, and inflame our desires towards Him, so that we may look to see Him fulfilling His mission among men as at the beginning.

I. First, I shall call your attention to THE INSTRUCTIVE SYMBOLS of the Holy Spirit, which were made prominent at Pentecost. They were two. There was a sound as of a rushing mighty wind, and there were cloven tongues as it were of fire.

Take the symbols separately. The first is *wind*—an emblem of Deity, and therefore a proper symbol of the Holy Spirit. Often under the Old Testament God revealed Himself under the emblem of breath or wind: indeed, as most of you know, the Hebrew word for "wind" and "spirit" is the same. So, with the Greek word, when Christ talked to Nicodemus, it is not very easy for translators to tell us when He said "spirit" and when He said "wind"; indeed, some most correctly render the original all the way through by the word "wind," while others with much reason have also used the word "spirit" in their translation. The original word signified either the one or the other, or both. Wind is, of all material things, one of the most spiritual in appearance; it is invisible, ethereal, mysterious; hence, men have fixed upon it as being nearest akin to spirit. In Ezekiel's famous vision, when he saw the valley full of dry bones, we all know that the Spirit of God was intended by that vivifying wind which came when the prophet prophesied and blew upon the withered relics till they were quickened into life. "The Lord hath His way in the whirlwind," thus He displays Himself when He works: "The Lord answered Job out of the whirlwind," thus He reveals Himself when He teaches His servants.

Observe that this wind was on the day of Pentecost accompanied with a sound—a sound as of a rushing mighty wind; for albeit the Spirit of God can work in silence, yet in saving operations He frequently uses sound. I would be the last to depreciate meetings in which there is nothing but holy silence, for I could wish that we had more reverence for silence, and it is in stillness that the inner life is nourished; yet the Holy Ghost does not work for the advancement of the kingdom of God by silence alone, for faith cometh by hearing. There is a sound as of a rushing, mighty wind, when the word is sounded forth throughout whole nations by the publishing of the gospel. The sound came on this occasion, no doubt, to call the attention of the assembly to what was about to occur, to arouse them, and to fill them with awe! There is something indescribably solemn about the rush of a rising tempest; it bows the soul before the sublime mystery of divine power. What more fitting as an attendant upon divine working than the deeply solemn rush of a mighty wind.

With this awe-inspiring sound as of a mighty wind, there was clear indication of its coming from heaven. Ordinary winds blow from this or that quarter of the skies, but this descended from heaven itself: it was distinctly like a down-draught from above. This sets forth the fact that the true Spirit, the Spirit of God, neither comes from this place nor that neither can His power be controlled or directed by human authority, but His working is ever from above, from God Himself. The work of the Holy Spirit is, so to speak, the breath of God, and His power is evermore in a special sense the immediate power of God. Coming downward, therefore, this mysterious wind passed into the chamber where the disciples were assembled, and filled the room. An ordinary rushing mighty wind would have been felt outside the room, and would probably have destroyed the house or injured the inmates, if it had been aimed at any one building, but this heavenly gust filled but did not destroy the room, it blessed but did not overthrow the waiting company.

The meaning of the symbol is that as breath, air, wind, is the very life of man, so is the Spirit of God the life of the spiritual man. By Him are we quickened at the first; by Him are we kept alive afterwards; by Him is the inner life nurtured, and increased, and perfected. The breath of the nostrils of the man of God is the Spirit of God.

This holy breath was not only intended to quicken them, but to invigorate them. They took in great draughts of heavenly life; they felt animated, aroused, and bestirred. A sacred enthusiasm came upon them, because they were filled with the Holy Ghost; and, girt with that strength, they rose into a nobler form of life than they had known before.

No doubt this wind was intended to show the irresistible power of the Holy Ghost; for simple as the air is, and mobile and apparently feeble, yet set it in motion, and you feel that a thing of life is among you; make that motion more rapid, and who knows the power of the restless giant who has been awakened. See, it becomes a storm, a tempest, a hurricane, a tornado, a cyclone. Nothing can be more potent than the wind when it is thoroughly roused, and so, though the Spirit of God be despised among men, so much so that they do not even believe in His existence, yet let Him work with the fullness of His power, and you will see what He can do. He comes softly, breathing like a gentle zephyr, which fans the flowers, but does not dislodge the insect of most gauzy wing, and our hearts are comforted. He comes like a stirring breeze, and we are quickened to a livelier diligence: our sails are hoisted and we fly before the gale. He comes with yet greater strength, and we prostrate ourselves in the dust as we hear the thunder of His power, bring down with a crash false confidences and refuges of lies! How the firm reliances of carnal men, which seemed to stand like rocks, are utterly cast down! How men's hopes, which appeared to be rooted like oaks, are torn up by the roots before the breath of the convincing Spirit! What can stand against Him? Oh! That we did but see in these latter days something of that mighty rushing wind which breaketh the cedars of Lebanon, and sweeps before it all things that would resist its power.

The second Pentecostal symbol was *fire*. Fire, again, is a frequent symbol of Deity. Abraham saw a burning lamp, and Moses beheld a burning bush. When Solomon had built his holy and beautiful house, its consecration lay in the fire of God descending upon the sacrifice to mark that the Lord was there; for when the Lord had dwelt aforetime in the tabernacle, which was superseded by the temple, He revealed Himself in a pillar of cloud by day and a pillar of fire by night. "Our God is a consuming fire." Hence the symbol of fire is a fit emblem of God the Holy Spirit. Let us adore and worship Him. Tongues of flame sitting on each man's head betoken a personal visitation to the mind and heart of each one of the chosen company. Not to consume them came the fires, for no one was injured by the flaming tongue; to men whom the Lord has prepared for His approach there is no danger in His visitations. They see God, and their lives are preserved; they feel His fires, and are not consumed. This is the privilege of those alone who have been prepared and purified for such fellowship with God.

The intention of the symbol was to show them that the Holy Spirit would illuminate them, as fire gives light. "He shall lead you into all truth." Henceforth they were to be no more children untrained, but to be teachers in Israel, instructors of the nations whom they were to disciple unto Christ: hence the Spirit of light was upon them. But fire doth more than give light: it inflames; and the flames which sat upon each showed them that they were to be ablaze with love, intense with zeal, burning with self-sacrifice; and that they were to go forth among men to speak not with the chill tongue of deliberate logic, but with burning tongues of passionate pleading; persuading and entreating men to come unto Christ that they might live. The fire signified inspiration. God was about to make them speak under a divine influence, to speak as the Spirit of God should give them utterance. Oh! Blessed symbol, would God that all of us experienced its meaning to the full and that the tongue of fire did sit upon every servant of the Lord. May a fire burn steadily within to destroy our sin, a holy sacrificial flame to make us whole burnt offerings unto God, a never-dying flame of zeal for God, and devotion to the cross.

Note that the emblem was not only fire, but a tongue of fire; for God meant to have a speaking church: not a church that would fight with the sword—with that weapon we have naught to do—but a church that should have a sword proceeding out of its mouth, whose one weapon should be the proclamation of the gospel of Jesus Christ. I should think from what I know of some preachers that when they had their Pentecost the influence sat upon them in the form of tongues of flowers, but the apostolic Pentecost knew not flowers, but flames. What fine preaching we have nowadays! What new thoughts, and poetical turns! This is not the style of the Holy Ghost. Soft and gentle is the flow of smooth speech which tells of the dignity of man, the grandeur of the century, the toning down of all punishment for sin, and the probable restoration of all lost spirits, including the archfiend himself. This is the Satanic ministry, subtle as the serpent, bland as his seducing words to Eve.

The Holy Ghost calls us not to this mode of speech. Fire, intensity, zeal, passion as much as you will, but as for aiming at effect by polished phrases and brilliant periods—these are fitter for those who would deceive men than for those who would tell them the message of the Most High. The style of the Holy Ghost is one which conveys the truth to the mind in the most forcible manner—it is plain but flaming, simple but consuming. The Holy Spirit has never written a cold period throughout the whole Bible, and never did He speak by a man a lifeless word, but evermore He gives and blesses the tongue of fire.

These, then, are the two symbols: He comes as the wind, which wafts the words we speak, and as fire which burns a way for the truth we utter. Our words are now full of life and flame; they are borne by the breath of the Spirit, and they fall like fire-flakes, and set the soul of men blazing with desire after God. If the Holy Spirit shall rest upon me or upon you, or upon any of us, to qualify us for service, it shall be after this fashion—not merely of life for ourselves, but of fiery energy in dealing with others. Come on us even now, O rushing mighty wind and tongue of fire, for the world hath great need. It lies stagnant in the malaria of sin and needs a healing wind; it is shrouded in dreadful night, and needs the flaming torch of truth. There is neither health nor light for it but from Thee, O blessed Spirit; come, then, upon it through Thy people.

Now put these two symbols together; only mind what you are at. Wind and fire together! I have kept them separate in my discourse hitherto; and you have seen power in each one; what are they together? Rushing mighty wind alone how terrible! Who shall stand against it? See how the gallant ships dash together, and the monarchs of the forest bow their heads. And fire alone! Who shall stand against it when it devours its prey? But set wind and fire to work in hearty union! Remember the old city of London. When first the flames began it was utterly impossible to quench them because the wind fanned the flame, and the buildings gave way before the fire-torrent. O God, send us the Holy Ghost in this fashion: give us both the breath of spiritual life and the fire of unconquerable zeal, till nation after nation shall yield to the sway of Jesus. O Thou who art our God, answer us by fire, we pray Thee. Answer us both by wind and fire, and then shall we see to be God indeed. The kingdom comes not, and the work is flagging. O that Thou wouldest send the wind and the fire! Thou wilt do this when we are all of one accord, all believing, all expecting, all prepared by prayer. Lord, bring us to this waiting state.

II. Secondly, my brethren, follow me while I call your attention to the immediate effects of this descent of the Holy Spirit, for these symbols were not sent in vain. There were two immediate effects: the first was filling, and the second was the gift of utterance. I call special attention to the first, namely, filling: "It filled all the house where they were sitting": and it did not merely fill the house, but the man—"They were all filled with the Holy Ghost." When they stood up to speak even the ribald mockers in the crowd noticed this, for they said, "These men are full," and though they added "with new wine," yet they evidently detected a singular fullness about them. We are poor, empty things by nature, and useless while we remain so: we need to be filled with the Holy Ghost. Where the Spirit of God is truly at work He first fills and then gives utterance: that is His way. Oh that you and I were at this moment filled with the Holy Ghost. "Full!" Then they were not cold, and dead, and empty of life as we sometimes are. "Full." Then there was no room for anything else in any one of them! They were too completely occupied by the heavenly power to have room for the desires of the flesh. Fear was banished, every minor motive was expelled: the Spirit of God as it flooded their very being drove out of them everything that was extraneous. They had many faults and many infirmities before, but that day, when they were filled with the Spirit of God, faults and infirmities were no more perceptible. They became different men from what they had ever been before: men full of God are the reverse of men full of self. Out of a full church the world shall receive salvation, but never out of an empty one. The first thing we want as a church is to be filled with the Holy Ghost: the gift of utterance will then come as a matter of course.

The next Pentecostal symbol was *utterance*. As soon as the Spirit of God filled them they began to speak at once. It seems to me that they began to speak before the people had come together. They could not help it; the inner forces demanded expression, and they must speak. So when the Spirit of God really comes upon a man, He does not wait till He has gathered an audience of the size which He desires, but He seizes the next opportunity. He speaks to one person, He speaks to two, He speaks to three, to anybody: He must speak, for He is full, and must have vent.

When the Spirit of God fills a man He speaks so as to be understood. The crowd spake different languages, and these Spirit-taught men spoke to them in the language of the country in which they were born. This is one of the signs of the Spirit's utterance. If my friend over yonder talks in Latinized style to a company of costermongers, I will warrant you the Holy Ghost has nothing to do with him. If a learned brother fires over the heads of his congregation with a grand oration, he may trace his elocution, if he likes, to Cicero and Demosthenes, but do not let him ascribe it to the Holy Spirit, for that is not after His manner. The Spirit of God speaks so that His words may be understood, and if there be any obscurity it lies in the language used by the Lord Himself.

The crowd not only understood, but they felt. There were lancets in this Pentecostal preaching, and the hearers "were pricked in the heart." The truth wounded men, and the slain of the Lord were many, for the wounds were in the most vital part. They could not make it out: they had heard speakers before, but this was quite a different thing. The men spake fire-flakes, and one hearer cried to his fellow, "What is this?" The preachers were speaking flame, and the fire dropped into the hearts of men till they were amazed and confounded.

Those are the two effects of the Holy Spirit—a fullness of the Spirit in the ministry and the church, and next, a fire ministry, and a church on fire, speaking so as to be felt and understood by those around. Causes produce effects like themselves, and this wind and fire ministry soon did its work. We read that this "was noised abroad." Of course it was, because there had been a noise as of a rushing mighty wind. Next to that we read that all the people came together, and were confounded. There was naturally a stir, for a great wind from heaven was rushing. All were amazed and astonished, and while some inquired believingly, others began to mock. Of course they did: there was a fire burning, and fire is a dividing thing, and this fire began to separate between the precious and the vile, as it always will do when it comes into operation. We may expect at the beginning of a true revival to observe a movement among the people, a noise, and a stir. These things are not done in a corner. Cities will know of the presence of God, and crowds will be attracted by the event.

This was the immediate effect of the Pentecostal marvel, and I shall now ask you to follow me to my third point, which is this:

III. The Holy Spirit being thus at work, what was THE MOST PROMINENT SUBJECT which these full men began to preach about with words of fire? Suppose that the Holy Spirit should work mightily in the church, what would our ministers preach about? "We do hear them speak in our own tongues the wonderful works of God." Their subject was the wonderful works of God. Oh, that this might be to my dying day my sole and only topic, "The wonderful works of God." For, first, they spoke of *redemption*, that wonderful work of God. Peter's sermon was a specimen of how they spoke of it. He told the people that Jesus was the Son of God, that they had crucified and slain Him, but that He had come to redeem men, and that there was salvation through His precious blood. He preached redemption. Oh, how this land will echo again and again with "Redemption, redemption, redemption, redemption by the precious blood," when the Holy Ghost is with us. This is fit fuel for the tongue of flame: this is something worthy to be wafted by the divine wind. "God was in Christ, reconciling the world unto himself, not imputing their trespasses unto them." "The blood of Jesus Christ his Son cleanseth us from all sin." This is one of the wonderful works of God of which we can never make too frequent mention.

They certainly spoke of the next wonderful work of God, namely, *regeneration*. There was no concealing of the work of the Holy Spirit in that primitive ministry. It was brought to the front. Peter said, "Ye shall receive the Holy Ghost." The preachers of Pentecost told of the Spirit's work by the Spirit's power: conversion, repentance, renewal, faith, holiness, and such things were freely spoken of and ascribed to their real author, the divine Spirit. If the Spirit of God shall give us once again a full and fiery ministry we shall hear it clearly proclaimed, "Ye must be born again," and we shall see a people forthcoming which are born, not of blood, nor of the will of the flesh, but of the will of God, and by the energy which cometh from heaven. A Holy Ghost ministry cannot be silent about the Holy Ghost and His sacred operations upon the heart.

And very plainly they spoke on a third wonderful work of God, namely, *remission* of sin. This was the point that Peter pushed home to them, that on repentance they should receive remission of sins. What a blessed message is this; Pardon for crimes of deepest dye, a pardon bought with Jesus' blood, free pardon, full pardon, irreversible pardon given to the vilest of the vile when they ground their weapons of rebellion, and bow at the feet that once were nailed to the tree. If we would prove ourselves to be under divine influence, we must keep to the divine message of fatherly forgiveness to returning prodigals. What happier word can we deliver?

These are the doctrines which the Holy Ghost will revive in the midst of the land when He worketh mightily—redemption, regeneration, remission. If you would have the Spirit of God resting on your labors, dear brothers and sisters, keep these three things ever to the front, and make all men hear in their own tongue the wonderful works of God.

IV. I shall close by noticing, in the fourth place, what were the GLORIOUS RESULTS of all this. Have patience with me, if you find the details somewhat long. The result of the Spirit coming as wind and fire, filling and giving utterance, was, first, in the hearers' *deep feeling*. There was never, perhaps, in the world such a feeling excited by the language of mortal man as that which was aroused in the crowds in Jerusalem on that day. You might have seen a group

here, and a group there, all listening to the same story of the wondrous works of God, and all stirred and affected; for the heavenly
wind and fire went with the preaching, and they could not help
feeling its power. We are told that they were pricked in the heart.
They had painful emotions, they felt wounds which killed their enmity. The word struck at the center of their being: it pierced the
vital point. Alas, people come into our places of worship nowadays
to hear the preacher, and their friends ask them on their return,
"How did you like him?" Was that your errand, to see how you liked
him? What practical benefit is there in such a mode of using the
servants of God? Are we sent among you to give opportunities for
criticism? Yet the mass of men seem to think that we are nothing
better than fiddlers or play actors, who come upon the stage to help
you while away an hour. O my hearers, if we are true to our God,
and true to you, ours is a more solemn business than most men
dream. The object of all true preaching is the heart: we aim at di-
vorcing the heart from sin, and wedding it to Christ. Our ministry
has failed, and has not the divine seal set upon it, unless it makes
men tremble, makes them sad, and then anon brings them to
Christ, and causes them to rejoice.

Then followed an *earnest inquiry*. "They were pricked in their
heart, and they said to Peter and the rest of the apostles, Men and
brethren, what shall we do?" Emotion is of itself but a poor result
unless it leads to practical action. To make men feel is well enough,
but it must be a feeling which impels them to immediate movement, or at least to earnest inquiry as to what they shall do. O spirit
of God, if Thou wilt rest on me, even, me, men shall not hear and
go their way and forget what they have heard! They will arise and
seek the Father, and taste His love. If Thou wouldst rest on all the
brotherhood that publish Thy word men would not merely weep
while they hear, and be affected while the discourage lasts, but they
would go their way to ask, "What must we do to be saved?" This is
what we need. We do not require new preachers, but we need a
new anointing of the Spirit. We do not require novel forms of service, but we want the fire Spirit, the wind Spirit to work by us till
everywhere men cry, "What must we do to be saved?"

Then came *a grand reception of the word.* We are told that they gladly received the word, and they received it in two senses: first, Peter bade them repent, and so they did. They were pricked to the heart from compunction on account of what they had done to Jesus, and they sorrowed after a godly sort, and quitted their sins. They also believed in Him whom they had slain, and accepted Him as their Savior there and then, without longer hesitancy. They trusted in Him whom God had set forth to be a propitiation, and thus they fully received the word. Repentance and faith make up a complete reception of Christ, and they had both of these. Why should we not see this divine result today? We shall see it in proportion to our faith.

But what next? Why, they were *baptized* directly. Having repented and believed, the next step was to make confession of their faith; and they did not postpone that act for a single day; why should they? Willing hands were there, the whole company of the faithful were all glad to engage in the holy service, and that same day were they baptized into the name of the Father, and of the Son, and of the Holy Spirit. If the Holy Ghost were fully with us, we should never have to complain that many believers never confess their faith, for they would be eager to confess the Savior's name in His own appointed way. Backwardness to be baptized comes too often of fear of persecution, indecision, love of ease, pride, or disobedience, but all these vanish when the heavenly wind and fire are doing their sacred work. Sinful diffidence soon disappears, sinful shame of Jesus is no more seen, and hesitancy and delay are banished forever when the Holy Spirit works with power.

Furthermore, there was not merely this immediate confession, but as a result of the Spirit of God there was *great steadfastness.* "They continued steadfastly in the apostles' doctrine." We have had plenty of revivals of the human sort, and their results have been sadly disappointing. Under excitement nominal converts have been multiplied: but where are they after a little testing? I am sadly compelled to own that, so far as I can observe, there has been much sown, and very little reaped that was worth reaping, from much of that which has been called revival. Our hopes were flattering as a

dream, but the apparent result has vanished like a vision of the
night. But where the Spirit of God is really at work the converts
stand: they are well rooted and grounded, and hence they are not
carried about by every wind of doctrine, but they continue steadfast in the apostolic truth.

We see next that there was *abundant worship of God*, for they
were steadfast not only in the doctrine, but in breaking of bread,
and in prayer, and in fellowship. There was no difficulty in getting a
prayer meeting then, no difficulty in maintaining daily communion
then, no want of holy fellowship then; for the Spirit of God was
among them, and the ordinance were precious in their eyes. "Oh,"
say some, "if we could get this minister or that evangelist we should
do well." Brothers, if you had the Holy Spirit you would have everything else growing out of His presence, for all good things are
summed up in Him.

Next to this there came *striking generosity*. Funds were not hard
to raise: liberality overflowed its banks, for believers poured all that
they had into the common fund. Then was it indeed seen to be true
that the silver and the gold are the Lord's. When the Spirit of God
operates powerfully there is little need to issue telling appeals for
widows and orphans, or go down on your knees and plead for missionary fields which cannot be occupied for want of money. When
the Spirit of God comes, those who have substance yield it to their
Lord: those who have but little grow rich by giving of that little, and
those who are already rich become happy by consecrating what
they have. There is no need to rattle the box when the rushing
mighty wind is heard, and the fire is dissolving all hearts in love.

Then came *continual gladness*. "They did eat their meat with
gladness." They were not merely glad at prayer meetings and sermons, but glad at breakfast and at supper. Whatever they had to eat
they were for singing over it. Jerusalem was the happiest city that
ever was when the Spirit of God was there. The disciples were
singing from morning to night, and I have no doubt the outsiders
asked, "What is it all about?" The temple was never so frequented
as then; there was never such singing before; the very streets of

Jerusalem, and the Hill of Zion, rang with the songs of the once despised Galileans.

They were full of gladness, and that gladness showed itself in *praising God*. I have no doubt they broke out now and then in the services with shouts of, "Glory! Hallelujah!" I should not wonder but what all propriety was scattered to the winds. They were so glad, so exhilarated that they were ready to leap for joy. Of course we never say "Amen," or "Glory!" now. We have grown to be so frozenly proper that we never interrupt a service in any way, because, to tell the truth, we are not so particularly glad, we are not so specially full of praise that we want to do anything of the sort. Alas, we have lost very much of the Spirit of God, and much of the joy and gladness which attend His presence, and so we have settled into a decorous apathy! We gather the pinks of propriety instead of the palm branches of praise. God send us a season of glorious disorder. Oh for a sweep of wind that will set the seas in motion, and make our ironclad brethren now lying so quietly at anchor to roll from stem to stern. As for us, who are as the little ships, we will fly before the gale if it will but speed us to our desired haven. Oh for fire to fall again, fire which shall affect the most stolid! This is a sure remedy for indifference. When a flake of fire falls into a man's bosom he knows it, and when the word of God comes home to a man's soul he knows it too. Oh that such fire might first sit upon the disciples and then fall on all around!

For, to close, there was then *a daily increase* of the church—"The Lord added to the church daily such as should be saved." Conversion was going on perpetually; additions to the church were not events which happened once a year, but they were everyday matters, "so mightily grew the word of God and prevailed." O Spirit of God, Thou art ready to work with us today even as Thou didst then! Stay not, we beseech Thee, but work at once. Break down every barrier that hinders the incoming of Thy might. Overturn, overturn, O sacred wind! Consume all obstacles, O heavenly fire, and give us now both hearts of flame and tongues of fire to preach thy reconciling word, for Jesus' sake. Amen.

9

The Indwelling and Outflowing of the Holy Spirit

He that believeth on me, as the scripture hath said, out of his belly shall flow rivers of living water. (But this spake he of the Spirit, which they that believe on him should receive: for the Holy Ghost was not yet given; because that Jesus was not yet glorified.) — John 7:38, 39.

Nevertheless I tell you the truth; It is expedient for you that I go away: for if I go not away, the Comforter will not come unto you, but if I depart, I will send him unto you — John 16:7.

It is essential, dear friends, that we should worship the living and true God. It will be ill for us if it can be said, "Ye worship ye know not what." "Thou shalt worship the Lord thy God, and him only shalt thou serve." The heathen err from this command by multiplying gods, and making this and that image to be the object of their adoration. Their excess runs to gross superstition and idolatry. I fear that sometimes we who "profess and call ourselves Christians" err in exactly the opposite direction. Instead of worshiping more than God I fear we worship less than God. This appears when we forget to pay due adoration to the Holy Spirit of God. The true God is triune, Father, Son, and Holy Spirit; and though there be but one

God yet that one God has manifested Himself to us in the trinity of His sacred persons. If, then, I worship the Father and the Son, but forget or neglect to adore the Holy Spirit, I worship less than God. While the poor heathen in his ignorance goes far beyond and transgresses, I must take care lest I fall short and fail too.

What a grievous thing it will be if we do not pay that loving homage and reverence to the Holy Spirit which is so justly His due. May it not be the fact that we enjoy less of His power and see less of His working in the world because the church of God has not been sufficiently mindful of Him? It is a blessed thing to preach the work of Jesus Christ, but it is an evil thing to omit the work of the Holy Ghost; for the work of the Lord Jesus itself is no blessing to that man who does not know the work of the Holy Spirit. There is the ransom price, but it is only through the Spirit that we know the redemption: there is the precious blood, but it is as though the fountain had never been filled unless the Spirit of God lead us with repenting faith to wash therein. The bandage is soft and the ointment is effectual, but the wound will never be healed till the Holy Spirit shall apply that which the great Physician has provided. Let us not therefore be found neglectful of the work of the divine Spirit, lest we incur guilt, and inflict upon ourselves serious damage.

You that are believers have the most forcible reasons to hold the Holy Ghost in the highest esteem; for what are you now without Him? What were you, and what would you still have been, if it had not been for His gracious work upon you? He quickened you, else you had not been in the living family of God today. He gave you understanding that you might know the truth, else would you have been as ignorant as the carnal work is at this hour. It was He that awakened your conscience, convincing you of sin: it was He that gave you abhorrence of sin, and led you to repent: it was He that taught you to believe, and made you see that glorious Person who is to be believed, even Jesus, the Son of God. The Spirit has wrought in you your faith and love and hope, and every grace. There is not a jewel upon the neck of your soul which he did not place there.

For every virtue we possess,
And every victory won,
And every thought of holiness,
   Are his alone.

Beloved brethren, notwithstanding all that the Spirit of God has already done in us, it is very possible that we have missed a large part of the blessing which He is willing to give, for He is able to "do exceeding abundantly above all that we ask or think." We have already come to Jesus, and we have drunk of the life-giving stream: our thirst is quenched, and we are made to live in Him. Is this all? Now that we are living in Him, and rejoicing to do so, have we come to the end of the matter? Assuredly not. We have reached as far as that first exhortation of the Master, "If any man thirst, let him come unto me and drink," but do you think that the generality of the church of God have ever advanced to the next, "He that believeth on me, as the Scripture hath said, out of his belly shall flow rivers of living water"? I think I am not going beyond the grievous truth if I say that only here and there will you find men and women who have believed up to that point. Their thirst is quenched, as I have said, and they live, and because Jesus lives they shall live also, but health and vigor they have not: they have life, but they have not life more abundantly. They have little life with which to act upon others: they have no energy welling up and overflowing to go streaming out of them like rivers. Brothers, let us go in to get of God all that God will give us: let us set our heart upon this, that we mean to have by God's help all that the infinite goodness of God is ready to bestow. Let us not be satisfied with the sip that saves, but let us go on to the baptism which buries the flesh and raises us in the likeness of the risen Lord: even that baptism into the Holy Ghost and into fire which makes us spiritual and sets us all on flame with zeal for the glory of God and eagerness for usefulness by which that glory may be increased among the sons of men.

Thus I introduce you to my texts, and by their guidance we will enter upon the further consideration of the operations of the Holy Spirit, especially of those to which we would aspire.

I. We will commence with the remark that THE WORK OF THE SPIRIT IS INTIMATELY CONNECTED WITH THE WORK OF CHRIST. It is a great pity when persons preach the Holy Spirit's work so as to obscure the work of Christ; and I have known some do that, for they have held up before the sinner's eye the inward experience of believers, instead of lifting up first and foremost the crucified Savior to whom we must look and live. The gospel is not "Behold the Spirit of God" but "Behold the Lamb of God." It is an equal pity when Christ is so preached that the Holy Spirit is ignored; as if faith in Jesus prevented the necessity of the new birth, and imputed righteousness rendered imparted righteousness needless. Have I not often reminded you that in the third chapter of John, where Jesus taught Nicodemus the doctrine, "Except a man be born again of water and of the spirit he cannot enter the kingdom of heaven," we also read those blessed words, "And as Moses lifted up the serpent in the wilderness, even so must the Son of man be lifted up: that whosoever believeth in Him should not perish, but have eternal life. For God so loved the world, that He gave His only begotten Son, that whosoever believeth in Him should not perish, but have everlasting life." The necessity for regeneration by the Spirit is there put very clearly, and so is the free promise that those who trust in Jesus shall be saved. This is what we ought to do: we must take care to let both these truths stand out most distinctly with equal prominence. They are intertwined with each other and are necessary each to each: what God hath joined together let no man put asunder.

They are so joined together that, first of all, *the Holy Spirit was not given until Jesus had been glorified*. Carefully note our first text; it is a very striking one: "This spake he of the Spirit which they that believe on Him should receive, for the Holy Ghost was not yet." The word "given" is not in the original: it is inserted by the translators to help out the sense, and they were perhaps wise in making such an addition, but the words are more forcible by themselves. How strong the statement, "For the Holy Ghost was not yet." Of course, none of us dreams that the Holy Spirit was not yet existing, for He is eternal and self-existent, being most truly God, but He was not yet in fellowship with man to the full extent in which He now is since Jesus Christ is glorified. The near and dear intercourse of God with man which is expressed by the indwelling of the Spirit could not take place till redeeming work was done and the Redeemer was exalted. As far as men were concerned, and the fullness of the blessing was concerned, indicated by the outflowing rivers of living water, the Spirit of God was not yet.

"Oh," say you, "but was not the Spirit of God in the church in the wilderness, and with the saints of God in all former ages?" I answer, Certainly, but not in the manner in which the Spirit of God now resides in the church of Jesus Christ. You read of the prophets, and of one and another gracious man, that the Spirit of God came upon them, seized the, moved them, spake by them, but He did not dwell in them. His operations upon men were a coming and going: they were carried away by the Spirit of God, and came under His power, but the Spirit of God did not rest upon them or abide in them. Occasionally the sacred endowment of the Spirit of God came upon them, but they knew not "the communion of the Holy Ghost." As a French pastor very sweetly puts it, "He appeared unto men; He did not incarnate Himself in man. His actions were intermittent: He went and came, like the dove which Noah sent forth from the ark and which went to and fro, finding no rest; while in the new dispensation He dwells, He abides in the heart, as the dove, His emblem, which John the Baptist saw descending and alighting upon the head of Jesus. Affianced of the soul, the Spirit went off to see His betrothed, but was not yet one with her; the marriage was not consummated until the Pentecost after the glorification of Jesus Christ."

You know how our Lord puts it, "He dwelleth with you and shall be in you." That indwelling is another thing from being *with* us. The Holy Spirit was with the Apostles in the days when Jesus was with them, but He was not in them in the sense in which He filled them at and after the Day of Pentecost. This shows how intimately the gift of the Holy Ghost is connected with our Lord Jesus Christ, inasmuch as in the fullest sense of His indwelling the Holy Ghost would not be with us until Christ had been glorified. It has been well observed that our Lord sent out seventy evangelists to preach the gospel, even as He had aforetime sent out the twelve; and no doubt they preached with great zeal and produced much stir, but the Holy Ghost never took the trouble to preserve one of their sermons, or even the notes of one. I have not the slightest doubt that they were very crude and incomplete, showing more of human zeal than of divine unction, and hence they are forgotten, but no sooner had the Holy Spirit fallen than Peter's first sermon is recorded, and henceforth we have frequent notes of the utterances of apostles, deacons and evangelists. There was an abiding fullness, and an overflowing of blessing, out of the souls of the saints after the Lord was glorified, which was not existing among men before that time.

Observe, too, that the Holy Spirit was given after the ascent of our divine Lord into His glory, partly *to make that ascent the more renowned.* When He ascended up on high He led captivity captive and gave gifts to men. These gifts were men in whom the Holy Spirit dwelt, who preached the gospel unto the nations. The shedding of the Holy Spirit upon the assembled disciples on that memorable day was the glorification of the risen Christ upon the earth. I know not in what way the Father could have made the glory of heaven so effectually to flow from the heights of the New Jerusalem and to come streaming down among the sons of men as by giving that chief of all gifts, the gift of the Holy Spirit when the Lord had risen and gone into His glory. With emphasis may I say of the Spirit at Pentecost that He glorified Christ by descending at such a time. What grander celebration could there have been? Heaven rang with hosannas, and earth echoed the joy. The descending Spirit is the noblest testimony among men to the glory of the ascended Redeemer.

Was not the Spirit of God also sent at the time *as an evidence of our divine Master's acceptance?* Did not the Father thus say to the church, "My Son has finished the work, and has fully entered into his glory; therefore give I you of the Holy Spirit"? If you would know what a harvest is to come of the sowing of the bloody sweat and of the death wounds, see the first fruits. Behold how the Holy Spirit is given, Himself to be the first fruits, the earnest of the glory which shall yet be revealed in us. I want no better attestation from

God of the finished work of Jesus than His blazing flaming seal of
tongues of fire upon the heads of the disciples. He must have done
His work, or such a boon as this would not have come from it.

Moreover, if you desire to see how the work of the Spirit come to
us in connection with the work of Christ, recollect that *it is the
Spirit's work to bear witness of Jesus Christ.* He does not take of a
thousand different matters and show them to us, but he shall take
"of mine," saith Christ, "and he shall show them unto you." The
Spirit of God is engaged in a service in which the Lord Jesus Christ
is the beginning and the end. He comes to men that they may
come to Jesus. Hence He comes to convince us of sin that He may
reveal the great sacrifice of sin: He comes to convince us of righteousness that we may see the righteousness of Christ; and of judgment that we may be prepared to meet Him when He shall come to
judge the quick and dead.

*It is by the gospel of Jesus Christ that the Spirit of God works in
the hearts of men.* "Faith cometh by hearing, and hearing by the
word of God": the Holy Spirit uses the hearing of the word of God
for the conviction, conversion, consolation, and sanctification of
men. His usual and ordinary method of operation is to fasten upon
the mind the things of God, and to put life and force into the consideration of them. He revives in men's memories things that have
long been forgotten, and He frequently makes these the means of
affecting the heart and conscience. The men can hardly recollect
hearing these truths, but still they were heard by them at some time
or other. Saving truths are such matters as are contained in their
substance in the word of God, and lie within the range of the teaching, or the person, or work, or offices of our Lord Jesus Christ. It is
the Spirit's one business here below to reveal Christ to us and in
us, and to that work He steadily adheres.

Moreover, *the Holy Spirit's work is to conform us to the likeness of
Jesus Christ.* He is not working us to this or that human ideal, but
He is working us into the likeness of Christ that He may be the first-
born among many brethren. Jesus Christ is that standard and
model to which the Spirit of God, by His sanctifying processes, is
bringing us till Christ be formed in us the hope of glory.

Evermore it is for the glory of Jesus that the Spirit of God works.
He works not for the glory of a church or of a community: He works
not for the honor of a man or for the distinction of a sect: His one
great object is to glorify Christ. "He shall glorify me" is our Savior's
declaration, and when He takes of the things of Christ and shows
them unto us, we are led more and more to reverence and love and
adore our blessed Lord Jesus Christ.

II. We will now advance another step, and here we shall need
our second text. THE OPERATIONS OF THE HOLY SPIRIT ARE OF IN-
COMPARABLE VALUE. They are of such incomparable value that the
very best thing we can think of was not thought to be so precious as
these are. Our Lord himself says, "It is expedient for you that I go
away: for if I go not away, the Comforter will not come unto you."
Beloved friends, the presence of Jesus Christ was of inestimable
value to his disciples, and yet it was not such an advantage to his
servants as the indwelling of the Holy Spirit. Is not this a wonderful
statement? Well might our Lord preface it by saying, "Now I tell
you the truth," as if He felt that they would find it a hard saying, for
a hard saying it is. Consider for a moment what Christ was to His
disciples while He was here, and then see what must be the value of
the Spirit's operations when it is expedient that they should lose all
that blessing in order to receive the Spirit of God. Our Lord Jesus
Christ was to them their teacher, they had learned everything from
His lips: He was their leader, they had never to ask what to do, they
had only to follow in His steps: He was their defender, whenever
the Pharisees or Sadducees assailed them He was like a brazen wall
to them: He was their comforter, in all times of grief they resorted to
Him, and His dear sympathetic heart poured out floods of comfort
at once. What if I were to say that the Lord Jesus Christ was everything to them, their all in all. What a father is to his children, ay,
what a mother is to her suckling, that was Jesus Christ to His disciples; and yet the Spirit of God's abiding in the church is better even
than all this.
    Now take another thought. What would you think if Jesus Christ
were to come among us now as in the days of His flesh: I mean not

as He will come, but as He appeared at His first advent. What joy it would give you! Oh, the delights, the heavenly joys, to hear that Jesus Christ of Nazareth was on earth again, a man among men! Should we not clap our hands for joy? Our one question would be, "Master, where dwellest thou?" for we should all long to live just where he lived. If Jesus lived anywhere, it would not matter where, if it were in the desert or on the bleakest of mountains, there would be a rush to the place. How would the spot be crowded; what rents they would pay for the worst of tenements if Jesus was but in the neighborhood. But do you not see the difficulty? We could not all get near Him in any literal or corporeal fashion. Now that the church is multiplied into millions of believers, some of the Lord's followers would never be able to see him, and the most could only hope to speak with him now and then. In the days of His flesh the twelve might see Him everyday, and so might the little company of disciples, but the case is altered now that multitudes are trusting in His name.

"But," you say, "surely it would thrill the church with enthusiasm." Fancy the Lord Himself standing on this platform this morning in the same garb as when He was upon earth. Oh, what rapturous worship! What burning zeal! What enthusiasm! We should go home in such a state of excitement as we never were in before. Yes, it is even so, but then the Lord is not going to carry on His kingdom by the force of mere mental excitement, not even by such enthusiasm as would follow the sight of His person. The work of the Holy Spirit is a truer work, a deeper work, a surer work, and will more effectually achieve the purposes of God than even would the enthusiasm to which we should be stirred by the bodily presence of our well-beloved Savior. The work is to be spiritual, and therefore the visible presence has departed. It is better that it should be so. We must walk by faith, and by faith alone; how could we do this if we could see the Lord with these mortal eyes? This is the dispensation of the unseen Spirit, in which we render glory to God by trusting in His word, and relying upon the unseen energy. Now, faith works and faith triumphs though the world seeth not the foundation upon which faith is built, for the Spirit who works in us cannot be discerned by carnal minds: the world seeth Him not, neither knoweth Him.

Thus you see that the operations of the Holy Spirit must be inestimably precious. There is no calculating their value, since it is expedient that we lose the bodily presence of Christ rather than remain without the indwelling of the Spirit of God.

III. Now go back to my first text again and follow me in the third head. Those operations of the Spirit of God, of which I am afraid some Christians are almost ignorant, are of wondrous power. The text says, "He that believeth on Me, out of the midst of him shall flow rivers of living water." THESE OPERATIONS ARE OF MARVELOUS POWER. Brethren, do you understand my text? Do rivers of living water flow out of you?

Notice, first, that this is to be *an inward work*: the rivers of living water are to flow out of the midst of the man. The words are according to our version, "Out of his belly"—that is, from his heart and soul. The rivers do not flow out of his mouth: the promised power is not oratory. We have had plenty of words, floods of words, but this is heart work. The source of the rivers is found in the inner life. It is an inward work at its fountain head. It is not a work of talent and ability, and show, and glitter, and glare: it is altogether an inward work. The life-flood is to come out of the man's inmost self, out of the bowels and essential being of the man. Homage is shown too generally to outward form and external observance, though these soon lose their interest and power, but when the Spirit of God rests within a man it exercises a home rule within him and he gives great attention to what an old divine was wont to call "the home department." Alas, many neglect the realm within which is the chief province under our care. O my brother in Christ, if you would be useful, begin with yourself. It is out of your very soul that a blessing must come. It cannot come out of you if it is not in you: and it cannot be in you unless God the Holy Ghost places it there.

Next, it is *life-giving work*. Out of the heart of the man, out of the center of his life, are to flow rivers of living water; that is to say, he is instrumentally to communicate to others the divine life. When he speaks, when he prays, when he acts, he shall so speak and pray and act that there shall be going out of him an emanation which is full of the life of grace and godliness. He shall be a light by which others shall see. His life shall be the means of kindling life in other men's bosoms. "Out of his belly shall flow rivers of living water."

Note *the plenitude* of it. The figure would have been a surprising one, if it had said, "Out of him shall flow a river of living water," but it is not so: it says rivers. Have you ever stood by the side of a very abundant spring? We have some such not far from London. You see the water bubbling up from many little mouths. Observe the sand dancing as the water forces its way from the bottom; and there, just across the road, a mill is turned by the stream which has just been created by the spring, and when the water-wheel is turned you see a veritable river flowing forward to supply Father Thames. Yet this is only one river; what would you think if you saw a spring yielding such supplies that a river flowed from it to the north, and a river to the south, a river to the east, and a river to the west; this is the figure before us: rivers of living water flowing out of the living man in all directions. What a word is this! Rivers of living water!! Oh that all professing Christians were such fountains.

See how *spontaneous* it is: "Out of the midst of him shall flow." No pumping is required; nothing is said about machinery and hydraulics; the man does not want exciting and stirring up, but, just as he is, influence of the best kind quietly flows away from him. Did you ever hear a great hubbub in the morning, a great outcry, a sounding of trumpets and drums, and did you ever ask, "What is it?" Did a voice reply, "The sun is about to rise, and he is making this noise that all may be aware of it"? No, he shines, but he has nothing to say about it; even so the genuine Christian just goes about flooding the world with blessing, and so far from claiming attention for himself, it may be that he himself is unconscious of what he is effecting. God so blesses him that his leaf does not wither, and whatsoever he doeth is prospering, for he is like a tree planted by the rivers of water that bringeth forth its fruit in its season: his verdure and fruit are the natural outcome of his vigorous life. Oh, the blessed spontaneity of the work of grace when a man gets into the fullness of it, for then he seems to eat and drink and sleep eternal life, and he spreads a savor of salvation all round.

And this is to be *perpetual*, not like intermittent springs which burst forth and flow in torrents, and then cease, but it is to be an everyday outgushing. In summer and winter, by day and by night, wherever the man is, he shall be a blessing, As he breathes, he shall breathe benedictions; as he thinks, his mind shall be devising generous things; and when he acts, his acts shall be as though the hand of God were working by the hand of man.

I hope I hear many sighs rising up in the place! I hope I hear friends saying, "Oh that I could get to that." I want you to attain the fullness of the favor. I pray that we may all get it; for because Jesus Christ is glorified, therefore the Holy Spirit is given in this fashion, given more largely to those in the kingdom of heaven than to all those holy men before the Lord's ascent to His glory. God gives no stinted blessing to celebrate the triumph of His Son: God giveth not the Spirit by measure unto Him. On such an occasion heaven's grandest liberality was displayed. Christ is glorified in heaven above, and God would have Him glorified in the church below by vouchsafing a baptism of the Holy Ghost to each of us.

So I close by this, which I hope will be a very comforting and inspiriting reflection:

IV. THESE OPERATIONS OF THE SPIRIT OF GOD ARE EASILY TO BE OBTAINED BY THE LORD'S CHILDREN. Did you say you had not received them? They are to be had, they are to be had at once. First, they are to be had by *believing in Jesus*. "This spake He of the Spirit, which they that believe on Him should receive." Do you not see that it is faith which gives us the first drink and causes us to live, and this second more abundant blessing of being ourselves made fountains from which rivers flow comes in the same way? Believe in Christ, for the blessing is to be obtained, not by the works of the law, nor by so much of fasting, and striving, and effort, but by belief in the Lord Jesus for it. With Him is the residue of the Spirit. He is prepared to give this to you, ay, to every one of you who believe on His name. He will not of course make all of you preachers; for who then would be hearers? If all were preachers, the other works of the church would be neglected, but He will give you this favor, that out of you there shall stream a divine influence all around you to bless your children, to bless your servants, to bless the workmen in the house where you are employed, and to bless the street you live in. In proportion as God gives you opportunity ,these rivers of living water will flow in this channel and in that, and they will be pouring forth from you at all times, if you believe in Jesus for the full blessing, and can by faith receive it.

But there is another thing to be done as well, and that is *to pray*; and here I want to remind you of those blessed words of the Master, "Everyone that asketh receiveth; and he that seeketh findeth; and to him that knocketh it shall be opened. If a son shall ask bread of any of you that is a father, will he give him a stone? Or if he ask a fish, will he for a fish give him a serpent? Or if he shall ask an egg, will he offer him a scorpion? If ye then, being evil, know how to give good gifts unto your children: how much more shall your heavenly Father give the Holy Spirit to them that ask him?" You see, there is a distinct promise to the children of God, that their heavenly Father will give them the Holy Spirit if they ask for His power; and that promise is made to be exceedingly strong by the instances joined to it. But he says, *"How much more* shall your heavenly Father give the Holy Spirit to them that ask him?" He makes it a stronger case than that of an ordinary parent. The Lord must give us the Spirit when we ask Him, for He has herein bound Himself by no ordinary pledge. He has used a simile which would bring dishonor on His own name, and that of the very grossest kind, if He did not give the Holy Spirit to them that asked Him.

Oh, then, let us ask Him at once, with all our hearts. Am I not so happy as to have in this audience some who will immediately ask? I pray that some who have never received the Holy Spirit at all may now be led, while I am speaking, to pray, "Blessed Spirit, visit me; lead me to Jesus." But especially those of you that are the children of God, to you is this promise especially made. Ask God to make you all that the Spirit of God can make you, not only a satisfied believer who has drunk for himself, but a useful believer, who overflows the neighborhood with blessing. I see here a number of friends from the country who have come to spend their holiday in London.

What a blessing it would be if they went back to their respective churches overflowing; for there are numbers of churches that need flooding; they are dry as a barn-floor, and little dew ever falls on them. Oh that they might be flooded!

What a wonderful thing a flood is! Go down to the river, look over the bridge, and see the barges and other craft lying in the mud. All the king's horses and all the king's men cannot tug them out to sea. There they lie, dead and motionless as the mud itself. What shall we do with them? What machinery can move them? Have we a great engineer among us who will devise a scheme for lifting these vessels and bearing them down to the river's mouth? No, it cannot be done. Wait till the tide comes in! What a change! Each vessel walks the water like a thing of life. What a difference between the low tide and the high tide. You cannot stir the boats when the water is gone, but when the tide is at the full, see how readily they move; a little child may push them with his hand. Oh, for a flood of grace! The Lord send to all our churches a great springtide! Then the indolent will be active enough, and those who were half dead will be full of energy. I know that in this particular dock several vessels are lying that I should like to float, but I cannot stir them. They neither work for God nor come out to the prayer meetings, nor give of their substance to spread the gospel. If the flood would come you would see what they are capable of: they would be active, fervent, generous, abounding in every good word and work. So may it be! So may it be! May springs begin to flow in all our churches, and may all of you who hear me this day get your share of the streams. Oh that the Lord may now fill you and then send you home bearing a flood of grace with you. It sounds oddly to speak of a man's carrying home a flood within him, and yet I hope it will be so, and that out of you shall flow rivers of living water. So may God grant for Jesus' sake. Amen.

10
The Abiding of the Spirit
The Glory of the Church

Yet now be strong, O Zerubbabel, saith the Lord; and be strong, O Joshua, son of Josedech, the high priest; and be strong, all ye people of the land, saith the Lord, and work: for I am with you, saith the Lord of hosts: according to the word that I covenanted with you when ye came out of Egypt, so my spirit remaineth among you: fear ye not— Haggai 2:4, 5.

S atan is always doing his utmost to stay the work of God. He hindered these Jews from building the temple; and today he endeavors to hinder the people of God from spreading the gospel. A spiritual temple is to be built for the Most High, and if by any means the evil one can delay its uprising he will stick at nothing: if he can take us off from working with faith and courage for the glory of God, he will be sure to do it. He is very cunning, and knows how to change his argument and yet keep to his design: little cares he how he works, so long as he can hurt the cause of God.

In the case of the Jewish people on their return from captivity he sought to prevent the building of the temple by making them selfish and worldly, so that every man was eager to build his own house and cared nothing for the house of the Lord. Each family

305

pleaded its own urgent needs. In returning to a long-deserted and neglected land, much had to be done to make up for lost time; and to provide suitably for itself every family needed all its exertions. They carried this thrift and self-providing to a great extreme and secured for themselves luxuries, while the foundations of the temple which had been laid years before remained as they were, or became still more thickly covered up with rubbish. The people could not be made to bestir themselves to build a house of God, for they answered to every exhortation, "The time is not come, the time that the Lord's house should be built." A more convenient season was always looming in the future, but it never came. Just now it was too hot, further on it was too cold; at one time the wet season was just setting in and it was of no use to begin, and soon after the fair weather required that they should be in their own fields. Like some in our day, they saw to themselves first, and God's turn was very long in coming; hence the prophet cried, "Is it time for you, O ye, to dwell in your ceiled houses, and this house lie waste?"

By the mouth of his servant Haggai stern rebukes were uttered, and the whole people were aroused. We read in verse twelve of the first chapter, "Then Zerubbabel the son of Shealtiel, and Joshua the son of Josedech, the high priest, with all the remnant of the people, obeyed the voice of the Lord their God, and the words of Haggai the prophet, as the Lord their God had sent him, and the people did fear before the Lord." All hands were put to the work; course after course of stone began to rise; and then another stumbling-block was thrown in the way of the workers. The older folks remarked that this was a very small affair compared with the temple of Solomon, of which their fathers had told them; in fact, their rising building was nothing at all, and not worthy to be called a temple.

The prophet describes the feeling in the verse which precedes our text. "Who is left among you that saw this house in her first glory?And how do ye see it now? Is it not in your eyes in comparison of it as nothing?" Feeling that their work would be very poor and insignificant, the people had little heart to go on. Being discouraged by the humiliating contrast, they began to be slack; and as they were quite willing to accept any excuse, and here was an excuse ready made for them, they would soon have been at a stand-still had not the prophet met the wiles of the arch-enemy with an-other word from the Lord. Nothing so confounds the evil one as the voice of the Eternal. Our Lord himself defeated Satan by the word of the Lord; and the prophet Haggai did the same. Twice the voice was heard—*"I am with you, saith the Lord of hosts."* They were also assured that what they built was accepted, and that the Lord meant to fill the new house with glory; yea, He meant to light it up with a glory greater than that which honored the temple of Solomon. They were not spending their strength for naught, but were laboring with divine help and favor. Thus they were encour-aged to put their shoulders to the work: the walls rose in due order, and God was glorified in the building up of His Zion.

The present times are, in many respects, similar to those of Hag-gai. History certainly repeats itself within the church of God as well as outside of it; and therefore the messages of God need to be re-peated also. The words of some almost-forgotten prophet may be re-delivered by the watchman of the Lord in these present days, and be a timely word for the present emergency. We are not free from the worldliness which put self first and God nowhere, else our var-ious enterprises would be more abundantly supplied with the sil-ver and the gold which are the Lord's, but which even professing Christians reserve for themselves. When this selfish greed is con-quered, then comes in a timorous depression. Among those who have escaped from worldliness there is apt to be too much despon-dency, and men labor feebly as for a cause which is doomed to fail-ure. This last evil must be cured. I pray that our text may this morning flame from the Lord's own mouth with all the fire which once blazed about it. May faint heart be encouraged and drowsy spirits be aroused, as we hear the Lord say, *"My spirit remaineth among you: fear ye not."*

I shall enter fully upon the subject, by the assistance of the Holy Spirit, by calling your attention to *discouragement forbidden.* Then I shall speak of *encouragement imparted;* and, having done so, I shall linger with this blessed text which overflows with comfort, and shall speak, in the third place, of *encouragement further applied.*

Oh that our Lord, who knows how to speak a word in season to him that is weary, may cheer the hearts of seekers by what shall be spoken under this last head of discourse!

I. To begin with, here is DISCOURAGEMENT FORBIDDEN. Discouragement comes readily enough to us poor mortals who are occupied in the work of God, seeing it is a work of faith, a work of difficulty, a work above our capacity, and a work much opposed.

Discouragement is very natural: it is a native of the soil of manhood. To believe is supernatural, faith is the work of the Spirit of God; to doubt is natural to fallen men; for we have within us an evil heart of unbelief. It is abominably wicked, I grant you, but still it is natural, because of the downward tendency of our depraved hearts.

Discouragement may come and does come to us, as it did to these people, from a consideration of the great things which God deserves at our hands, and the small things which we are able to render. When in Haggai's days the people thought of Jehovah, and of a temple for Him, and then looked upon the narrow space which had been enclosed, and the common stones which had been laid for foundations, they were ashamed. Where were those hewn stones and costly stones which, of old, Solomon brought from far? They said within themselves, "This house is unworthy of Jehovah: what do we by laboring thus?" Have you not felt the depressing weight of what is so surely true? Brethren, all that we do is little for our God; far too little for Him that loved us and gave Himself for us. For Him that poured out His soul unto death on our behalf the most splendid service, the most heroic self-denial, are all too little; and we feel it is so. Alabaster boxes of precious ointment are too mean a gift. When we have done our utmost in declaring the glory of Jesus, we have felt that words are too poor and mean to set before our adorable Lord.

When we have prayed for His kingdom, we have been disgusted with our own prayers; and all the efforts we have put forth in connection with any part of His service have seemed too few, too feeble for us to hope for acceptance. Thus have we been discouraged. The enemy has worked upon us by this means, yet he has made us argue very wrongly. Because we could not do much, we have half resolved to do nothing! Because what we did was so poor, we were inclined to quit the work altogether! This is evidently absurd and wicked. The enemy can use humility for his purpose as well as pride. Whether he makes us think too much or too little of our work, it is all the same so long as he can get us off from it.

It is significant that the man with one talent went and hid his Lord's money in the earth. He knew that it was but one, and for that reason he was less afraid to bury it. Perhaps he argued that the interest on one talent could never come to much, and would never be noticed side by side with the result of five or ten talents; and he might as well bring nothing at all to his Lord as bring so little. Perhaps he might not have wrapped it up if it had not been so small that a napkin could cover it. The smallness of our gifts may be a temptation to us. We are consciously so weak and so insignificant, compared with the great God and His great cause, that we are discouraged, and think it vain to attempt anything.

Moreover, the enemy contrasts our work with that of others and with that of those who have gone before us. We are doing so little as compared with other people, therefore let us give up. We cannot build like Solomon, therefore let us not build at all. Yet, brethren, there is a falsehood in all this; for, in truth, nothing is worthy of God. The great works of others, and even the amazing productions of Solomon, all fell short of His glory. What house could man build for God? What are cedar, and marble, and gold as compared with the glory of the Most High? Though the house was "exceeding magnifical," yet the Lord God has of old dwelt within curtains, and never was His worship more glorious than within the tent of badgers' skins; indeed, as soon as the great house was built, true religion declined. What of all human work can be worthy of the Lord? Our little labors do but share the insignificance of greater things, and therefore we ought not to withhold them: yet here is the temptation from which we must pray to be delivered.

The tendency to depreciate the present because of the glories of the past is also injurious. The old people looked back to the days of the former temple, even as we are apt to look upon the times of the great preachers of the past. What work was done in those past days! What Sabbaths were enjoyed then! What converts were added to the church! What days of refreshing were then vouchsafed! Everything had declined, decreased, degenerated!

But, brethren, we must not allow this sense of littleness to hamper us; for God can bless our littleness, and use it for His glory. I notice that the great men of the past thought of themselves even as we think of ourselves. Certainly they were not more self-confident than we are. Let us throw our heart and soul into the work of the Lord, and yet do something more nearly in accordance with our highest ideal of what our God deserves of us. Let us excel our ancestors. Let us aspire to be even more godly, more conscientious, and more sound in the faith than they were, for the Spirit of God remaineth with us.

Wherever discouragement comes in it is dreadfully weakening. I am sure it is weakening, because the prophet was bidden to say three times to the governor, high priest, and people, "Be strong." This proves that they had become weak. Being discouraged, their hands hung down, and their knees were feeble. Faith girds us with omnipotence, but unbelief makes everything hang loose and limp about us. Distrust, and thou wilt fail in everything; believe and according to thy faith so shall it be unto thee. To lend a discouraged people to the Holy War is a difficult as for Xerxes' commanders to conduct the Persian troops to battle against the Greeks. The vassals of the great king were driven to the conflicts by whips and sticks, for they were afraid to fight: do you wonder that they were defeated? A church that needs constant exhorting and compelling accomplishes nothing. The Greeks had no need of blows and threats, for each man was a lion, and courted the encounter, however great the odds against him. Each Spartan fought *con amore*; he was never more at home than when contending for the altars and the hearths of his country. We want Christian men of this same sort, who have faith in their principles, faith in the doctrines of grace, faith in God the Father, God the Son, and God the Holy Ghost; and who therefore contend earnestly for the faith in these days when piety is mocked at from the pulpit, and the gospel is sneered at by professional preachers. We need men who love the truth, to whom it is dear as their lives; men into whose hearts the old doctrine is burned by the hand of God's Spirit through a deep experience of its necessity and of its power. We need no more of those who will parrot what they are taught, but we want men who will speak what they know. Oh, for a troop of men like John Knox, heroes of the martyr and covenanter stock! Then would Jehovah of hosts have a people to serve Him who would be strong in the Lord and in the power of His might.

Discouragement not only weakens men, but *it takes them off from the service of God*. It is significant that the prophet said to them, "Be strong, all ye people of the land, saith the Lord, *and work*." They had ceased to build: they had begun to talk and argue, but they had laid down the trowel. They were extremely wise in their observations, and criticisms, and prophecies, but the walls did not rise. It is always so when we are discouraged: we cease from the work of the Lord, and waste time in talk and nonsensical refinements. May the Lord take away discouragement from any of you who now suffer from it! I suppose some of you feel it, for at times it creeps over my heart and makes men to with heaviness to my work. I believe that God's truth will come to the front yet, but it hath many adversaries today. All sorts of unbeliefs are being hatched out from under the wings of "modern thought." The gospel seems to be regarded as a nose of wax, to be altered and shaped by every man who wishes to show his superior skill. Nor is it in doctrine alone, but in practice also, that the times are out of joint. Separateness from the world, and holy living, are to give place to gaiety and theater-going. To follow Christ fully has gone out of fashion with many of those from whom we once hoped better things. Yet are there some who waver not, some who are willing to be in the right with two or three. Blessed is the man who shall be able to stand fast by his God in these evil days. Let us not in any wise be discouraged. "Be strong; be strong; be strong," sounds as a threefold voice from the triune God. "Fear not" comes as a sweet cordial to the faint: therefore let no man's heart fail him. Thus much about the discouragement.

II. Secondly, here is THE ENCOURAGEMENT IMPARTED, which is the grand part of our text. "According to the word that I covenanted with you when ye came out of Egypt, so my spirit remaineth among you: fear ye not." God remembers His covenant and stands to His ancient promises. When the people came out of Egypt the Lord was with them by His Spirit: hence He spoke to them by Moses, and through Moses He guided, and judged, and taught them. He was with them also by His Spirit in inspiring Bezaleel and Aholiab, as to the works of art which adorned the tabernacle. God always finds workmen for his work, and by His Spirit fits them for it. The Spirit of God rested upon the elders who were ordained to relieve Moses of his great burden.

The Lord was also with His people in the fiery cloudy pillar which was conspicuous in the midst of the camp. His presence was their glory and their defense. This is a type of the presence of the Spirit with the church. At the present day, if we hold the truth of God, if we live in obedience to His holy commands, if we are spiritually-minded, if we cry unto God in believing prayer, if we have faith in His covenant and in His Son, the Holy Spirit abideth among us. The Holy Ghost descended upon the church at Pentecost, and He has never gone back again: there is no record of the Spirit's return to heaven. He will abide with the true church evermore. This is our hope for the present struggle. The Spirit of God remaineth with us.

To *what end*, my brethren, is this Spirit with us? Let us think of this, that we may be encouraged at this time. The Spirit of God remaineth among you *to aid and assist the ministry which He has already given*. Oh, that the prayers of God's people would always go up for God's ministers, that they may speak with a divine power and influence which none shall be able to gainsay! We look too much for clever men; we seek out fluent and flowery speakers; we sigh for men cultured and trained in all the knowledge of the heathen: nay, but if we sought more for unction, for divine authority, and for that power which doth hedge about the man of God, how much wiser should we be! Oh, that all of us who profess to preach the gospel would learn to speak in entire dependence upon the direction of the Holy Spirit, not daring to utter our own words, but even trembling lest we should do so, and committing ourselves to that secret influence without which nothing will be powerful upon the conscience or converting to the heart.

Know ye not the difference between the power that cometh of human oratory, and that which cometh by the divine energy which speaks so to the heart that men cannot resist it? We have forgotten this too much. It were better to speak six words in the power of the Holy Ghost than to preach seventy years of sermons without the Spirit. He who rested on those who have gone to their reward in heaven can rest this day upon our ministers and bless our evangelists, if we will but seek it of Him. Let us cease to grieve the Spirit of God, and look to Him for help to the faithful ministers who are yet spared to us.

This same Spirit who of old gave to His church eminent teachers *can raise up other and more useful men.* The other day, a brother from Wales told me of the great men he remembered: he said that he had never heard such a one as Christmas Evans, who surpassed all men when he was in the *hwyl.* I asked him if he knew another Welsh minister who preached like Christmas Evans. "No," he said, "we have no such man in Wales in our days." So in England we have neither Wesley nor Whitefield, nor any of their order; yet, as with God is the residue of the Spirit, He can fetch out from some chimney-corner another Christmas Evans, or find in our Sunday school another George Whitefield, who shall declare the gospel with the Holy Ghost sent down from heaven. Let us never fear for the future, to despair for the present, since the Spirit of God remaineth with us. What if the growing error of the age should have silenced the last tongue that speaks out the old gospel, let not faith be weakened. I hear the tramp of legions of soldiers of the cross. I hear the clarion voices of hosts of preachers. "The Lord gave the word; great was the company of those that published it." Have faith in God through our Lord Jesus Christ! When He ascended on high He led captivity captive, and received gifts for men. He then gave apostles, teachers, preachers and evangelists, and He can do the like again. Let us fall back upon the eternal God, and never be discouraged for an instant.

Nor is this all. The Holy Spirit being with us, *He can move the whole church to exercise its varied ministries.* This is one of the things we want very much—that every member of the church should recognize that he is ordained to service. Everyone in Christ, man or woman, hath some testimony to bear, some warning to give, some deed to do in the name of the holy child Jesus; and if the Spirit of God be poured out upon our young men and our maidens, each one will be aroused to energetic service. Both small and great will be in earnest, and the result upon the slumbering masses of our population will surprise us all. Sometimes we lament that the churches are so dull. There is an old proverb which says of So-and-so, that he was "as sound asleep as a church." I suppose there is nothing that can sleep so soundly as a church. But yet the Spirit of God still remaineth, and therefore churches go to be awakened. I mean that not only in part but as a whole, a church may be quickened. The dullest professor, the most slovenly believer, the most captious and useless member of a church, may yet be turned to good account. I see them like a stack of sticks, piled up, dead, and dry. Oh for the fire! We will have a blaze out of them yet.

Come, Holy Spirit, heavenly Dove, brood over the dark, disordered church as once Thou didst over chaos, and order shall come out of confusion, and the darkness shall fly before the light. Only let the Spirit be with us, and we have all that is wanted for victory. Give us His presence, and everything else will come in its due season for the profitable service of the entire church.

If the Spirit be with us, there will come multitudinous conversions. We cannot get at "the lapsed masses," as they are pedantically called. We cannot stir the crass infidelity of the present age: no, *we* cannot, but *He* can. All things are possible with God. If you walk down to our bridges at a certain hour of the day you will see barges and vessels lying in the mud; and all the king's horses and all the king's men cannot stir them. Wait until the tide comes in, and they will walk the water like things of life. The living flood accomplishes at once what no mortals can do. And so today our churches cannot stir. What shall we do? Oh, that the Holy Spirit would come with a flood-tide of His benign influences, as He will if we will but believe in Him; as He must if we will but cry unto Him; as He shall if we will cease to grieve Him. Everything will be even as the saints desire when the Lord of saints is with us. The hope of the continuance and increase of the church lies in the remaining of the Spirit with us. The hope of the salvation of London lies in the wonder-working Spirit. Let us bow our heads and worship the omnipotent Spirit who deigns to work in us, by us, and with us.

Then, brethren, if this should happen — and I see not why it should not — then we may expect to see *the church put on her beautiful garments*; then shall she begin to clear herself of the errors which now defile her; then shall she press to her bosom the truths which she now begins to forget; then will she go back to the pure fount of inspiration and drink from the Scriptures of truth; and then out of the midst of her shall flow no turbid streams, but rivers of living water. If the Holy Ghost will work among us we shall rejoice in the Lord, and glory in the name of our God.

When once the Spirit of God putteth forth His might all things else will be in accord with Him. Notice that in the rest of the chapter — which I shall read now, not as relating to that temple at all, but to the church of God — there is great comfort given to us. If the Holy Spirit be once given, then we may expect providence to cooperate with the church of God. Read verse 6: "Yet once, it is a little while, and I will shake heaven and the earth, and the sea, and the dry land. I will shake all nations." Great commotions will cooperate with the Holy Spirit. We may expect that God will work for His people in an extraordinary fashion if they will but be faithful to Him. Empires will collapse, and times will change, for the truth's sake. Expect the unexpected, reckon upon that which is unlikely, if it be necessary for the growth of the kingdom. Of old the earth helped the woman when the dragon opened his mouth to drown her with the floods that he cast forth: unexpected help shall come to us when affairs are at their worst.

And next, the Lord in this chapter promises His people that they shall have all the supplies they need for His work. They feared that they could not build His house, because of their poverty, but, saith the Lord of hosts, "The silver and the gold are mine." When the church of God believes in God, and goes forward bravely, she need not trouble as to supplies. Her God will provide for her. He that gives the Holy Ghost will give gold and silver according as they are needed; therefore, let us be of good courage. If God is with us, why need we fear? One of our English kings once threatened the great city of London that if its councilors talked so independently, he would—yes—he would, indeed he would—take his court away from the city. The Lord Mayor on that occasion replied, that if his majesty would graciously leave the river Thames behind him, the citizens would try to get on without his court. If any say, "If you hold to these old-fashioned doctrines you will lose the educated, the wealthy, the influential," we answer: But if we do not lose the godly and the presence of the Holy Ghost we are not in the least alarmed. If the Holy Ghost remaineth with us, there is a river the streams whereof make glad the city of God. Brethren, my heart leaps within me as I cry, "The Lord of hosts is with us; the God of Jacob is our refuge." "Therefore will we not fear, though the earth be removed, and though the mountains be carried unto the midst of the sea."

The best comfort of all remained: "The desire of all nations shall come." This was in a measure fulfilled when Jesus came into that latter house and caused all holy hearts to sing for gladness, but it was not wholly fulfilled in that way; for if you notice in the ninth verse it is written, "The glory of this latter house shall be greater than of the former; *and in this place will I give peace,*" which the Lord did not fully do to the second temple, since that was destroyed by the Romans. But there is another advent, when "the desire of all nations shall come" in power and glory; and this is our highest hope. Though truth may be driven back, and error may prevail, Jesus comes, and He is the great Lord and patron of truth: He shall judge the world in righteousness, and the people in equity. Here is our last resource; here are God's reserves. He whom we serve liveth and reigneth forever and ever; and He saith, "Behold, I come quickly; and my reward is with me, to give every man according as his work shall be." "Therefore, my beloved brethren, be ye steadfast, unmoveable, always abounding in the work of the Lord, foras-much as ye know that your labor is not in vain in the Lord."

III. I should have done if it had not been that this text seemed to me to overflow so much, that it might not only refresh God's people, but give drink to thirsty sinners who are seeking the Lord. For a moment or two I give myself to ENCOURAGEMENT FURTHER APPLIED.

It is at the beginning of every gracious purpose that men have most fear, even as these people had who had newly begun to build. When first the Holy Spirit begins to strive with a man and to lead him to Jesus, he is apt to say—"I cannot; I dare not; it is impossible. How can I believe and live?" Now I want to speak to some of you here who are willing to find Christ, and to encourage you by the truth that the Spirit lives to help you. I would even like to speak to those who are *not* anxious to be saved. I remember that Dr. Payson, an exceedingly earnest and useful man of God, once did a singular thing. He had been holding inquiry meetings with all sorts of people, and great numbers had been saved. At last, one Sunday he gave out that he should have a meeting on Monday night of those persons who did not desire to be saved; and, strange to say, some twenty persons came who did not wish to repent or believe. He spoke to them and said, "I am sure that if a little film, thin as the web of the gossamer, were let down by God from heaven to each one of you, you would not push it away from you. Although it were almost invisible, you would value even the slightest connection between you and heaven. Now, your coming to meet me tonight is a little link with God. I want it to increase in strength till you are joined to the Lord forever." He spoke to them most tenderly, and God blessed those people who did not desire to be saved, so that before the meeting was over they were of another mind. The film had become a thicker thread, and it grew and grew until the Lord Christ held them by it forever.

Dear friends, the fact of your being in the Tabernacle this morning is like that filmy thread: do not put it away. Here is your comfort, the Holy Spirit still works with the preaching of the word. Do

I hear you say, "I cannot feel my need of Christ as I want to feel it?" The Spirit remaineth among us. He can make you feel more deeply the guilt of sin and your need of pardon. "But I have heard so much about conviction and repentance; I do not seem to have either of them." Yet the Spirit remaineth with us, and that Spirit is able to work in you the deepest conviction and the truest repentance. "O sir, I do not feel as if I could do anything": but the Spirit remaineth with us, and all things that are needful for godliness He can give. He can work in you to will and to do of His own good pleasure. "But I want to believe in the Lord Jesus Christ unto eternal life." Who made you want to do that? Who but the Holy Spirit? Therefore He is still at work with you; and though as yet you do not understand what believing is, or else I am persuaded you would believe at once, the Spirit of God can instruct you in it. You are blind, but He can give you sight; you are paralyzed, but He can give you strength—the Spirit of God remaineth.

"Oh, but that doctrine of regeneration staggers me: you know, we must be born again." Yes, we are born again of the Spirit, and the Spirit remaineth still with us; He is still mighty to work that wondrous change, and to bring you out of the kingdom of Satan into the kingdom of God's dear Son. The Spirit remaineth with us, blessed be His name! "Ah, dear sir," says one, "I want to conquer sin!" Who made you desire to conquer sin? Who, but the Spirit that remaineth with us? He will give you the sword of the Spirit and teach you how to use it, and He will give you both the will and the power to use it successfully. Through the Spirit's might you can overcome every sin, even that which has dragged you down and disgraced you. The Spirit of God is still waiting to help you. When I think of the power of the Spirit of God, I look hopefully upon every sinner here this morning. I bless His name that He can work in you all that is pleasing in His sight. Some of your may be very careless but He can make you thoughtful. Coming up to London to see the Exhibition, I hope you may yourselves become an exhibition of divine grace. You think not about things, but He can make you feel at this moment a sweet softness stealing over you, until you long to be alone and to get home to the old armchair and there seek the Lord. You can thus be led to salvation.

I thought when I came in here that I should have a picked congregation; and so I have. You are one of them. Wherever you come from, I want you now to seek the Lord. He has brought you here, and He means to bless you. Yield yourselves to Him while His sweet Spirit pleads with you. While the heavenly wind softly blows upon you open wide every window. You have not felt that you wanted it, but that is the sure proof that you need it; for he that does not know his need of Christ, is most in need. Open wide your heart that the Spirit may teach you your need; above all, breathe the prayer that He would help you this morning to look to the Lord Jesus Christ, for "there is life in a look at the Crucified One—there is life at this moment for you."

"Oh," you say, "if I were to begin I should not keep on." No; if *you* began perhaps you would not, but if *He* begins with you *He* will keep on. The final perseverance of saints is the result of the final perseverance of the Holy Spirit; He perseveres to bless, and we persevere in receiving the blessing. If He begins, you have begun with a divine power that fainteth not neither is weary. I wish it might so happen that on this fifth day of the ninth month, not the prophet Haggai, but I, God's servant, may have spoken to you such a word as you shall never forget; and may the Lord add to the word, by the witness of the Holy Ghost, "From this day will I bless you!" Go away with that promise resting upon you. I would like to give a shake of the hand to every stranger here this morning, and say, "Brother, in the name of the Lord I wish you from this day a blessing." Amen and amen.

11

The Covenant Promise of the Spirit

And I will put my spirit within you—Ezekiel 36:27.

No preface is needed; and the largeness of our subject forbids our wasting time in beating about the bush. I shall try to do two things this morning: first, I would *commend the text*; and secondly, I would in some measure *expound the text.*

I. First, as for THE COMMENDATION OF THE TEXT, the tongues of men and of angels might fail. To call it a golden sentence would be much too commonplace: to liken it to a pearl of great price would be too poor a comparison. We cannot feel, much less speak, too much in praise of the great God who has put this clause into the covenant of His grace. In that covenant every sentence is more precious than heaven and earth; and this line is not the least among His choice words of promise: "I will put my spirit within you."

I would begin by saying that *it is a gracious word.* It was spoken to a graceless people, to a people who had followed "their own way," and refused the way of God; a people who had already provoked something more than ordinary anger in the Judge of all the earth; for He Himself said (verse 18), "I poured my fury upon them." These people, even under chastisement, caused the holy name of God to be profaned among the heathen, whither they went. They had been highly favored, but they abused their privileges, and behaved worse than those who never knew the Lord. They sinned wantonly, willfully, wickedly, proudly and presumptuously; and by this they greatly provoked the Lord. Yet to them He made such a promise as this—"I will put my spirit within you." Surely, where sin abounded grace did much more abound.

Clearly this is a word of grace, for the law saith nothing of this kind. Turn to the law of Moses, and see if there be any word spoken therein concerning the putting of the Spirit within men to cause them to walk in God's statutes. The law proclaims the statutes, but the gospel alone promises the spirit by which the statutes will be obeyed. The law commands and makes us know what God requires of us, but the gospel goes further, and inclines us to obey the will of the Lord, and enables us to walk in His ways practically. Under the dominion of grace the Lord worketh in us to will and to do of His own good pleasure.

So great a boon as this could never come to any man by merit. A man might so act as to deserve a reward of a certain kind, in measure suited to His commendable action, but the Holy Spirit can never be the wage of human service: the idea verges upon blasphemy. Can any man deserve that Christ should die for him? Who would dream of such a thing? Can any man deserve that the Holy Ghost should dwell in him, and work holiness in him? The greatness of the blessing lifts it high above the range of merit, and we see that if the Holy Ghost be bestowed, it must be by an act of divine grace—grace infinite in bounty, exceeding all that we could have imagined. "Sovereign grace o'er sin abounding" is here seen in clearest light. "I will put my spirit within you" is a promise which drops with graces as the honeycomb with honey. Listen to the divine music which pours from this word of love. I hear the soft melody of grace, grace, grace, and nothing else but grace. Glory be to God, who gives to sinners the indwelling of His Spirit.

Note, next, that *it is a divine word:* "I will put my spirit within you." Who but the Lord could speak after this fashion? Can one man put the Spirit of God within another? Could all the church combined breathe the Spirit of God into a single sinner's heart? To put any good thing into the deceitful heart of man is a great achievement, but to put the Spirit of God into the heart, truly this is the finger of God. Nay, here I may say, the Lord has made bare His arm, and displayed the fullness of His mighty power. To put the Spirit of God into our nature is a work peculiar to the Godhead, and to do this within the nature of a free agent, such as man, is marvelous. Who but Jehovah, the God of Israel, can speak after this royal style, and, beyond all dispute, declare, "I will put my spirit within you?" Men must always surround their resolves with conditions and uncertainties, but since omnipotence is at the back of every promise of God, He speaks like a king; yea, in a style which is only fit for the eternal God. He purposes and promises, and He as surely performs. Sure, then, is this sacred saying, "I will put my spirit within you." Sure, because divine.

O sinner, if we poor creatures had to save of you, we should break down in the attempt, but, behold the Lord Himself comes on the scene, and the work is done! All the difficulties are removed by this one sentence, "I will put my spirit within you." We have wrought with our spirit, we have wept over you, and we have entreated you, but we have failed. Lo, there cometh One into the matter who will not fail, with whom nothing is impossible; and He begins His work by saying, "I will put my spirit within you." The word is of grace and of God; regard it, then, as a pledge from the God of grace.

To me there is much charm in the further thought that *this is an individual and personal word.* The Lord means, "I will put my spirit within you": that is to say, within *you*, as individuals. "I will put my spirit within you" one by one. This must be so since the connection requires it. We read in verse 26, "A new heart also will I give you." Now, a new heart can only be given to one person. Each man needs a heart of his own, and each man must have a new heart for himself. "And a new spirit will I put within you." Within each one this must be done. "And I will take away the stony heart out of your flesh, and I will give you a heart of flesh"—these are all personal, individual operations of grace. God deals with men one by one in the solemn matters of eternity, sin, and salvation. We are born one by one, and we die one by one: even so we must be born again one by one, and each one for himself must receive the Spirit of God Without this a man has nothing. He cannot be caused to walk in God's statutes except by the infusion of grace into him as an individual. I think I see among my hearers a lone man, or woman, who feels himself, or herself, to be all alone in the world, and therefore hopeless. You can believe that God will do great things for a nation, but how shall the solitary be thought of? You are an odd person, one that could not be written down in any list; peculiar sinner, with constitutional tendencies all your own. Thus saith God, "I will put my spirit within you"; within *your* heart—even *yours.*

My dear hearers, you who have long been seeking salvation, but have not known the power of the Spirit—this is what you need. You have been striving in the energy of the flesh, but you have not understood where your true strength lieth. God saith to you "Not by might, nor by power, but by my Spirit, saith the Lord"; and again, "I will put my spirit within you." Oh, that this word might be spoken of the Lord to that young man who is ready to despair; to that sorrowful woman who has been looking into herself for power to pray and believe! You are without strength or hope in and of yourself, but this meets your case in all points. "I will put my spirit within you"—within *you* as an individual, Inquire of the Lord for it. Lift up your heart in prayer to God, and ask Him to pour upon you the Spirit of grace and of supplications. Plead with the Lord, saying, "Let thy good Spirit lead me. Even me." Cry, "Pass me not, my gracious Father, but in me fulfill this wondrous word of thine, 'I will put my spirit within you.'"

Note, next, that *this is a separating word.* I do not know whether you will see this readily, but it must be so: this word separates a man from his fellows. Men by nature are of another spirit from that of God, and they are under subjection to that evil spirit, the Prince of the power of the air. When the Lord comes to gather out His own, fetching them out from among the heathen, He effects the separation by doing according to this word, "I will put my spirit within you." This done, the individual becomes a new man. Those who have the Spirit are not of the world, nor like the world; and they soon have to come out from among the ungodly, and to be separate; for difference of nature creates conflict. God's Spirit will not dwell with the evil spirit: you cannot have fellowship with Christ and with Belial; with the kingdom of heaven and with this world.

I wish that the people of God would again wake up to the truth that to gather out a people from among men is the great purpose of the present dispensation. It is still true, as James said at the Jerusalem Council, "Simeon hath declared how God at the first did visit the Gentiles, to take out of them a people for his name." We are not to remain clinging to the old wreck with the expectation that we shall pump the water out of her and get her safe into port. No; the cry is very different—"Take to the lifeboat! Take to the lifeboat!" You are to quit the wreck, and then you are to carry away from the sinking mass that which God will save. You must be separate from the old wreck, lest it suck you down to sure destruction. Your only hope of doing good to the world is by yourselves being "not of the world," even as Christ was not of the world. For you to go down to the world's level will neither be good for it nor for you. That which happened in the days of Noah will be repeated; for when the sons of God entered into alliance with the daughters of men, and there was a league between the two races, the Lord could not endure the evil mixture, but drew up the sluices of the lower deep and swept the earth with a destroying flood.

Surely, in that last day of destruction, when the world is overwhelmed with fire, it will be because the church of God shall have degenerated, and the distinctions between the righteous and the wicked shall have been broken down. The Spirit of God, wherever He comes, doth speedily make and reveal the difference between Israel and Egypt; and in proportion as His active energy is felt, there will be an ever-widening gulf between those who are led of the Spirit and those who are under the dominion of the flesh. It is a separating word this. Has it separated you? Has the Holy Spirit called you alone and blessed you? Do you differ from your old companions? Have you a life they do not understand? If not, may God in mercy put into you that most heavenly deposit, of which He speaks in our text: "I will put my spirit within you"!

But now notice, that *it is a very uniting word*. It separates from the world, but it joins to God. Note how it runs: "I will put *my* Spirit within you." It is not merely *a* spirit, or *the* spirit, but My spirit. Now when God's own Spirit comes to reside within our mortal bodies, how near akin we are to the Most High! "Know ye not that your body is the temple of the Holy Ghost?" Does not this make a man sublime? Have you never stood in awe of your own selves, O ye believers? Have you enough regarded even this poor body, as being sanctified and dedicated, and elevated into a sacred condition, by being set apart to be the temple of the Holy Ghost? Thus are we brought into the closest union with God that we can well conceive of. Thus is the Lord our light and our life; while our spirit is subordinated to the divine Spirit. "I will put my spirit within you" — then God Himself dwelleth in you. The Spirit of Him that raised up Christ from the dead is in you. With Christ in God your life is hid, and the Spirit seals you, anoints you, and abides in you. By the Spirit we have access to the Father; by the Spirit we perceive our adoption, and learn to cry, "Abba, Father"; by the Spirit we are made partakers of the divine nature, and have communion with the thrice holy Lord.

I cannot help adding here that *it is a very condescending word* — "I will put my spirit within you." Is it really so, that the Spirit of God who displays the power and energetic force of God, by whom God's Word is carried into effect — that the Spirit who of old moved upon the face of the waters, and brought order and life from chaos and death — can it be so that He will deign to sojourn in men? God in our nature is a very wonderful conception! God in the babe at Bethlehem, God in the carpenter of Nazareth, God in the "man of sorrows," God in the Crucified, God in Him who was buried in the tomb — this is all marvelous.

The incarnation is an infinite mystery of love, but we believe it. Yet, if it were possible to compare one illimitable wonder with another, I should say that God's dwelling in His people and that repeated ten thousand times over, is more marvelous. That the Holy

Ghost should dwell in millions of redeemed men and women, is a miracle not surpassed by that of our Lord's espousal of human nature. For our Lord's body was perfectly pure, and the Godhead, while it dwells with His holy manhood, does at least dwell with a perfect and sinless nature, but the Holy Spirit bows Himself to dwell in sinful men; to dwell in men who, after their conversion, still find the flesh warring against the spirit, and the spirit against the flesh; men who are not perfect, though they strive to be so; men who have to lament their shortcomings, and even to confess with shame a measure of unbelief. "I will put my spirit within you" means the abiding of the Holy Spirit in our imperfect nature. Wonder of wonders! Yet is it as surely a fact as it is a wonder. Believers in the Lord Jesus Christ, you have the Spirit of God, for "if any man have not the Spirit of Christ, he is none of his." You could not bear the suspicion that you are not His; and therefore, as surely as you are Christ's, you have His Spirit abiding in you.

The Savior has gone away on purpose that the Comforter might be given to dwell in you, and He does dwell in you. Is it not so? If it be so, admire this condescending God, and worship and praise His name. Sweetly submit to His rule in all things. Grieve not the Spirit of God. Watch carefully that nothing comes within you that may defile the temple of God. Let the faintest monition of the Holy Spirit be law to you. It was a holy mystery that the presence of the Lord was specially within the veil of the Tabernacle, and that the Lord God spake by Urim and Thummim to His people; it is an equally sacred marvel that now the Holy Ghost dwells in our spirits and abides within our nature and speaks to us whatsoever He hears of the Father. By divine impressions which the opened ear can apprehend, and the tender heart can receive, He speaketh still. God grant us to know His still small voice so as to listen to it with reverent humility and loving joy: then shall we know the meaning of these words, "I will put my spirit within you."

Nor have I yet done with commending my text, for I must not fail to remind you that *it is a very spiritual word*. "I will put my spirit within you" has nothing to do with our wearing a peculiar garb—that would be a matter of little worth. It has nothing to do with affectations of speech—those might readily become a deceptive peculiarity. Our text has nothing to do with outward rites and ceremonies, but goes much further and deeper. It is an instructive symbol when the Lord teaches us our death with Christ by burial in baptism: it is to our great profit that He ordains bread and wine to be tokens of our communion in the body and blood of His dear Son, but these are only outward things, and if they are unattended with the Holy Spirit they fail of their design.

There is something infinitely greater in this promise—"I will put my spirit within you." I cannot give you the whole force of the Hebrew, as to the words "within you," unless I paraphrase them a little, and read "I will put my spirit in the midst of you." The sacred deposit is put deep down in our life's secret place. God puts His Spirit not upon the surface of the man, but into the center of his being. The promise means—"I will put my spirit in your bowels, in your hearts, in the very soul of you." This is an intensely spiritual matter, without admixturing of anything material and visible. It is spiritual, you see, because it is the Spirit that is given; and He is given internally within our spirit.

Observe once more that *this Word is a very effectual one.* "I will put my spirit within you, and cause you to walk in my statutes, and ye shall keep my judgments and do them." The Spirit is operative—first upon the inner life, in causing you to love the law of the Lord; and then it moves you openly to keep His statutes concerning Himself, and His judgments between you and your fellow-men. Obedience, if a man should be flogged to it, would be of little worth, but obedience springing out of a life within, this is a priceless breastplate of jewels. If you have a lantern, you cannot make it shine by polishing the glass outside, you must put a candle within it: and this is what God does, He puts the light of the Spirit within us, and then our light shines. He puts His Spirit so deep down into the heart, that the whole nature feels it: it works upward, like a spring from the bottom of a well. It is, moreover, so deeply implanted that there is no removing it. If it were in the memory, you might forget it; if it were in the intellect, you might err in it, but "within you" it touches the whole man, and has dominion over you without fear of failure.

When the very kernel of your nature is quickened into holiness, practical godliness is effectually secured. Blessed is he who knows by experience our Lord's words—"The water that I shall give him shall be in him a well of water springing up into everlasting life."

II. But now I must work upon THE EXPOSITION OF THE TEXT. I trust the Holy Spirit will aid me therein. Let me show you how the good Spirit manifests the fact that He dwells in men. I have to be very brief on a theme that might require a great length of time; and can only mention a part of His ways and workings.

One of the first effects of the Spirit of God being put within us is *quickening*. We are dead by nature to all heavenly and spiritual things, but when the Spirit of God comes, then we begin to live. The man visited of the Spirit begins to feel; the terrors of God make him tremble, the love of Christ makes him weep. He begins to fear, and he begins to hope: a great deal of the first and a very little of the second, it may be. He learns spiritually to sorrow: he is grieved that he has sinned, and that he cannot cease from sinning. He begins to desire that which once he despised: he especially desires to find the way of pardon, and reconciliation with God. Ah, dear hearers! I cannot make you feel, I cannot make you sorrow for sin, I cannot make you desire eternal life, but it is all done as soon as this is fulfilled by the Lord, "I will put my spirit within you." The quickening Spirit brings life to the dead in trespasses and sins.

This life of the Spirit shows itself by causing the man to pray. The cry is the distinctive mark of the living child. He begins to cry in broken accents, "God be merciful to me." At the same time that he pleads, he feels the soft relentings of repentance. He has a new mind towards sin, and he grieves that he should have grieved his God. With this comes faith; perhaps feeble and trembling, only a touch of the hem of the Savior's robe, but still Jesus is his only hope and his sole trust. To Him he looks for pardon and salvation. He dares to believe that Christ can save even him. Then has life come into the soul when trust in Jesus springs up in the heart.

Remember, dear friends, that as the Holy Spirit gives quickening at the first, so He must revive and strengthen it. Whenever you become dull and faint, cry for the Holy Spirit. Whenever you cannot feel in devotion as you wish to feel, and are unable to rise to any heights of communion with God, plead my text in faith, and beg the Lord to do as He hath said, namely, "I will put my spirit within you." Go to God with this covenant clause, even if you have to confess, "Lord, I am like a log, I am a helpless lump of weakness. Unless thou come and quicken me I cannot live to Thee." Plead importunately the promise, "I will put my spirit within you." All the life of the flesh will gender corruption; all the energy that comes of mere excitement will die down into the black ashes of disappointment; the Holy Ghost alone is the life of the regenerated heart. Have you the Spirit? And if you have Him within you, have you only a small measure of His life, and do you wish for more? Then go still where you went at first. There is only one river of the water of life: draw from its floods. You will be lively enough, and bright enough, and strong enough, and happy enough when the Holy Spirit is mighty within your soul. AMEN

When the Holy Spirit enters, after quickening He gives *enlightening*. We cannot make men see the truth, they are so blind, but when the Lord puts His Spirit within them their eyes are opened. At first they may see rather hazily, but still they do see. As the light increases, and the eye is strengthened, they see more and more clearly. What a mercy it is to see Christ, to look unto Him, and so to be lightened! By the Spirit, souls see things in their reality: they see the actual truth of them, and perceive that they are facts. The Spirit of God illuminates every believer, so that he sees still more marvelous things out of God's law, but this never happens unless the Spirit opens his eyes. The apostle speaks of being brought "out of darkness into His marvelous light"; and it is a marvelous light, indeed, to come to the blind and dead. Marvelous because it reveals truth with clearness. When you get into a puzzle over the Word of the Lord, do not give up in despair, but believingly cry, "Lord, put thy Spirit within me." Here lies the only true light of the soul.

The Spirit also works *conviction*. Conviction is more forcible than illumination: it is the setting of a truth before the eye of the soul, so as to make it powerful upon the conscience. I speak to many here who know what conviction means; still I will explain it from my own experience. I knew what sin meant by my reading, and yet I never knew sin in its heinousness and horror, till I found myself bitten by it as by a fiery serpent, and felt its poison boiling in my veins. When the Holy Ghost made sin to appear sin, then was I overwhelmed with the sight, and I would fain have fled from myself to escape the intolerable vision. A naked sin stripped of all excuse, and set in the light of truth, is a worse sight than to see the devil himself. When I saw sin as an offense against a just and holy God, committed by such a proud and yet insignificant creature as myself, then was I alarmed. Sirs, did you ever see and feel yourselves to be sinners? "Oh, yes," you say, "we are sinners." O sirs, do you mean it? Do you know what it means? The beggar who exhibits a sham sore knows not disease; if he did he would have enough of it without pretenses. To kneel down and say, "Lord, have mercy upon us miserable sinners," and then to get up and feel yourself a very decent sort of body, worthy of commendation, is to mock Almighty God. It is by no means a common thing to get hold of a real sinner, one who is truly so in his own esteem; and it is as pleasant as it is rare, for you can bring to the real sinner the real Savior, and He will welcome him. I do not wonder that Hart said:

> A sinner is a sacred thing,
> The Holy Ghost hath made him so.

The point of contact between a sinner and Christ is sin. The Lord Jesus gave Himself for our sins, He never gave Himself for our righteousnesses. He comes to heal the sick, and the point He looks to is our sickness. No one ever knows sin as his own personal ruin till the Holy Spirit shows it to him. Conviction as to the Lord Jesus comes in the same way. We do not know Christ as our Savior till the Holy Spirit is put within us. Our Lord says—"He shall receive of mine, and shall show it unto you," and you never see the things of the Lord Jesus till the Holy Ghost shows them to you. To know Jesus Christ as your Savior, as one who died *for you* in particular, is a knowledge which only the Holy Spirit imparts. To apprehend present salvation,

as your own personally, comes by your being convinced of it by the
Spirit. Oh, to be convinced of righteousness, and convinced of acceptance in the Beloved! This conviction cometh only of Him that
hath called you, even of Him of whom the Lord saith, "I will put
my Spirit within you."

Furthermore, the Holy Spirit comes into us for *purification.* "I
will put my spirit within you, and cause you to walk in my statutes,
and ye shall keep my judgments, and do them." When the Spirit
comes, He infuses a new life, and that new life is a fountain of holiness. The new nature cannot sin, because it is born of God, and
"it is a living and incorruptible seed." This life produces good fruit,
and good fruit only. The Holy Ghost is the life of holiness. At the
same time, the coming of the Holy Ghost into the soul gives a mortal stab to the power of sin. The old man is not absolutely dead, but
it is crucified with Christ. It is under sentence, and before the eye of
the law it is dead, but as a man nailed to a cross may linger long,
but yet he cannot live, so the power of evil dies hard, but die it
must. Sin is an executed criminal: those nails which fasten it to the
cross will hold it fast till no breath remains in it. God the Holy
Ghost gives the power of sin its death wound. The old nature strug-
gles in its dying agonies, but it is doomed, and die it must.

But you never will overcome sin by your own power, nor by any
energy short of that of the Holy Spirit. Resolves may bind it, as Samson was bound with cords, but sin will snap the cords asunder. The
Holy Spirit lays the ax at the root of sin, and fall it must. The Holy
Ghost within a man is "the Spirit of judgment, the Spirit of burning." Do you know Him in that character? As the Spirit of judgment, the Holy Spirit pronounces sentence on sin, and it goes out
with the brand of Cain upon it. He does more: He delivers sin over
to burning. He executes the death penalty on that which He has
judged. How many of our sins have we had to burn alive! And it has
cost us no small pain to do it. Sin must be got out of us by fire, if no
gentler means will serve; and the Spirit of God is a consuming fire.
Truly, "our God is a consuming fire." They paraphrase it, "God out
of Christ is a consuming fire," but that is not Scripture: it is, "*our*
God," our covenant God, who is a consuming fire to refine us from

sin. Has not the Lord said, "I will purely purge away all thy dross, and take away all thy sin"? This is what the Spirit does, and it is by no means easy work for the flesh, which would spare many a flattering sin if it could.

The Holy Spirit bedews the soul with purity till He saturates it. Oh, to have a heart saturated with holy influences till it shall be as Gideon's fleece, which held so much dew that Gideon could wring out a bowl full from it! Oh, that our whole nature were filled with the Spirit of God; that we were sanctified wholly, body, soul, and spirit! Sanctification is the result of the Holy Spirit being put within us.

Next, the Holy Ghost acts in the heart as the Spirit of *preservation*. Where He dwells men do not go back unto perdition. He works in them a watchfulness against temptation day by day. He works in them to wrestle against sin. Rather than sin a believer would die ten thousand deaths. He works in believers union to Christ, which is the source and guarantee of acceptable fruitfulness He creates in the saints those holy things which glorify God, and bless the sons of men. All true fruit is the fruit of the Spirit. Every true prayer must be "praying in the Holy Ghost." He helpeth our infirmities in prayer. Even the hearing of the Word of the Lord is of the Spirit, for John says, "I was in the Spirit on the Lord's day, and heard behind me a great voice." Everything that comes of the man, or is kept alive in the man, is first infused and then sustained and perfected of the Spirit. "It is the spirit that quickeneth; the flesh profiteth nothing."

We never go an inch towards heaven in any other power than that of the Holy Ghost. We do not even stand fast and remain steadfast except as we are upheld by the Holy Spirit. The vineyard which the Lord hath planted He also preserves; as it is written, "I the Lord do keep it; I will water it every moment: lest any hurt it, I will keep it night and day." Did I hear that young man say, "I should like to become a Christian, but I fear I should not hold out? How am I to be preserved?" A very proper inquiry for "He that endureth to the end, the same shall be saved." Temporary Christians are no Christians: only the believer who continues to believe will enter heaven. How, then, can we hold on in such a world as this?

Here is the answer. "I will put my spirit within you." When a city has been captured in war, those who formerly possessed it seek to win it back again, but the king who captured it sends a garrison to live within the walls, and he said to the captain, "Take care of this city that I have conquered, and let not the enemy take it again." So the Holy Ghost is the garrison of God within our redeemed humanity, and he will keep us to the end. "May the peace of God, which passeth all understanding, keep your hearts and minds through Christ Jesus." For preservation, then, we look to the Holy Spirit.

Lest I weary you, I will be very brief upon the next point: the Holy Spirit within us is for *guidance*. The Holy Spirit is given to lead us into all truth. Truth is like a vast grotto, and the Holy Spirit brings torches, and shows us all the splendor of the roof; and since the passage seems intricate, He knows the way, and He leads us into the deep things of God. He opens up to us one truth after another, by His light and by His guidance, and thus we are "taught of the Lord." He is also our practical guide to heaven, helping and directing us on the upward journey. I wish Christian people would inquire more often of the Holy Ghost as to guidance in their daily life. Know ye not that the Spirit of God dwelleth in you? You need not always be running to this friend and that one to get direction: wait upon the Lord in silence, sit still in quiet before the oracle of God. Use the judgment God has given you, but when that suffices not, resort to Him whom Mr. Bunyan calls "the Lord High Secretary," who lives within, who is infinitely wise, and who can guide you by making you to "hear a voice behind you saying, This is the way, walk ye in it." The Holy Ghost will guide you in life; He will guide you in death; and He will guide you to glory. He will guard you from modern error, and from ancient error, too. He will guide you in a way that you know not; and through the darkness He will lead you in a way you have not seen: these things will He do unto you, and not forsake you.

Oh, this precious text! I seem to have before me a great cabinet full of jewels rich and rare. May God the Holy Ghost Himself come and hand these out to you, and may you be adorned with them all the days of your life!

Last of all, "I will put my spirit within you," that is, by way of *consolation*, for His choice name is "The Comforter." Our God would not have His children unhappy, and therefore, He Himself, in the third Person of the blessed Trinity, has undertaken the office of Comforter. Why does your face such mournful colors wear? God can comfort you. You that are under the burden of sin; it is true no man can help you into peace, but the Holy Ghost can. O God, to every seeker here who has failed to find rest, grant Thy Holy Spirit! Put Thy Spirit within him, and he will rest in Jesus. And you dear people of God, who are worried, remember that worry and the Holy Ghost are very contradictory one to another. "I will put my spirit within you" means that you shall become gentle, peaceful, resigned, and acquiescent in the divine will. Then you will have faith in God that all is well. David says—"God my exceeding joy"; and such He is to us. "Yea, mine own God is he!" Can you say, "My God, my God"? Do you want anything more? Can you conceive of anything beyond your God? Omnipotent to work all forever! Infinite to give! Faithful to remember! He is all that is good. Light only: "in him is no darkness at all." I have all light, yea, all things, when I have my God. The Holy Spirit makes us apprehend this when He is put within us. Holy Comforter, abide with us, for then we enjoy the light of heaven. Then are we always peaceful and even joyful; for we walk in unclouded light. In Him our happiness sometimes rises into great waves of delight, as if it leaped up to the glory. The Lord make this text your own—"I will put my Spirit within you." Amen.

12
"Honey in the Mouth!"

He shall glorify me: for He shall receive of mine, and shall show it unto you. All things that the Father hath are mine: therefore said I, that He shall take of mine, and shall show it unto you—John 16:14, 15.

Beloved friends, here you have the Trinity, and there is no salvation apart from the Trinity. It must be the Father, the Son, and the Holy Ghost. "All things that the Father hath are mine," saith Christ, and the Father hath all things. They were always His; they are still His; they always will be His; and they cannot become ours till they change ownership, till Christ can say, "All things that the Father hath are mine"; for it is by virtue of the representative character of Christ standing as the surety of the Covenant that the "all things" of the Father are passed over to the Son, that they might be passed over to us. "It pleased the Father that in Him should all fullness dwell; and of His fullness have all we received." But yet we are so dull that, though the conduit-pipe is laid on to the great fountain, we cannot get at it. We are lame; we cannot reach thereto; and in comes the third Person of the divine unity, even the Holy Spirit, and He receives of the things of Christ, and then delivers them over to us. So we do actually receive, through Jesus Christ, by the Spirit, what is in the Father.

Ralph Erskine, in his preface to a sermon upon the fifteenth verse, has a notable piece. He speaks of grace as honey—honey for the cheering of the saints, for the sweetening of their mouths and hearts, but he says that in the Father "the honey is in the flower, which is at such a distance from us that we could never extract it." In the Son "the honey is in the comb, prepared for us in our Immanuel, God-Man, Redeemer, the Word that was made flesh, saying, 'All things that the Father hath are mine; and mine for your use and behoof': it is in the comb. But then, next, we have honey in the mouth; the Spirit taking all things, and making application thereof, by showing them unto us, and making us to eat and drink with Christ, and share of these 'all things'; yea, not only eat the honey, but the honeycomb with the honey; not only His benefits, but Himself." It is a very beautiful division of the subject. Honey in the flower in God, as in mystery; really there. There never will be any more honey than there is in the flower. There it is. But how shall you and I get at it? We have not wisdom to extract the sweetness. We are not as the bees that are able to find it out. It is bee-honey, but not man-honey. Yet you see in Christ it becomes the honey in the honeycomb, and hence He is sweet to our taste as honey dropping from the comb. Sometimes we are so faint that we cannot reach out a hand to grasp that honeycomb; and, alas! there was a time when our palates were so depraved that we preferred bitter things, and thought them sweet. But now the Holy Ghost has come, we have got the honey in the mouth, and the taste that enjoys it; yea, we have now so long enjoyed it, that the honey of grace has entered into our constitution, and we have become sweet unto God; His sweetness having been conveyed by this strange method unto us.

Beloved friends, I scarcely need say to you, do keep the existence of the Trinity prominent in your ministry. Remember, you cannot pray without the Trinity. If the full work of salvation requires a Trinity, so does that very breath by which we live. You cannot draw near to the Father except through the Son, and by the Holy Spirit. There is a trinity in nature undoubtedly. There certainly constantly turns up the need of a Trinity in the realm of grace; and when we get to heaven we shall understand, perhaps, more fully what is meant by the Trinity in unity. But if that is a thing never to be understood, we shall at least apprehend it more lovingly; and we shall rejoice more completely as the three tones of our music shall rise up in perfect harmony unto HIM who is one and indivisible, and yet is three, forever blessed, Father, Son, and Holy Ghost, one God.

Now for the point which I am to open up to you this morning; though *I* cannot do it, but *He* must do it. We must sit here, and have the text acted out upon ourselves. "He shall glorify me. He shall take of mine, and shall show it unto you." May it be so just now!

First, *what the Holy Spirit does:* "He shall take of mine, and shall show it unto you." Secondly, *what the Holy Spirit aims at and really effects:* "He shall glorify me." And then, thirdly, *how in doing both these things He is the Comforter.* It is the Comforter that does this; and we shall find our richest, surest comfort in this work of the Holy Spirit, who shall take of the things of Christ, and show them unto us.

I. First, WHAT THE HOLY SPIRIT DOES. It is clear, beloved friends, that the Holy Spirit *deals with the things of Christ.* Do not let us strain at anything new. The Holy Ghost could deal with anything in heaven above, or in the earth beneath—the story of the ages past, the story of the ages to come, the inward secrets of the earth, the evolution of all things, if there be an evolution. He could do it all. Like the Master, He could handle any topic He chose, but He confines himself to the things of Christ, and therein finds unutterable liberty and boundless freedom.

The Holy Spirit still exists, and works, and teaches in the church, but we have a test by which to know whether what people claim to be revelation is revelation or not: "He shall receive of mine." The Holy Ghost will never go farther than the cross, and the coming of the Lord. He will go no farther than that which concerns Christ. "He shall receive of mine." His one vocation is to deal with the things of Christ. If we do not remember this, we may be carried away by vagaries, as many have been. When you have been the whole Sunday morning whittling away a text to the small end of nothing, what have you done? A king spent a day in trying to make a portrait on a cherry-stone—a king, who was ruling empires; and here is a minister, who professes to have been called of the Holy Ghost to the employ of taking of the things of Christ, who spent a whole morning with precious souls, who were dying while he spoke to them, in handling a theme concerning which it did not signify the turn of a hair whether it was so or not. Oh, imitate the Holy Spirit! If you profess to have Him dwelling in you, be moved by Him. Let it be said of you in your measure, as of the Holy Ghost without measure, "He shall receive of mine, and shall show it unto you."

But, next, what does the Holy Ghost do? Why, *He deals with feeble men,* yea, He dwells with us poor creatures. I can understand the Holy Ghost taking the things of Christ, and rejoicing therein, but the marvel is, that He should glorify Christ by coming and showing these things to us. And yet, brethren, it is among us that Christ is to get His glory. Our eyes must see Him. An unseen Christ is little glorious; and the things of Christ unknown, the things of Christ untasted and unloved, seem to have lost their brilliance to a high degree. The Holy Spirit, therefore, feeling that to show a sinner the salvation of Christ glorifies Him, spends His time, and has been spending these centuries, in taking of the things of Christ, and showing them to us. Ah! It is a great condescension on His part to show them to us, but it is a miracle, too. If it were reported that suddenly stones had life, and hills had eyes, and trees had ears, it would be a strange thing, but for us who were dead and blind and deaf in an awful sense—for the spiritual is more emphatic than the natural—for us to be so far gone, and for the Holy Ghost to be able to show the things of Christ to us, is to His honor. But He does do it. He comes from heaven to dwell with us. Let us honor and bless His name.

I never could make up my mind which to admire most as an act of condescension; the incarnation of Christ, or the indwelling of the Holy Ghost. The incarnation of Christ is marvelous—that He should dwell in human nature, but, observe, the Holy Ghost dwells in human nature in its sinfulness; not in perfect human nature, but in imperfect human nature; and He continues to dwell, not in one body, which was fashioned strangely for Himself, and was pure and without taint, but He dwells in *our* body. Know ye not that they are the temples of the Holy Ghost, which were defiled by nature, and in which a measure of defilement still remains, despite His indwelling? And this He has done these multitudes of years, not in one instance, nor in thousands of instances only, but in a number that no man can number. He continues still to come into contact with sinful humanity. Not to the angels, nor to the seraphim, not to the cherubim, nor to the host who have washed their robes, and made them white in the blood of the Lamb, does he show the things of Christ, but He shall show them unto *us*.

I suppose that it means this, that *He takes of the words of our Lord*—those which He spoke personally, and by His apostles. Let us never allow anybody to divide between the word of the apostles and the word of Christ. Our Savior has joined them together. "Neither pray I for these alone, but for them also which shall believe on me through their word." And if any begin rejecting the apostolic word, they will be outside the number for whom Christ prays; they shut themselves out by that very fact. I wish that they would solemnly recollect that the word of the apostles is the word of Christ. He tarried not long enough, after He had risen from the dead, to give us further exposition of His mind and will; and He could not have given it before His death because it would have been unsuitable. "I have yet many things to say unto you, but ye cannot bear them now." After the descent of the Holy Ghost, the disciples were prepared to receive that which Christ spoke by His servants Paul and Peter, and James and John. Certain doctrines which we are sometimes taunted about as being not revealed by Christ, but by His apostles, were all revealed by Christ, every one of them. They can all be found in His teaching, but they are very much in the parabolic form. It is after He has gone up into glory, and has prepared a people by His Spirit to understand the truth more fully, that He sends his apostles, and says, "Go forth, and open up to those whom I have chosen out of the world the meaning of all

I said." The meaning is all there, just as all the New Testament is in the Old.

Well, now, the words of the Lord Jesus, and the words of His apostles, are to be *expounded* to us by the Holy Spirit. We shall never get at the center of their meaning apart from His teaching. We shall never get at their meaning at all, if we begin disputing about the words, saying, "Now, I cannot accept the words." If you will not have the shell, you will never have the chick. It is impossible. "The words are not inspired," they say. If we have no inspiration in the words, we have got an impalpable inspiration that oozes away between your fingers, and leaves nothing behind. You must go and say, "Great Master, we thank Thee for the Book with all our hearts; and we thank Thee for putting the Book into words, but now, good Master, we will not cavil over the letter, as did the Jews and the rabbis and the scribes of old, and so miss Thy meaning. Open wide the door of the words, that we may enter into the secret closet of the meaning; and teach us this, we pray Thee. Thou hast the key. Lead us in."

Dear friends, whenever you want to understand a text of Scripture, try to read the original. Consult anybody who has studied what the original means, but remember that the quickest way into a text is praying in the Holy Ghost. Pray the chapter over. I do not hesitate to say that, if a chapter is read upon one's knees, looking up at every word to Him that gave it, the meaning will come to you with infinitely more light than by any other method of studying it. "He shall glorify me: for he shall receive of mine, and shall show it unto you." He shall re-deliver the Master's message to you in the fullness of its meaning.

But I do not think that is all that the text means. "He shall receive of mine." In the next verse the Lord goes on to say, "All things that the Father hath are mine." I do think that it means, therefore, that *the Holy Spirit will show us the things of Christ.* Here is a text for us — "The things of Christ." Christ speaks as if He had not any things just then which were specially His own, for He had not died then; He had not risen then; He was not pleading then as the great Intercessor in heaven: all that was to come. But still, He says, "Even now all things that the Father hath are mine: all His attributes, all His glory, all His rest, all His happiness, all His blessedness. *All that is mine, and the Holy Ghost shall show that to you."*

But I might almost read my text in another light; for He has died, and risen, and gone on high, and lo, He cometh. His chariots are on the way. Now, there are certain things which the Father hath, and which Jesus Christ hath, which are truly the things of Christ, emphatically the things of Christ; and my prayer is, that you and I, preachers of the gospel, might have this text fulfilled in us: "He shall take of mine—my things—and shall show them unto you."

Suppose, dear brethren, that we are going to preach the word again, and the Holy Spirit shows to us our Master in His Godhead. Oh, how we will preach Him as divine—how surely He can bless our congregation! How certainly He must be able to subdue all things unto Himself, seeing that He is very God of very God! It is equally sweet to see Him as Man. Oh, to have the Spirit's view of Christ's manhood! distinctly to recognize that He is bone of my bone, and flesh of my flesh, and that in His infinite tenderness He will make me compassionate, and deal with my poor people, and with the troubled consciences that are round me; that I have still to go to them, and tell them of One who is touched with the feeling of their infirmities, having been tempted in all points like as they still are! Oh, my brothers, if we once, nay, if every time before we preach, we get a view of Christ in His divine and human natures, and come down fresh from that vision to speak about Him, what glorious preaching it would be for our people!

It is a glorious thing to get a view of the offices of Christ by the Holy Spirit, but especially of His office as a Savior. I have often said to Him, "You must save my people. It is no business of mine. I never set up in that line, or put over my door that I was a savior, but Thou hast been apprenticed to this trade. Thou hast learned it by experience, and Thou dost claim it as Thine own honor. Thou art exalted on high to be a Prince and a Savior. Do Thine own work, my Lord." I took this text, and used it with sinners the other Sunday night, and I know that God blessed it when I said to them,

"May the Holy Ghost show you that Christ is a Savior! A physician does not expect you to make any apologies when you call upon him because you are ill, for he is a physician, and he wants you in order that he may prove his skill; so Christ is a Savior, and you need not apologize for going to Him, because He cannot be a Savior if there is not somebody to be saved." The fact is, Christ cannot get hold of us anywhere except by our sin. The point of contact between the sick one and the physician is the disease. Our sin is the point of contact between us and Christ. Oh, that the Spirit of God would take of Christ's divine offices, especially that of a Savior, and show them unto us!

Did the Holy Ghost ever show to you these things of Christ, namely, His covenant engagements? When He struck hands with the Father, it was that He would bring many sons unto glory; that of those whom the Father gave Him He would lose none, But that they should be saved; for He is under bonds to His Father to bring his elect home. When the sheep have to pass again under the hand of Him that telleth them, they will go under the rod one by one, each one having the blood-mark; and He will never rest till the number in the heavenly fold shall tally with the number in the book. So I believe; and it has seemed delightful to me to have this shown to me when I have gone to preach. It is a dull, dreary, wet foggy morning. There are only a few present. Yes, but they are picked people, whom God hath ordained to be there, and there will be the right number there. I shall preach, and there will be some saved. We do not go at a peradventure, but, guided by the blessed Spirit of God, we go with a living certainty, knowing that God has a people that Christ is bound to bring home, and bring them home He will; and while He shall see of the travail of His soul, His Father shall delight in every one of them. If you get a clear view of that, it will give you backbone, and make you strong. "He shall take of mine, and shall show you my covenant engagements, and when you see them you shall be comforted."

But, beloved, the Holy Ghost favors you by taking what is peculiarly Christ's, namely, His love, and showing that to you. We have seen it, sometimes more vividly than at other times. But if the full blaze of the Holy Spirit were to be concentrated upon the love of Christ, and our eyesight enlarged to its utmost capacity, it would be such a vision that heaven could not excel it. We should sit with our Bible before us in our study, and feel, "Well now, here is a man, whether in the body or out of the body, I cannot tell. Such a man is caught up into the third heaven." Oh, to see the love of Christ in the light of the Holy Ghost! When it is so revealed to us, it is not merely the surface which we see, but the love of Christ itself. You know that you never saw anything yet, strictly speaking. You only see the appearance of the thing—the light reflected by it; that is all you see. But the Holy Ghost shows us the naked truth, the essence of the love of Christ; and what that essence is—that love without beginning, without change, without limit, without end; and that love set upon His people simply from motives within Himself, and from no motive *ab extra*—what must be, what tongue can tell? Oh, it is a ravishing sight!

I think that if there could be one sight more wonderful than the love of Christ, it would be the blood of Christ.

> Much we talk of Jesu's blood,
> But how little's understood!

It is the climax of God. I do not know of anything more divine. It seems to me as if all the eternal purposes worked up to the blood of the Cross, and then worked from the blood of the cross towards the sublime consummation of all things. Oh, to think that He should become man! God has made spirit, pure spirit, embodied spirit; and then materialism; and somehow, as if He would take all up into one, the Godhead links Himself with the material, and He wears dust about Him even as we wear it; and taking it all up, He then goes, and, in that fashion, redeems His people from all the evil of their soul, their spirit, and their body, by the pouring out of a life which, while it was human, was so in connection with the divine, that we speak correctly of "the blood of God."

Turn to the twentieth chapter of the Acts, and read how the apostle Paul puts it: "Feed the church of God, which he hath purchased with his own blood." I believe that Dr. Watts is not wrong when he says—"God that loved and died." It is an incorrect accuracy, a strictly absolute accuracy of incorrectness. So it must be ever when the finite talks of the Infinite. It was a wonderful sacrifice that could absolutely obliterate, annihilate, and extinguish sin, and all the traces that could possibly remain of it; for "He hath finished the transgression, made an end of sins, made reconciliation for iniquity, and brought in everlasting righteousness."

Ah, dear friends! You have seen this, have you not? but you have to see more of it yet; and when we get to heaven, we shall then know what that blood means, and with what vigor shall we sing, "Unto him that loved us, and washed us from our sins in his own blood!" Will anybody be there to say, "Is not that the religion of the shambles?" as they blasphemously call it. Ah, my friends! They will find themselves where they will wish they had believed "the religion of the shambles"; and I think that it will burn like coals of juniper into the soul of any man that has ever dared to talk like that, that he did despite the blood of God, and so, by his own willful deeds, will be cast away forever.

May the Holy Spirit show unto you Gethsemane, and Gabbatha, and Golgotha! and then, may it please Him to give you a sight of what our Lord is now doing! Oh, how it would cheer you up at any time when you were depressed, only to see Him standing and pleading for you! Do you not think that if your wife is ill, and your child is sick, and there is scant food in the cupboard, if you were to go out at the back door, and you saw Him with the breastplate on, and all the stones glittering, and your name there, and Him pleading for you, you would go in and say, "There, wife, it is all right. He is praying for us"? Oh, it would be a comfort if the Holy Ghost showed you a pleading Christ! And then, to think that He is reigning as well as pleading. He is at the right hand of God, even the Father, who hath put all things under His feet. And He waits till the last enemy shall lie there. Now, you are not afraid, are you, of those who have said, "All power is given unto me in heaven and in earth. Go ye therefore, and teach all nations; and lo, I am with you alway, even unto the end of the world."

Next, and best of all, may the Holy Spirit give you a clear view of His coming. This is our most brilliant hope: "Lo, He cometh!" The more the adversary waxes bold, and the less of faith there is, and when zeal seems almost extinct, these are the tokens of His coming. The Lord always said so; and that He would not come unless there was a falling away first; and so the darker the night grows, and the fiercer the storm becomes, the better will we remember that He at the lake of Galilee came to them upon the waves in the night when the storm was wildest. Oh, what will His enemies say when He comes? When they behold the nail-prints of the Glorified, and the Man with the thorn crown — when they see Him really come — they that have despised His word, and His ever-blessed blood, how will they flee before that face of injured love! And we, on the contrary, through His infinite mercy, will say, "This is what the Holy Ghost showed us; and now we behold it literally. We thank Him for the foresights which He gave us of the beatific vision."

I have not done on the first head yet, because there is one point which I want you to recollect. When the Holy Ghost takes of the things of Christ, and shows them to us, He has a purpose in so doing. It is with you, with regard to the Spirit showing you things, as it was with Jacob. You know Jacob lay down, and went to sleep, and the Lord said to him, "The land whereon thou liest, to thee will I give it." Now, wherever you go, throughout the whole of Scripture, if you can find a place where you can lie down, that is yours. If you can sleep on a promise, that promise is yours. "Lift up now thine eyes," said God to Abraham, "and look from the place where thou art northward, and southward, and eastward, and westward: for all the land which thou seest, to thee will I give it." The Lord increase our holy vision of delighted faith; for there is nothing you see but you may also enjoy; all that is in Christ is there for you.

II. Now, secondly, WHAT THE HOLY SPIRIT AIMS AT, AND WHAT HE REALLY ACCOMPLISHES. "He shall glorify me."

Ah, brothers! The Holy Ghost never comes to glorify *us*, or to glorify a denomination, or, I think, even to glorify a systematic arrangement of doctrines. He comes to glorify Christ. If we want to be in accord with Him, we must preach in order to glorify Christ. May we never have this thought, "I will put that bit in; it will tell well. The friends will feel that oratory is not quite extinct, that Demosthenes lives again in this village." No, no. I should say, brother, though it is a very delightful piece, strike that out ruthlessly, because if you have had a thought of that kind about it, you had better not put yourself in the way of temptation by using it. "Yes, that is a magnificent sentence! I do not know where I met with it, or whether it is my own. I am afraid that most of our friends will not understand it, but then it will give them an impression that they have a deep thinker in their pulpit." Well then, it may be very admirable, and further, it might be a very right thing, to give them that precious piece, but if you have that thought about it, strike it out. Strike it out ruthlessly. Say, "No, no, no! If it is not distinctly my aim to glorify Christ, I am not in accord with the aim of the Holy Ghost, and I cannot expect His help. We shall not be pulling the same way, and therefore I will have nothing of which I cannot say that I am saying it simply, sincerely, and only that I may glorify Christ."

How, then, does the Holy Spirit glorify Christ? It is very beautiful to think that He glorifies Christ *by showing Christ's things*. If you wanted to do honor to a man, you would perhaps take him a present to decorate his house. But here, if you want to glorify Christ, you must go and take the things out of Christ's house, "the things of Christ." Whenever we have to praise God, what do we do? We simply say what He is. "Thou art this, and Thou art that." There is no other praise. We cannot fetch anything from elsewhere, and bring it to God, but the praises of God are simply the facts about Himself. If you want to praise the Lord Jesus Christ, tell the people about Him. Take of the things of Christ, and show them to the people, and you will glorify Christ. Alas! I know what you will do. You will weave words together, and you will form and fashion them, in a marvelous manner, till you have produced a charming piece of literature. When you have carefully done that, put it in the fire under the oven, and let it burn. Possibly you may help to bake some bread with it. Brethren, it is better for us to tell what Christ is, than to invent ten thousand fine words of praise in reference to Him. "He shall glorify me, for He shall receive of mine, and shall show it unto you."

Again I think that the blessed Spirit glorifies Christ by showing us the things of Christ *as Christ's*. Oh, to be pardoned! Yes, it is a great thing, but to find that pardon in His wounds, that is a great thing! Oh, to get peace! Yes, but to find that peace in the blood of His cross! Brethren, have the blood-mark very visibly on all your mercies. They are all marked with the blood of the cross, but sometimes we think so much of the sweetness of the bread, or of the coolness of the waters, that we forget whence these came, and how they came, and then they lack their choicest flavor. That it came from Christ is the best thing about the best thing that ever came from Christ. That He saves me is, somehow, better than my being saved. It is a blessed thing to go to heaven, but I do not know that it is not a better thing to be in Christ, and so, as the result of it, to get into heaven. It is Himself, and that which comes of Himself, that becomes best of all, because it comes of Himself. So the Holy Ghost shall glorify Christ by making us see that these things of Christ are indeed of Christ, and completely of Christ, and still are in connection with Christ; and we only enjoy them because *we* are in connection with Christ.

Then it is said in the text, "He shall glorify me: for He shall take of mine, and shall show it *unto you*." Yes, it does glorify Christ for the Holy Spirit to show Christ *to us*. How often I have wished that we could have a few Miltons, and such like men, to sing of the love of Christ; a few mighty men, who teach politics, and the like, to consecrate their talent to the preaching of the gospel. Why is it not so? Well, because the Holy Ghost does not seem to think that that would be the way to glorify Christ supremely; and He prefers, as a better way, to take us common-place sort of persons, and to take the things of Christ, and to show them to *us*. He does glorify Christ; and blessed be His name that ever my bleary eyes should look upon His infinite loveliness; that ever such a wretch as I, who can understand everything but what I ought to understand, should be made to comprehend the heights and depths, and to know, with all saints,

the love of Christ, that passeth knowledge. You see in a school that
clever boy. Well, it is not much for the master to have made a scholar
of him. But here is one who shines as a scholar, and his mother says
that he was the greatest dolt in the family. All his schoolfellows say,
"Why, he was our butt! He seemed to have no brains, but our master,
somehow, got some brain into him, and made him know something
which he appeared, at one time, incapable of knowing." Somehow, it
does seem to be as if our very folly, and impotence, and spiritual
death—if the Holy Ghost shows to us the things of Christ—will go
towards the increase of that great glorifying of Christ at which the
Holy Spirit aims.

Then, beloved brethren, since it is for the honor of Christ for
His things to be shown to men, He will show them to us, *that we
may go and show them to other people.* This we cannot do, except as
He is with us to make the others to see, but He will be with us while
we tell forth what He has taught us; and so the Holy Ghost will really be showing to others while He is showing to us. A secondary
influence will flow from this service, for we shall be helped to *use
the right means* to make others see the things of Christ.

III. Our time is almost gone, but in the third place I must just
point out to you HOW HE IS IN BOTH OF THESE THINGS OUR COM-
FORTER.

He is so, firstly, for this reason—that *there is no comfort in the
world like the sight of Christ.* He shows to us the things of Christ.
Oh, brethren, if you are poor, and if the Holy Ghost shows you that
Christ had no where to lay His head, what a sight for you! And if
you are sick, and if the Holy Ghost shows you what sufferings Christ
endured, what comfort comes to you! If you are made to see the
things of Christ, each thing according to the condition which you
are in, how speedily you are delivered out of your sorrow!

And then, if the Holy Ghost glorifies Christ, *that is the cure for
every kind of sorrow.* He is the Comforter. I may have told you before, but I cannot help telling you again, that many years ago, after
the terrible accident in the Surrey Gardens, I had to go away into
the country, and keep quite still. The very sight of the Bible made

me cry. I could only keep alone in the garden; and I was heavy and sad, for people had been killed in the accident; and there I was, half dead myself; and I remember how I got back my comfort, and I preached on the Sabbath after I recovered. I had been walking round the garden, and I was standing under a tree. If it is there now, I should know it; and I remember these words: "Him hath God exalted with his right hand to be a Prince and a Savior." "Oh," I thought to myself, "I am only a common soldier. If I die in a ditch, I do not care. The king is honored. He wins the victory"; and I was like those French soldiers in the old times, who loved the emperor; and you know how, when they were dying, if he rode by, the wounded man would raise himself up on his elbow, and cry once more, *"Vive l' Empereur!"* for the emperor was graven on his heart. And so, I am sure, it is with every one of you, my comrades, in this holy war. If our Lord and King is exalted, then let other things go which way they like: if He is exalted, never mind what becomes of us. We are a set of pygmies; it is alright if *He* is exalted. God's truth is safe, we are perfectly willing to be forgotten, derided, slandered, or anything else that men please. The cause is safe, and the King is on the throne, Hallelujah! Blessed be His name!